RUSSIA, BRICS, AND THE DISRUPTION OF GLOBAL ORDER

RUSSIA, BRICS, AND THE DISRUPTION OF GLOBAL ORDER

Rachel S. Salzman

Georgetown University Press / Washington, DC

The publisher is not responsible for third-party websites or their content. URL links were active at time of publication.

Library of Congress Cataloging-in-Publication Data

Names: Salzman, Rachel S., author.
Title: Russia, BRICS, and the disruption of global order / Rachel S. Salzman.
Description: Washington, DC : Georgetown University Press, 2019. | Includes
    bibliographical references and index.
Identifiers: LCCN 2018023022 (print) | LCCN 2018034075 (ebook) | ISBN
    9781626166615 (pbk. : alk. paper) | ISBN 9781626166608 (hardcover : alk. paper) |
    ISBN 9781626166622 (ebook)
Subjects: LCSH: Russia (Federation)—Foreign relations—BRIC countries. |
    BRIC countries—Foreign relations—Russia (Federation)
Classification: LCC JZ1616.A57 (ebook) | LCC JZ1616.A57 B757 2019 (print) |
    DDC 327.47—dc23
LC record available at https://lccn.loc.gov/2018023022

♾ This book is printed on acid-free paper meeting the requirements of the American National Standard for Permanence in Paper for Printed Library Materials.

20 19   9 8 7 6 5 4 3 2   First printing

Printed in the United States of America.

Cover design by Martyn Schmoll.
Cover image by Frederic Legrand—COMEO/Shutterstock.com.

For my parents

Contents

List of Figures   ix
Acknowledgments   xi
A Note on Transliteration and Sources   xiii
Abbreviations   xv
Introduction: Russia, the West, and BRICS   xvii

1   Status Quo Revisionism: Post-Soviet Russia
    and the International System   1

2   From BRIC to BRICS: An Institutional History   23

3   Laying the Rhetorical Foundation for BRICS:
    The Evolution of the Concepts of Sovereignty and
    National Identity, 2000–2007   44

4   Potemkin Villages and Rhetorical Bridges:
    BRICS in Russian Policy, 2008–13   63

5   From Bridge to Bulwark (and Back Again):
    Russia and BRICS after the Onset of the Ukraine Crisis   88

6   BRICS from Other Perspectives: The Views from India
    and China   118

Conclusion: Russia and BRICS in an Age of Strategic Uncertainty   138
Bibliography   145
Index   165
About the Author   175

Figures

2.1. BRICS GDP Growth   35

2.2. G7 GDP Growth   36

2.3. BRICS GDP Per Capita   37

2.4. G7 GDP Per Capita   37

Acknowledgments

THIS BOOK BEGAN AS A DISSERTATION, AND SO I FIRST OWE A DEBT OF gratitude to my committee. My dissertation adviser, Bruce Parrott, provided thoughtful, incisive, and helpful comments, and his patience throughout was indispensable. Charles Gati always pushed me to consider the opposing argument. Andrew Kuchins was the first to propose that I look into BRICS. Martin Gilman provided an economist's eye and kept me focused on the topic at hand. Angela Stent was instrumental in helping me draw out the macro themes of the research. Without the unique contribution of each committee member, this process would have been much the poorer.

Further thanks go to Angela and Andy, who selected me for a postdoctoral fellowship at the Center for Eurasian, Russian, and East European Studies at Georgetown University. They provided support and guidance throughout the process of transforming the dissertation into a book. The fellowship, sponsored by the Carnegie Corporation of New York as part of the Russia Futures Project, also afforded me the opportunity to do additional fieldwork in Russia, China, and India to enrich and expand my argument.

It is not only faculty advisers and senior scholars who helped bring this project to fruition. Madina Bizhanova provided invaluable support as a research assistant in the final stages, and Hillel Smith offered design inspiration. Thanks are also due to Don Jacobs at Georgetown University Press for his help in shepherding the early manuscript through peer review and the publishing committee, and to Kathryn Owens for making it publication-ready. Finally, there would have been no manuscript to review without the support of the inimitable librarians at the SAIS library, who offered support from the inception of the project through to its very final stages.

In addition to the support from Carnegie Corporation of New York, I am thankful to the Cosmos Scholars Foundation and the National Security Education Program Boren Fellowship for their support of my dissertation fieldwork. On the substantive and personal side, I am especially grateful to Robert H. Legvold and Amb. James F. Collins for their guidance and support. I would not be where I am today had it not been for them.

Finally, I owe more to my parents than words can express. Faced with a child deeply interested in Russia since the age of thirteen, my parents have patiently supported my steps and missteps as I found my way. My father has read every word I have written, whether on education under Tsar Nicholas I or contemporary Russian foreign policy. He and my mother have provided untold assistance and guidance. I will be forever grateful.

A Note on Transliteration and Sources

I USE THE LIBRARY OF CONGRESS SYSTEM OF TRANSLITERATION WITHOUT diacritics, except in instances of proper names with English equivalents, such as Alexander, or where there is an accepted English spelling of a name, such as Yeltsin. "Ы" is rendered as "y." Both "Й" and "И" are written as "i." "Я" is "ia."

The Kremlin and the Russian Ministry of Foreign Affairs often provide English translations of speeches and documents. When these were available, I cite the English version since it is the translation of record. In places where the English translation may have missed some of the nuance in the Russian original or needs clarification, I provide the transliterated Russian in brackets and cite both versions.

Abbreviations

AIIB	Asian Infrastructure and Investment Bank
BRI	Belt and Road Initiative
BRIC	Brazil Russia India China
BRICS	Brazil Russia India China South Africa
BTTC	BRICS Think Tanks Council
CIS	Commonwealth of Independent States
CRA	Contingency Reserve Arrangement
CSCE	Conference for Security and Cooperation in Europe
CSTO	Collective Security Treaty Organization
DCFTA	Deep and Comprehensive Free Trade Area
EEU	Eurasian Union
EST	European Security Treaty
GDP	gross domestic product
G7	Group of Seven
G8	Group of Eight
G20	Group of Twenty
IBSA	India-Brazil–South Africa Dialogue Forum
IMF	International Monetary Fund
MER	market exchange rate
MGIMO	Moscow State Institute of International Affairs
MID	Ministerstvo innostranykh del (Russian Ministry of Foreign Affairs)
NATO	North Atlantic Treaty Organization
NDB	New Development Bank
NKI BRIKS	National Committee on BRICS Research (Russia)
O5	Outreach 5
OSCE	Organization for Security and Cooperation in Europe
PPP	purchasing power parity
RAN	Russian Academy of Sciences

RIC	Russia India China ("Strategic Triangle")
SCO	Shanghai Cooperation Organization
UN	United Nations
UNSC	UN Security Council
WTO	World Trade Organization

Introduction

Russia, the West, and BRICS

THIS BOOK TELLS THE STORY OF HOW RUSSIA'S BRICS (BRAZIL, RUSSIA, India, China, and South Africa) initiative led to substantive changes in global governance at both rhetorical and practical levels. It is the story of why Russia began to search for non-Western partners, how Russian leaders have framed the idea of BRICS and Russia's role in the international system in their rhetoric over time, and how BRICS has changed during its first decade on the global stage. BRICS is not exclusively a Russian story, but understanding the role BRICS has played in Russian foreign policy is critical to understanding the group itself.

In some ways, this is also the story of the rise and fall in Russia's relations with the geographical and ideological West. Increasing strain between Russia and its Western partners since 2004 has influenced how Russian leaders speak publicly about Russia's national identity and international relationships. BRICS, with its membership of (then) fast-growing, non-Western economies, provided a useful rhetorical counterpoint for Russian leaders to emphasize over continuing to cooperate within Western-dominated institutions. The development of BRICS from an investment strategy to an informal political grouping to an association building its own international institutions lent credence to Russia's claim that BRICS constitutes an alternative institutional option to those led by the West.

An interrogation of how Russian leaders conceptualize their relations with the West and the non-West is especially important in the wake of the biggest rupture in relations between Russia and the rest of the Euro-Atlantic community since the end of the Cold War. There is no shortage of analysis about how the outbreak of the crisis in Eastern Ukraine in February 2014 altered Russia's relationship with Europe and the United States, or of how the crisis changed the balance in Russia's relations with countries elsewhere, especially China. Less studied, however, is the impact of the crisis on how Russia conceives of its global institutional alignments, particularly in the context of new groupings such as BRICS. This study fills that gap. Taking a long-term perspective, this book answers the question of how the Russian foreign policy elite has framed Russia's approach to BRICS over time and how that framing altered as a consequence of the

Ukrainian crisis. Using the story of BRICS as a proxy, the study reveals how Russia became a revolutionary actor intent on not only contesting US hegemony but also upending the current international system. I choose BRICS as the proxy not because it is consistently Russia's most valued institutional alignment but because, among the new institutions Russia has created, it is the only one to achieve global prominence and global interest.

It must be stated explicitly that this is a story about words more than deeds.[1] It is an investigation of what Russian leaders have said more than an analysis of what they have done. In part, this is because the story is so new that declarations have not always had time to translate into actions. It also is because much of the power of BRICS comes from words and symbolism. More importantly, however, I focus on rhetoric because it is significant in its own right. Words are themselves political choices. They have meaning apart from whether what is said does or does not come to pass. Words shape policy choices, and they can be used to lead and mislead the audience. Political rhetoric is an indication of what leaders would have the public understand to be true, even if it is not. When the rhetoric changes, it gives insight into a shift in how leaders wish their positions to be perceived. When that shift is precipitated by dramatic changes in a country's internal or external environment, an adjustment in rhetoric can be indicative of where policy may be headed even before those concrete changes are visible. Rhetoric, therefore, is an integral part of the policy process. It must be taken seriously as such.

At the same time, this is not a story of words without deeds. Changes in how Russia has talked about BRICS have been accompanied by very real shifts in both the relationship with the West and the international environment. Repeated cycles of deterioration and renewal in the US-Russian relationship have been caused by a mutually reinforcing cycle of policy adjustment and changes in rhetoric.[2] For example, the period between the terrorist attacks of September 11, 2001, and the US invasion of Iraq in 2003 witnessed both productive cooperation and conciliatory framing of the relationship on the part of the Russian leadership. By contrast, the negative impact of US unilateralism in the Iraq war on US-Russian relations was exacerbated by shifts in Russia's domestic politics that necessitated a more pessimistic official framing of Russia's place in the Euro-Atlantic order by that country's leaders.

Similarly, BRICS did not come together simply because Russia found it useful to emphasize rhetorically an alliance of non-Western economies. There is a strong political economy rationale underpinning BRICS, and the other BRICS countries would have abstained from cooperation were the group not worth their while. Changes in the distribution of global economic power and mistrust of US leadership of international institutions laid the foundation for cooperation among these unlikely partners. This cooperation has proved durable through changes in leadership as well as economic downturns across the group. The drive toward institutional creation in BRICS stalled following the 2014 creation of a BRICS development bank and contingency currency pool, but these two institutions are open and functioning. Even with slowing momentum, BRICS cooperation is sufficiently entrenched to constitute an association worthy of attention.

The story begins with Russia's failed integration into the Euro-Atlantic order following the end of the Cold War and the reasons for that failure. Anti-Westernism in Russia traces to centuries-old debates over national identity but also links directly to modern conflicts over how post-Soviet Russia should engage with the international system. The origins of BRICS lie in the economic rise of the non-West and growing anger at US foreign policy that occurred over the course of the late 1990s and early to mid-2000s. The intersection of these stories is the topic of the first chapter, which lays the foundation for understanding what BRICS has been both to Russia and to its other members.

The second chapter presents an institutional and intellectual history of the development of BRICS on the international stage. The chapter details the main milestones of cooperation, beginning with the first informal meeting in 2005 and running through the 2014 summit in Fortaleza, Brazil. It also includes a short quantitative examination of the development of trade and investment relationships among the BRICS countries as well as a quantitative depiction of BRICS institutionalization. The primary conclusion of chapter 2 is that BRICS has progressed from being a private-sector catchphrase to an independent group with non-economic aims and elements of deep cooperation in certain sectors.

The third chapter gives a prehistory of BRICS in Russian foreign policy. Looking primarily at presidential speeches and foreign policy concepts from the Russian Ministry of Foreign Affairs, chapter 3 traces how the meanings of the ideas of sovereignty and national identity evolved during Vladimir Putin's first two presidential terms. The chapter traces how, between 2000 and 2007, Putin relied on increasingly exclusionary definitions of these terms. The goal of the redefinition was to separate Russia rhetorically from the West and establish Russia as an independent pole in international affairs. The primary argument of the third chapter is that the rhetorical separation of Russia from the political West was a key inflection point that allowed for the incorporation of BRICS into Russian political rhetoric when the group burst forth in 2008.

Russian efforts to reframe its foreign policy orientation collided with global discontent over power in the current economic order during the 2008 global financial crisis. This is the topic of the fourth chapter. During 2008, the world witnessed the simultaneous emergence of BRICS in the international arena and the beginning of a volatile period in Russian-Western relations, marked by the low of the 2008 war between Russia and Georgia and the high of the Obama administration "reset." The chapter considers the impact of these developments from two angles: the official and the unofficial. On the official level, I analyze Russian government policy and rhetoric on BRICS in the context of improving relations with the West and President Medvedev's emphasis on economic modernization as opposed to political status. On the unofficial level, I consider the proliferation of analyses of BRICS between 2008 and 2013 in Russian state universities and research institutions. This two-level analytical approach reveals the chasm between the potential BRICS held for Russia and the role it actually played: while BRICS cooperation was increasing, Russian leadership continued to conceive of the group as strictly a rhetorical balance against the West. This further underscores the extent to which relations with the West have determined how Russian leaders conceive of BRICS.

The connection between relations with the West and Russia's approach to BRICS was brought out in sharp relief with the onset of the crisis in Crimea and southeastern Ukraine in February 2014. The Ukrainian crisis and its aftereffects are the subject of the fifth chapter, which analyzes how the crisis and the economic and political rupture with the West affected Russia's attitude toward BRICS. It looks in particular at the change in political rhetoric following the March 2014 annexation of Crimea and the role of anti-Western sentiment in Russia's BRICS policy and in the BRICS group as a whole. The chapter also explores Russian efforts to increase economic ties with the BRICS countries after the imposition of both Western sanctions and Russian "anti-sanctions" (self-imposed bans on agricultural imports from the EU and several other countries). The main argument of this chapter is that BRICS immediately after Crimea served important political and economic functions for Russia. That shift in perspective did not last, however, and by the end of 2015 Russian leadership had reverted to its shallow engagement with BRICS and focused instead on moving other projects forward, especially the Eurasian Economic Union and the Greater Eurasian Partnership.

The reasons for Russia's shift in focus away from BRICS after 2015 leads to the sixth and final chapter, which steps back from the Russian perspective to look at how BRICS operates in Indian and Chinese foreign policy. The goal here is twofold: the first is to offer a comparative perspective on BRICS to act as a corrective against Russian rhetoric about the group. As discussed in more depth at various points throughout the text, Russia's capacity to shape BRICS is constrained by the goals and national interests of the other members. Understanding how India and China approach the group gives further insight into how the group developed and where main intra-BRICS tensions lie. This in turn leads to the second goal: understanding the likely future course of BRICS in the midst of major policy changes among what Russia views as the group's three core members.

The stories in this study are still ongoing. They are also unfolding in the midst of profound global uncertainty about international order and leadership. The conclusion contextualizes Russia's BRICS initiative and Chinese and Indian responses to it within the broader story about concerns over global order. Contemporary strategic uncertainty is better attributed to dramatic political developments in the West than to BRICS, but the uncertainty has been magnified by

Russian and BRICS success in hollowing out the foundations of the current system. What follows is the story of how we reached this point.

Notes

1. On words versus deeds in foreign policy, see Bell, *Reagan Paradox*, chap. 1.
2. On the cyclical nature of US-Russian relations, see Stent, *Limits of Partnership*.

1

Status Quo Revisionism

Post-Soviet Russia and the International System

> [Russia] is ready to take a part in international relations, but she prefers other countries to abstain from taking an interest in her affairs: that is to say, to insulate herself from the rest of the world without remaining isolated from it.
> —Isaiah Berlin

> Over the next 10 years, the weight of the BRICs . . . in world GDP will grow. . . . In line with these prospects, world policymaking forums should be re-organised and in particular, the G7 should be adjusted to incorporate BRIC representatives. . . . It is time for the world to build better global economic BRICs.
> —Jim O'Neill, 2001

RUSSIA'S PLACE VIS-À-VIS THE WEST AND, INDEED, REGARDING THE INTERnational system has long been unsettled. The discomfort comes from an ongoing internal struggle between a desire to engage with the international system—that is, to play a leading role in its formation and administration—while still maintaining complete control over domestic development and national identity.[1] National identity, further, has been divided between identification with Europe and the (ideological) West and the idea of Russia as a civilization apart. The latter conception dictates that Russia is required by virtue of geography and culture to follow its own developmental path.[2]

This divide has produced a foreign policy approach that sometimes attempts to position Russia as an alternative center of power and undermine the legitimacy of the reigning system. An alternate tactic is to present Russia as a bridge between old and new structures. The result is a country that, until the onset of the Ukraine crisis, was at once both a status quo and a revisionist power. Post-Soviet Russia has attempted to maintain the status quo wherein its power is magnified. However, when efforts to join established organizations have proven unsuccessful or the requirements for entry were unacceptable, the government has retreated and created alternative organizations. This institutional creation has been accompanied by efforts to undermine rhetorically the legitimacy of the organizations from which Russia is excluded.

This chapter establishes a framework within which to understand Russia's BRICS diplomacy. It therefore has two tasks. The first is to trace how Russia has interacted with leading global institutions, and the international order more generally, since the collapse of the Soviet Union in 1991. The second is a discussion of the changes the international system has undergone during that era, with particular emphasis on the period before 2008. This sets the backdrop for understanding why BRICS was so appealing to Russia and locates BRICS within the evolving international system.

The chapter begins with a discussion of methodology and the vagaries of analyzing political rhetoric. It then moves to a review of the main foreign policy perspectives that have predominated among the post-Soviet Russian elite. That overview is followed by a two-part examination of Russia's relationship with the West: first, why the relationship has remained strained since the end of the Cold War, and second, how Russia has responded to that strain. Finally, the discussion broadens to an evaluation of seminal global changes in the past twenty-five years that have markedly affected the international order. This discussion contextualizes Russia's debates and actions within broader international trends.

Methodology: The Meaning of Political Rhetoric

Much of the argument here rests on the analysis of elite political rhetoric. Methodologically, these are tricky waters. As Stacie Goddard and Ronald Krebs argue in a special issue of *Security Studies* devoted to the study of political rhetoric, "scholars of international relations often dismiss rhetorical contestation as meaningless posturing, unworthy of serious analysis."[3] It is not hard to see why. Politicians say so much to so many different audiences that it seems logical to focus more on what gets done than on what gets said.

That approach, however, misses a critical piece of the creation of foreign policy. As Goddard and Krebs argue, "public talk is essential to the process of how states coalesce around collective intention and how institutions shape their members' subsequent behavior."[4] Put differently, the process of rhetorical contestation—of politicians talking and shaping the debate—is a fundamental piece of how a government arrives at a foreign policy that has public support.

This is not a new consideration. The post–World War II generation of realists understood that rhetoric is an important component of foreign policy action both domestically and internationally.[5] They saw rhetoric as fundamental to responsible and responsive policy creation.[6] These scholars were also aware of the potential abuses of rhetoric. Indeed, concern that "American grand strategy . . . became dependent on rhetorics of fear or destiny" was part of what motivated them to consider the role of rhetoric in policy and search for alternative sources for rhetorical flourishes.[7] They saw danger in rhetoric based in fear.

Indeed, these scholars were concerned about the practical implications of reckless words. Hans Morgenthau wrote in an indictment of the Truman Administration's foreign policy,

> You have deceived once: now you must deceive again, for to tell the truth would be to admit having deceived. If your better judgment leads you near the road of rational policy, your critics will raise the ghost of your own deception, convict you out of your own mouth as appeaser and traitor, and stop you in your tracks.
>
> You have falsified the real issue between the United States and the Soviet Union into a holy crusade to stamp out Bolshevism everywhere on earth, for this seemed a good way of arousing the public: now you must act as though you meant it. . . . You have told the people that American power has no limits, for flattery of the people is "good politics": now you must act as though you meant it.[8]

This is an almost causal argument. Morgenthau does not see speeches and doctrines that appealed to the national ego and national morality as window dressing on concrete national interests. Instead, he and some of his contemporaries saw political rhetoric as having "important and even determining" influence on foreign policy behavior.[9]

Morgenthau was not simply fear-mongering about the dangers of fear-mongering. As Charles Gati argues in his book on the 1956 uprising against the Soviets in Hungary, US promises had real impact on the ground. Gati writes, "Combining the best techniques of Hollywood with those of Madison Avenue, the United States was offering a product—liberation—it could not deliver. The advertising was misleading, but it convinced the oppressed peoples of Eastern Europe that their cause was America's cause, and it reinforced the Soviet oppressors' belief that in America they had an implacable enemy."[10] In Gati's estimation, US rhetoric about intentions to liberate Eastern Europe inculcated in its audience false beliefs that spurred tangible outcomes. On US government directive, Radio Free Europe did not use its platform to press for any moderation among the Hungarian audience, and it even offered advice on how to manufacture weapons.[11] Hungarians took up arms in Budapest at least in part because US rhetoric made them believe they would be supported in their struggle.[12] The US government, moreover, believed that those words were sufficient support. Documents indicate that while material support was never meant to be forthcoming, US officials seem to have "had an excessive, almost religious faith in the power of words."[13]

As Gati rightly notes, however, there was a domestic context to what he terms the US "huffing and puffing" about rolling back the Soviet armies.[14] Democrats and Republicans were as concerned about demonstrating their superior fitness to rule as they were about the national security threat that the USSR posed to the United States and its allies.[15] Another way of understanding the role of the domestic context in shaping US Cold War rhetoric is to posit that as much as rhetoric can have a determinant influence on policy, it does not work free of constraints.

The clearest constraint on rhetoric is the extent to which it has a receptive audience. This ties the discussion to the question of the role of national identity in setting the boundaries of debate. In answer to the question of why some identity narratives catch on while others do not, Anne Clunan proposes that "whether . . . national self-images and their behavioral orientations towards the outside world come to be epistemically dominant rests on their perceived legitimacy among the majority of political elites."[16] National identity cannot be derived de novo; it is bound by what the political elite understands as a "legitimate" interpretation. What this means in practical terms is that the debate over national identity, and by extension national interest, is bounded by what the audience is willing to hear. Goddard and Krebs make a similar point. They argue that certain strategic options, regardless of their technical merits, will never come up for debate because cultural or historical reasons preclude the legitimation of the policy.[17]

The preceding argument demonstrates that rhetoric has practical influence on policy adoption and operates within understood and bounded constraints. Rhetorical analysis, therefore, is methodologically sound and potentially quite revealing. This is not an argument that rhetoric is the same as policy. Indeed, it is a softer claim than that made by Morgenthau, wherein rhetoric has discernable concrete effects. My argument is that if rhetoric helps shape policy, then analysis of the rhetorical roots of policy must be part of analyzing policy. Tracing how the framing of ideas and arguments evolves over time offers new depth and nuance in understanding foreign policy actions.

This is not the same as the literature on the influence of ideas on policy, although that literature is related. The difference between that literature and the work presented here is that ideational analysis is fundamentally concerned in one way or another with ideas as causal variables. As Daniel Béland and Robert Henry Cox write, "ideas are causal beliefs."[18] Although they group under this umbrella the process of the dissemination of ideas and political discourse, their ultimate concern is with how ideas effect change. My concern is how the framing of fluid concepts moves the bounds of acceptable policy options and creates space for policy changes. Put differently, my interest is more in how rhetoric changes ideas than how ideas change policy.

Russia offers fertile ground for this analytical approach. Speeches and foreign policy concepts play an unusually large role in the Russian foreign policy process. Most Western states, for example, do not define a specific, codified foreign policy concept.[19] The USSR relied heavily on programmatic policy documents, but Andrei Kozyrev was initially reluctant for post-Soviet Russia to follow that tradition.[20] However, as the debate over whether or how much to orient westward became more heated, foreign policy elites (governmental and otherwise) argued that the government needed to "provide a framework for its foreign policy."[21] The first post-Soviet Foreign Policy Concept was published in January 1993.[22] Since then, the government has approved new official concepts in 2000, 2008, 2013, and 2016. While these concepts are not the definitive statement on the foreign policy that a given leader will conduct, they can be seen as setting the bounds of the debate. Foreign policy documents and their ilk (e.g., the National Security Concept) "define the mental universe within which policy decisions are made."[23] Changes in the documents over time therefore indicate shifts in the acceptable parameters of foreign policy.

Similarly, presidential speeches indicate intentions and agenda setting, as Gordon Hahn argues: "In Russia, the words of the country's leader mean something; they are taken as important signals throughout the bureaucracy and cannot be used to promise important plans that the leadership has no intent of fulfilling. Often cryptic and cautious, they nevertheless provide political orientation to politicians and bureaucrats alike."[24] As with the Foreign Policy Concepts, most speeches are not direct indications of coming policy actions. Instead they reflect how a leader conceptualizes current challenges and how he would have Russia react to those challenges. Taken together, therefore, official policy documents and presidential speeches show how the government wishes to see foreign policy evolve.

In addition, analysis of annual addresses to the Federal Assembly gives a more nuanced perspective on attitude evolution. For example, Vladimir Putin approved a Foreign Policy Concept and a national security concept at the beginning of his first term as president, in 2000. The next formal foreign policy document was not produced until 2007. There are significant differences between the 2000 and 2007 documents, however, and the annual presidential addresses give a window into the source of those differences. Put another way, the 2000 and 2007 documents show a beginning and an end to a process; the annual speeches show the interim steps.

Finally, it is worth noting that Putin himself viewed the annual addresses as policy-setting events. In his 2006 address, he stated that "today's and previous addresses provide the basis for domestic and foreign policy for the next decades."[25] If these speeches, as Putin argued, set the basis for policy, then they can be analyzed to illuminate how policy aims were articulated and how that articulation changed over time.

One final note: given Putin's centrality to shaping policy, this analysis depends heavily on his speeches. This is not the result of a mistaken belief that there are no competing interests among the Russian elite or that Putin is unconstrained by either domestic politics or public opinion. Instead, it is because—especially in the realm of discourse and rhetoric about an issue—what he says matters most. The ideas that influence what he says and how he balances between competing groups are beyond the purview of this study. Instead, the emphasis is on the speeches that are finally given and the policy concepts that are adopted.

Russian Foreign Policy Orientations

With the collapse of the Soviet Union, a fierce debate began over how to formulate the foreign policy of the new Russian Federation. Debate soon turned on efforts to identify and protect national interests. How different sections of the Russian elite chose to define the national interest was intertwined with the broader competing foreign policy orientations under discussion in the early 1990s. The most traditional divide is that between Westernizers and Slavophiles. Dating back to the debates among the members of the proto-intelligentsia of the 1840s, the two groups agreed that Russia needed to modernize and develop economically. They disagreed on the correct method for doing so. Westernizers advocated development according to European principles and pathways. Slavophiles, by contrast, argued that Russia has a special historical and cultural mission and could develop only in accordance with native-born traditions. Since the end of the Cold War, this has been reframed as a debate between Atlanticists and Eurasianists, in which the core question is whether (or how much) to orient toward the institutional and ideological West.[26] Like the original Westernizer/Slavophile debate, the Atlanticist/Eurasianist divide also encompasses debates about whether Russian economic and political development should directly emulate the Western model or if it should instead follow a unique Russian path.[27] While Atlanticism reigned in the very early post–Cold War years, by October 1993 it was no longer the dominant paradigm.[28]

There are different ways of parsing the spectrum of foreign policy perspectives in Russia since the end of the Cold War, but the specifics of the classification schema are less important than the directional drift that took place over the course of the 1990s. While much of the foreign policy elite was initially predisposed to close cooperation with the West and a drive toward liberal ideas, many of those early Atlanticists ultimately moved away from those ideals.[29] By the end of the 1990s foreign policy consensus settled on the group alternately called the Great Power Balancers or the Pragmatic Nationalists.[30] This was the group that was willing to work with the West in areas of coinciding interests, but unwilling to do so at the perceived expense of Russian national interests or sovereignty.

The drift away from the Atlanticist consensus by the elite is important for two reasons. First, it demonstrates that the ongoing prevalence of Pragmatic Nationalists in positions of power is not just a story of loss of power by those inclined to close cooperation with the West. Instead, it is demonstrative of an overall shift in views among the Russian foreign policy elite toward a more nationalistic conception of Russian identity and national interests.[31] This has serious implications for analysis: if the Pragmatic Nationalists had grown primarily from an opposition group, then it might be fair to conclude that there remained a strong basis of Atlanticist elites. Since many of the Atlanticists themselves became Pragmatic Nationalists, it suggests that the views they espouse—moderate Eurasianism, cordial but not subordinate relations with the West, and the pursuit of great power status—represent a broad swath of the Russian foreign policy establishment. That the Pragmatic Nationalist group has persisted in power since 1993 but now allies more closely with nationalists indicates that the shift away from the Atlanticist view has continued and intensified.

It is also significant that it is precisely the Atlanticists who changed their minds. The shift away from the Atlanticist view has strong elements of political disillusionment. Indeed, one reason Kozyrev and his coterie lost ideological control was public and official disappointment with the level of assistance (monetary and otherwise) that Russia received from the West, especially the United States, in managing the detritus of the dissolution of the Soviet Union.[32] The sense that Russia was held to different standards than, for example, Estonia, and that the West had no sympathy for Russian security concerns in its border regions left a bad taste in the collective mouth of the Russian elite.[33] Whether or not this was a fair perception of the realities on the ground (the next section takes up this question), Russian disappointment with the West is a fundamental variable for understanding Russian foreign policy rhetoric and behavior.

Twenty-five years after the collapse of the Soviet Union, the core debate within the Russian foreign policy establishment remains the extent to which Russia should engage with the existing (Western-led) international system and what policy orientation best supports Russian development. Indeed, even the simple Westernizer/Slavophile dichotomy distills down to the same question. No matter how it is parsed, the foreign policy–making elite is in agreement that Russia's main task is development, in pursuit of becoming (or staying) a great power. The crisscrossing debates are over how best to accomplish this aim.

Russia and the West: A Failed Experiment?

As noted above, there was a brief window before the end of 1992 when those in favor of joining the West were politically ascendant and capable of implementing their policy vision without crippling domestic opposition.[34] It is worth posing the question, therefore, of why the debate over Russia's "special path" renewed itself so quickly following dissolution of the Soviet Union. It is an important question because the international institutional choices made during this era have had long-lasting and far-reaching consequences for how Russia engages with the international system.[35]

There are three basic reasons that Russia did not integrate into the Western order in the early 1990s. First, there was an ambiguous embrace from the West. Second, Russia was unwilling to join the existing order as a supplicant with no agency in how the existing organizations operated. Finally, domestic opposition quickly became sufficiently intense to preclude integration while domestic policy choices further closed off international opportunities.

Following the fall of the Berlin Wall and the collapse of the Soviet outer empire in Eastern Europe, there existed a brief opportunity to utterly remake the international system. Mikhail Gorbachev spoke of the need to build "a common European home," and US president George H. W. Bush spoke of "a Europe whole and free."[36] The obvious institutional organ to accomplish this goal was the Conference for Security and Cooperation in Europe (CSCE, later OSCE). Formed as part of the 1975 Helsinki Final Act, the CSCE gave all the major players a seat at the table and an equal voice. Alternatively, the Soviets and the West could have agreed on some type of a new pan-European security structure, including both the North Atlantic Treaty Organization (NATO) and the Warsaw Treaty Organization. This was the path that Gorbachev advocated, especially after he realized the Soviet Union would have no role in a united Germany.[37] For a variety of reasons, including concerns over the dangers of creating new institutions as well as US interests in maintaining power and a footprint on the continent, neither of those options panned out. Instead, the post–Cold War Euro-Atlantic security order was built around the persistence of NATO along with parallel efforts to increase partnership between the Alliance and Soviet successor states, including Russia.

The decision not to disband NATO and the Alliance's subsequent enlargement to former members of the Eastern Bloc are points of bitter disagreement between Russia and the West. Russian leaders, especially since the middle 2000s, argue that NATO's enlargement beyond Germany violates an agreement brokered between the West and the Soviet Union during the negotiations over the reunification of Germany. Most Western scholars disagree with that perspective. Who is right in this debate, however, is ultimately much less important than what the debate signifies. At its root, the disagreement reveals a larger truth that is essential to understanding Russian foreign policy thinking and behavior. From the very beginning there existed profound misunderstandings between the two former Cold War enemies about the future of the European security order and Russia's place in it. From the Russian perspective, these misunderstandings have never been sufficiently addressed. The result has been a Russia that is on the margins of the European order and, more importantly, a Russia that feels itself to be marginalized by the European order.

Samuel Charap terms this stalemate an "integration dilemma."[38] Applying the theory of the security dilemma to the integration processes in post–Cold War Europe, Charap and his coauthor, Jeremy Shapiro, argue that Russia could never have been absorbed into either NATO or the European Union (EU).[39] As a result, "barring a realistic prospect of joining itself, Moscow viewed Euro-Atlantic integration for Russia's neighbors as inherently threatening to Russian interests."[40] In the language of the security dilemma, the West's effort to secure Europe—which was remarkably successful—made Russia feel less secure.

Whether or not the right decisions were made in the early 1990s, those decisions cast a long shadow. The extent to which the Russian elite feels that Russian interests have been encroached on in the post–Cold War institutional settlement, particularly but not exclusively in Europe, remains a key driver of how its leaders conceive of and execute foreign policy. It is important to remember, however, that the Russian leadership has also found it useful to heighten that threat perception for domestic political aims.[41] This leads to the second and third parts of the story: Russian unwillingness to join international organizations as a supplicant and the domestic drivers of that unwillingness.

The basis of Charap and Shapiro's argument that Russia could never have joined either NATO or the EU is that Russia could not agree to a nonnegotiable accession process.[42] This is a problem not only in the Euro-Atlantic context but globally as well. Post-Soviet Russia's circuitous path to membership in organs of global economic governance provides a case in point.

Russia applied for membership in the General Agreement on Tariffs and Trade in 1993, shortly before it became the World Trade Organization (WTO) following the 1994 Uruguay Round.[43] However, Russia's early enthusiasm for membership soon dwindled, and meetings during the 1990s were more about show than substance.[44] Russian negotiators refused to meet their negotiating partners' demands about lowering tariffs and were unwilling to make other concessions required for WTO membership.[45] Russia ultimately would not join the WTO until August 2012.

One reason that successive Russian governments (other than the early years of Putin's first term) were reluctant to pursue WTO membership aggressively is that Russian elites tend to hold economic ideas that run counter to the liberalism ingrained in the WTO.[46] Indeed, a key aspect of the story of Russia's tortuous WTO accession was the shaky support among elites for the economic values the WTO promotes. Despite the efforts of early reformers such as Yegor Gaidar, international experts during the 1990s, longtime Putin adviser and minister of finance Alexei Kudrin, and at times Putin himself, Russia has never accepted the neoliberal economic program that underpins much of global economic governance. Instead, development has depended on large, state-owned enterprises, primarily in the natural resources sector. The average external tariff actually increased throughout the 1990s, beginning at 6.25 percent in 1993 and going as high as nearly 12 percent by 1997.[47] During the 2000s, tariff rates fluctuated considerably but remained higher than the global average tariff until after accession to the WTO in 2012.

Disagreement with liberal economic norms is part of the explanation. So are strong domestic lobbies in Russia, particularly agriculture, which stood to lose from WTO accession. However, it is not the whole story. Equally important is the political side of the story. Russia's unwillingness to join the WTO is an example of a broader phenomenon in the Russian approach to the international system.

Aspirant countries have very little bargaining power with respect to WTO membership terms: accession "primarily involves unilateral tariff or market-access concessions by the prospective member in an effort to secure support for entry."[48] Essentially, joining the WTO means acceding to the demands of other countries, with no ability to change how negotiations are conducted. This is not just a feature of WTO accession. As Russia realized to its dismay throughout the 1990s, aspirants to many dominant international institutions have no agency; they must either accept the rules as written or stay outside the club.[49] All post-Soviet Russian leaders, however, have been generally unwilling to join institutions and organizations that Russia has not helped design.[50]

The story of Russia's integration into the International Monetary Fund (IMF) offers an interesting counterpoint to the WTO accession story. It is further indication of how and when Russia is willing to be incorporated into an existing order. Immediately after the collapse of the Soviet Union, Russia applied for and was granted membership in the IMF. It also succeeded in obtaining a sole directorship, a privilege normally reserved for the most powerful economies.[51]

According to senior IMF officials, it was made clear from the beginning that Russia should get special treatment in its dealings with the IMF.[52] In this case, it was coordinated pressure from Group of Seven (G7) countries (in part as a way of redirecting aid to Russia through the IMF) rather than Russian expectations of special treatment that produced the final outcome.[53] Indeed, Russia had very complicated feelings toward the institution since Soviet leaders had long portrayed it "as a tool of Western capitalism and especially U.S. foreign policy."[54] The IMF is also firmly in the same neoliberal tradition as the WTO. Nevertheless, once G7 leaders decided that aid to Russia should be channeled through the IMF, the country benefited from special treatment in its accession and received preferential membership terms that its economic performance did not necessarily justify.[55] In addition, this was not all due to coordinated pressure from G7 members; Russia actively lobbied G7 members to get its own seat on the executive board.[56]

The reason for Russia's preference for not joining international institutions in which its special status is not recognized leads to the third main reason for its failure to integrate fully into the Western order following the collapse of the Soviet Union. By the middle of 1992, domestic political pressures in Russia had reached a point at which the Yeltsin government could no longer pursue an explicitly pro-Western policy without fear of reprisal at home.[57] Part of the problem was a sense that the post–Cold War order looked very much like the Cold War order, most notably in the persistence of NATO.[58] Economic reform also proved disastrous for the majority of the Russian population, with real wages falling by over one third and personal consumption dropping by 40 percent.[59] These reforms were associated in the popular mind with Western economic advisers.[60] Combined with the rampant corruption during the course of privatization, the process destroyed much public support for the Yeltsin government's perceived deference to Western interests.[61] Simultaneously, Western states had a fiercely negative reaction to Russia's activities during the First Chechen War in 1994. Taken together, these factors opened up space for a renewal of the longstanding debate about Russia's distinctiveness from the West and the wisdom of pursuing a foreign policy not entirely oriented westward.[62]

There was also an ideational aspect to the rise in domestic opposition to the Yeltsin-Kozyrev program: agreement that Russia is a great power and should be treated as such in international affairs.[63] There is a consensus among the Russian elite that the goal of Russian foreign policy should be to return the state to its historic position as a great power with independence of maneuver on the international stage.[64] While the wisdom of this approach remained a subject of public debate throughout the 1990s, the consensus has gone largely unchallenged since 1999.[65] The result of this foreign policy consensus has been a Russia unwilling to embrace the institutional order that emerged after the Cold War because of a sense that to do so would run counter to the core of Russian national identity. That conflict is partly to do with disagreement over norms. It also, however, is intricately tied to the fact that the postwar and post–Cold War institutional order gives the United States, as the order's progenitor and main underwriter, extraordinary political powers.[66] To accede to the order is to accept the United States as the preeminent international power. For Russia, this has always been a bridge too far.

There are several factors in the explanation above that raise questions about whether opportunities were missed or different outcomes might have been achieved with different choices. For example, had NATO not persisted, would Russia have felt so alienated so early? Alternatively, had economic reform been administered better and with less corruption on the part of the Yeltsin government, would there have been such susceptibility to the renewal of the distinctiveness narrative? Ultimately, however, these counterfactuals are useful for interrogation of what went wrong in the 1990s, but they do not change the ending. As a result of Western choices, Russia's unwillingness to accept its newly weakened international position, and the resurgence of domestic opposition, Russian integration with Western institutional structures was essentially off the table (at least in the short and medium term) by the middle of the 1990s. The logical next question, then, is what Russia did instead.

Russian Responses to the Post–Cold War Order

One of Russia's primary objectives following the collapse of the Soviet Union was to maintain those elements of the previous world order in which Russia, as the largest Soviet successor state, would play a leading role—first and foremost the United Nations (UN) because of Russia's permanent seat and veto power in the UN Security Council (UNSC).[67] Indeed, Russian preference for maintaining the primacy of the UNSC as the main arbiter of international legitimacy has been a hallmark of the post–Cold War era.[68] Russia's rhetorical support for the institution has been consistent regardless of the government's willingness to act counter to UN directives or its refusal to allow issues to come before the UNSC when it suited the perceived national interest.

Russia also continued its advocacy for the CSCE (later the Organization for Security and Cooperation in Europe, OSCE) into the 1990s, even after it was clear that NATO would persist and predominate as the prime organ of Euro-Atlantic security. That support declined as Russia perceived that the focus of what was now the OSCE had shifted to human rights and elections in the former Soviet republics while NATO and the European Union took over the competencies of security and economics on the continent.[69] As Foreign Minister Sergei Lavrov explained during the 2010 Munich Security Conference,

> With the disintegration of the Soviet Union and the Warsaw Treaty Organization a real opportunity emerged to make the OSCE a full-fledged organization providing equal security for all states of the Euro-Atlantic area. However, this opportunity was missed, because the choice was made in favor of the policy of NATO expansion, which meant not only preserving the lines that separated Europe during the cold war into zones with different levels of security, but also moving those lines eastward. The role of the OSCE was, in fact, reduced to servicing this policy by means of supervision over humanitarian issues in the post-Soviet space.[70]

It is unlikely that further Russian action would have reversed the preeminence of NATO over the OSCE. It is worth recognizing, however, that Russian support for the institution diminished when it became apparent that the OSCE would no longer serve to maintain or magnify Russian influence.

Parallel to the efforts to maintain and elevate the UN and the OSCE, Russia also pursued a policy of new institutional creation designed to amplify its dominance of the post-Soviet space. First but weakest among these was the Commonwealth of Independent States (CIS), which was established as part of the agreement that dissolved the Soviet Union. However, since the original purpose of the CIS was to facilitate Russian independence from the former Soviet republics, it proved an ineffective mechanism for reviving Russian power once foreign policy objectives shifted in that direction.[71] Nevertheless, the CIS did (and does) provide a very loose framework for regional cooperation.[72]

In the 1990s attention shifted to furthering economic integration among the New Independent States. In 1995, at Kazakhstan's initiative, Russia, Belarus, and Kazakhstan agreed to form a customs union.[73] The agreement was implemented fairly well initially, but backsliding began in 1996, in part because of disagreements over the common external tariff.[74] Economic cooperation continued, however, and in 2000 the initial trade agreement morphed into the Eurasian Economic Community, which included Russia, Kazakhstan, Belarus, Tajikistan, and Kyrgyzstan.[75] In 2003 Russia, Ukraine, Kazakhstan, and Belarus also signed an agreement on creating a common economic space.[76] After being rejuvenated by Putin in very public fashion in 2009, the Customs Union implemented common customs duties in July 2010, and further integration has proceeded apace.[77]

In addition to economic organizations, Russia has also attempted to coordinate regional security cooperation through the creation in 2002 of the Collective Security Treaty Organization (CSTO). CSTO member states include Russia, Belarus, Kazakhstan, Kyrgyzstan, Tajikistan, and (since 2006) Uzbekistan.[78] Putin has consistently attempted to use the CSTO as a basis for cooperation with NATO (especially in Afghanistan), an approach that recalls Gorbachev's argument for cooperation between NATO and the Warsaw Pact.[79] NATO has been unwilling to cooperate with the CSTO, however, and many in the West assume that the CSTO is a mechanism for projecting Russian power among former Soviet republics rather than a legitimate security organization. Whether or not this is the case, and regardless of how effectively the agreements of both the CSTO and the Customs Union are implemented among their members, both organizations have provided Russia with platforms from which to compete rhetorically with Western-led alternatives.[80]

Alternative institutional formation has extended beyond the states of the former Soviet Union. Most notable among these is the Shanghai Cooperation Organization (SCO). The SCO was established in 2001 out of the grouping formerly known as the "Shanghai Five" (Russia, China, Kazakhstan, Tajikistan, and Kyrgyzstan).[81] The SCO has been a useful mechanism for managing the relationship between Russia and China and has been effective at promoting regional economic cooperation (although Russia historically preferred to keep the SCO focused on security to prevent China from gaining the upper hand in leadership).[82] The organization has also attracted interest from other regional powers, notably Iran, India, and Pakistan.[83] During the 2015 SCO summit in Ufa, Russia (held in conjunction with the BRICS summit), India and Pakistan were accepted as full members in the organization.[84] Despite its many failings, the SCO is one of the best examples of Russia's larger institutional approach to its perceived alienation from the post–Cold War Euro-Atlantic order. The SCO has attracted not just former Soviet republics and China but, with the inclusion of India and Pakistan and the participation of Iran and Turkey, other major regional and global powers.[85]

While the SCO has attracted interest from other powers in greater Eurasia, it is regional in scope. BRICS is a signal and singular global element of Russia's creation of parallel institutions. Despite numerous shortcomings, the group "offers both exclusivity and a central role for Russia, regardless of the issues being discussed or the quality of its contributions."[86] It also draws in powers from beyond Eurasia, lending the group the patina of being a global movement. Russian efforts to turn BRICS into a (seemingly) cohesive and organized structure in global governance, important in their own right, also tell the story of Russia's broader efforts to engage with and reshape the world it found itself in following the end of the Cold War.

That story nests the institutional approach within a larger strategic approach: working toward the creation of a multipolar world. Evgenii Primakov was the first to articulate multipolarity as a grand strategy for post-Soviet Russia during his time as foreign minister in the mid-1990s.[87] Primakov put a great deal of emphasis on the importance of building ties with non-Western powers, particularly China and India.[88] The aims of this strategy were to maintain Russian influence in the former Soviet region and to contain US hegemony. The goal of multipolarity has been official Russian doctrine since 1997 and was formally enshrined in the 2000 Foreign Policy Concept that Putin approved in his first year in office.[89]

Multipolarity in its most basic meaning is "the ability of sovereign powers to take political decisions of their own."[90] Implicit in this definition is the idea of balance of power: in a multipolar world, the poles balance against one another to prevent hegemony. In Kremlin usage, multipolarity is specifically a counterbalance to Western "collective unilateralism" and, more broadly, an alternative to globalization.[91] Essentially, Kremlin leaders use the idea of multipolarity to lobby against Western dominance of the international system and for a system in which sovereign states remain the principal actors. Its closest analog is a concert of great powers along the lines of that established by the Congress of Vienna.[92] In the Kremlin's conception, a multipolar world would also provide for the competitive coexistence of different value systems rather than the value homogenization that Western discourse envisions.[93] The homogenization refers not only to values but development profile as well; each country should be able to find a culturally appropriate development system rather than following one uniform model.[94] This is a core feature of the civilizational approach that emerged in Russian rhetoric in the later years of President Putin's second presidential term (discussed in more depth in chapter 4).[95]

The idea of multipolarity as a system based on the actions of sovereign states is critical for understanding one of the primary links between Russia's foreign policy and its domestic context. The domestic twin of multipolarity is sovereign democracy. As Andrei Zagorski argues, "The concept of sovereign democracy . . . does not stipulate the peculiar Russian understanding of democracy but, rather, the principle of state sovereignty."[96] In the Russian view, few states are fully sovereign, meaning few states are able to conduct the foreign policy they wish without fear of repercussions from other global actors.[97] Sovereign states are the leading nations—those that are able to pursue their own national interests and that play a role in shaping and coordinating global governance.[98] In addition, Russia understands sovereignty as the right to control territory, not responsibility to the population.[99] Therefore, sovereign democracy is about the Russian government's right to administer its domestic affairs as it sees fit, without interference, while maintaining the rights of an independent sovereign actor on the international stage.

A corollary to the preference for unfettered freedom of action on the international stage is a preference for informal as opposed to formal alliances. Russian leaders often appeal rhetorically to the primacy of international law and show a preference for legally binding agreements on some specific issues (notably on US plans for ballistic missile defense in Europe).[100] In terms of coalitions and long-term partnership agreements, however, Russia's preference is clearly in favor of informality and flexibility.[101] Indeed, none of the new organizations whose creation Russia has spearheaded includes binding action clauses analogous to Article V of the North Atlantic Treaty. While there are benefits to retaining freedom of action, the penchant for flexibility also creates a situation in which Russia has no guaranteed partners in times of need.

In contrast to the Soviet era, post-Soviet Russia, especially since 2000, has also integrated the need for a strong economy into its conception of power.[102] There is no question that military strength remains a big part of how Russia conceives of power on the international stage. However, by the time Dmitry Medvedev was in power, Russians increasingly associated being a great power with economic development rather than military might.[103] That shift in appreciation of economic power was also evident in government policy. By the end of Putin's second term in office, Russia used economic might more than military prowess to project power.[104] Both the August 2008 war with Georgia and the ongoing conflict in Ukraine are ample evidence that military power remains important. However, economic and political concerns in Russia are intertwined, and economics, whether through energy or otherwise, plays a central role in how Russia engages with the international system. In addition, especially since the 2008 financial crisis, imbalances in the global economic order have taken a more central place in the overall Russian narrative about general imbalance in global governance, as have more explicit criticisms of Western economic norms.

The combination of sovereign democracy at home, a preference for strategic independence and loose partnerships abroad, and an increasing understanding of economics as a source of power provide a further explanation for Russia's lukewarm approach to global economic governance institutions. Under Putin's leadership, Russia has pursued what Nigel Gould-Davies terms "sovereign globalization."[105] The essence of sovereign globalization is an effort to integrate into the global economy enough to reap the benefits of economic growth and exert economic power abroad without sacrificing domestic control to foreign actors. In other words, Putin pursued international economic integration to achieve geopolitical goals.

The concept of "sovereign globalization" offers a useful gloss for understanding myriad components of Putin's approach to the international system. Most important to this investigation, however, is what it means for Russia's relationship with organs of global economic governance. Russia has eschewed membership in international organizations that lessen strategic independence. Consider the two organizations discussed in the previous section: the WTO comes with binding rules about foreign economic policy that curtail the use of trade policy toward political ends and mandate minimum equal treatment of other WTO members through the "Most Favored Nation" clause. The IMF, by contrast, imposes very little on the conduct of foreign economic policy. It therefore offers the image of international economic integration without infringing on freedom of action.

Indeed, all the groups and organizations in global economic governance in which Russia has actively sought membership are characterized by high prestige and low obligations.[106]

Russia has sought minimal international obligations throughout its engagement with the post–Cold War system. That it has done so contrasts sharply with its professed desire to be a great power because "since the nineteenth century, a view has taken hold that being a Great Power in the international arena entails *responsibilities* as well as rights."[107] What Russia seeks, in fact, is not to be a great power but to be recognized as one: to be included as a matter of course in all the high table forums and accorded appropriate *droit de regard*.[108] Bobo Lo explains, "In the end, the value of 'indispensability' comes not from being expected to deliver results—indeed, this is an unwelcome burden—but from others accepting Russia's importance and greatness as incontestable truths."[109]

Post-Soviet Russia's tepid engagement with the international system, its search for prestige without obligations, its efforts to exploit the benefits of global economic integration without paying the costs of openness itself, and its institutional creation in its own neighborhood should all be understood in this context. So too should the push to make BRICS an activist part of the global system without imposing membership costs on BRICS members. Ultimately, post-Soviet Russia wishes to help control the conversation about global governance without assuming the costs of participation in the system.

Seminal Changes in the International System since 1991

Changing relations with the West, and especially the United States, were the primary determinant of Russia's foreign policy posture following the end of the Cold War and the collapse of the Soviet Union. Those interactions, however, took place in a wider context. That broader story is important for understanding why Russia's efforts to bring BRICS together as a political group were ultimately successful.

Immediately following the collapse of the Soviet Union, the columnist Charles Krauthammer famously declared the beginning of the "unipolar moment."[110] He argued that with the end of the Cold War and the demise of the only other power capable of countering the United States, the coming period would be one of unparalleled US dominance in the international arena.[111] The next year Francis Fukuyama proclaimed "the end of history."[112] The scholar argued that democracy had proved itself the only sustainable form of government, the market the only viable basis for an economy, and liberal democracy the victorious "ideology of potentially universal validity."[113] The United States had won the Cold War not only in its material aspect but its ideational one as well.[114]

In some ways the 1990s bore out those arguments. US dominance on all metrics of power, including military, economic, and soft power, made the United States seem untouchable. At the same time, crises around the world sowed discontent with US management of the international system. The Asian financial crisis of 1997, which helped fuel the Russian default in 1998, called into question the wisdom of neoliberal economics. The crises also fueled anger at the United States and the IMF for the harsh remedies imposed in the aftermath of the crises. The war in Kosovo in 1999, pursued without UNSC authorization, was perceived abroad (especially in Russia) as the United States ignoring and breaking international law.

The discontent planted by the policies of the 1990s blossomed in the 2000s, in the wake of the unilateral US invasion of Iraq and George W. Bush's Freedom Agenda. A Pew survey published in June 2007 concluded that international distrust of American leadership had increased overall and that, since 2002, favorable global impressions of the United States had declined worldwide. Those unfavorable impressions were not just about US military activities but were also related to a sense that US policies widened the divide between rich and poor countries and took little account of the desires of other actors.[115]

The Pew survey revealed that the mistrust ran deeper than discrete US policies. It concluded, "In much of the world there is broad and deepening dislike of American values and a global backlash against the spread of American ideas and customs. Majorities or pluralities in most countries surveyed say they dislike American ideas about democracy—and this sentiment has increased in most regions since 2002."[116] In part, this burgeoning mistrust of American values was related to the perception that US democracy became militarized during the Bush presidency.[117] Regardless of the precise cause, the results of this poll are an important indication of the extent to which much of what the United States symbolizes internationally had become a matter of debate and distaste even before the onset of the 2008 financial crisis.[118] This decline, combined with the economic rise of Brazil, Russia, India, and China, opened the door to serious challenges to the US hegemony in the post–Cold War system. Russia's BRICS diplomacy, which began in earnest in 2005, must be understood in this context.[119]

Anger against US global leadership was not the only catalyst for BRICS efforts to reform global economic governance. Profound changes in the distribution of economic power rendered the allocation of effective power in organizations such as the IMF obsolete. For example, in 2007, Indian gross domestic product (GDP) grew at a rate of 9.8 percent and composed 5.3 percent of global GDP as measured in purchasing power parity (PPP). By contrast, French GDP grew at a rate of 1.9 percent and composed 2.9 percent of global GDP (PPP).[120] Nevertheless, France had its own executive director seat on the IMF executive board and 4.87 percent of total IMF votes. India, on the other hand, represented a constituency of four countries that received only 2.36 percent of total votes for the whole group.[121]

The underrepresentation of emerging economies was not just a problem in terms of quota weights; it also had deep effects on the influence of these countries on IMF governance. Ngaire Woods explains, "Executive directors from the United

States, Japan, Germany, France, and the United Kingdom are held directly to account by the government that appoints each. If a director fails to perform . . . he or she can be summarily removed and replaced. By contrast no country in a constituency can require their executive director to resign. Once elected a director stays in office until his or her two-year term has expired."[122] Underrepresentation, therefore, has knock-on effects. Not only do countries have less raw power in the form of voting weight, they also have less power over how their interests are represented in the IMF. The imbalance also tended to make IMF management less responsive to the demands of non–agenda setting countries for information or support as compared to the demands of G7 countries.[123] Finally, in addition to consequences of numeric underrepresentation, there is a long-standing agreement that the head of the IMF would always be European, while the head of the World Bank would be American.[124] This agreement closes off avenues for equally qualified candidates from the developing world to take the helm of either organization.

BRICS is both an antihegemonic project and a logical outgrowth of a changing global political economy. As is discussed in later chapters, for Russia political motivations for BRICS cooperation have mostly outstripped economic motivations. Nevertheless, when BRICS began to coalesce, Russia was one of the new global creditors that desired more say in global economic governance. Russia found common cause with the other BRIC countries because all, to a greater or lesser degree, found global economic governance unfair and counter to their interests. Had there not been an existing and increasing imbalance between economic weight and political power, the BRICS project would have withered before it began. The effort to bring BRICS together as a political group is therefore representative of how post-Soviet Russia has engaged with the international system, but it is also a multicountry response to outdated global economic governance.

Conclusion

Russia has long had a complicated relationship with integration into the dominant international system. A combination of conflicted national identity, a widely held consensus on the importance of the country being accepted as a great power, and a profound disappointment with the West following the end of the Cold War magnified these complications. By the middle of the 2000s, Russian policy had settled into a balance between cooperation and competition with Western-led institutions and a search for influence without obligation.

The Russian dialectic between cooperation and competition with the West took place within an international environment that was also rapidly changing. By the middle of the first decade of the 2000s, US global leadership was increasingly unpopular. At the same time, rapid growth in countries underrepresented in global economic governance forced the question of reform of some international institutions. As a result of these twin processes, long-simmering discontent in the developing world began to manifest as outright efforts to block Western domination of international decision-making. The unipolar moment, if it had ever existed, was over, and history was back.

It was not a political scientist who first grouped together the countries that would go on to symbolize the rise of the developing world. Instead, it was an economist at the investment bank Goldman Sachs. Since the 2001 release of the report "Building Better Global Economic BRICs" heralded the rise of Brazil, Russia, India, and China, the term "BRIC" has spread far beyond Wall Street. The next chapter details that process, examining the history of how Jim O'Neill's BRICs became a political association and what that association has achieved.

Notes

Epigraphs: Berlin, *Soviet Mind*, 85; and O'Neill, "Building Better Global Economic BRICs," S.01–S.03.

    1. Sakwa, "Problem of 'the International,'" 451.

    2. Dubin, "Myth of the 'Special Path'"; and Magaril, "Mythology of the 'Third Rome.'"

    3. Goddard and Krebs, "Rhetoric, Legitimation, and Grand Strategy," 6.

    4. Ibid., 31.

    5. Tjalve and Williams, "Reviving the Rhetoric of Realism," 37.

    6. Ibid., 40.

    7. Ibid., 46.

    8. Morgenthau, *In Defense of the National Interest*, 239–40.

    9. Tjalve and Williams, "Reviving the Rhetoric of Realism," 44.

  10. Gati, *Failed Illusions*, 72.

  11. Ibid., 219.

  12. Scott, "Cold War and Rhetoric," 12.

  13. Gati, *Failed Illusions*, 218.

  14. Ibid., 71.

  15. Ibid.

  16. Clunan, *Social Construction of Russia's Resurgence*, 204.

  17. Goddard and Krebs, "Rhetoric, Legitimation, and Grand Strategy," 11.

  18. Béland and Cox, introduction to *Ideas and Politics*, 3.

  19. Light, "Foreign Policy Thinking," 38.

  20. Ibid., 38–39; and Lo, *Vladimir Putin*, 69.

  21. Light, "Foreign Policy Thinking," 38.

  22. Ibid., 61.

  23. Mankoff, *Russian Foreign Policy*, 16.

  24. Hahn, "Medvedev, Putin, and Perestroika 2.0," 244.

  25. Putin, "Poslanie k Federalnomu Sobraniiu Rossiiskoi Federatsii," May 10, 2006.

  26. Stent, "Reluctant Europeans," 418; and Talbott, "Dangerous Leviathans."

  27. Dubin, "Myth of the 'Special Path,'" 36.

28. Light, "Foreign Policy Thinking," 35.

29. Ibid., 51.

30. Kuchins and Zevelev, "Russia's Contested National Identity," 197; and Light, "Foreign Policy Thinking," 35.

31. Light, "Foreign Policy Thinking," 51.

32. Shiraev and Zubok, *Anti-Americanism in Russia*, 53; and Light, "Foreign Policy Thinking," 84–85.

33. Light, "Foreign Policy Thinking," 84–85.

34. This is not to argue that there was no domestic opposition, merely that Boris Yeltsin and his government were strong enough to override it.

35. Sarotte, *1989*, 5.

36. Nation, *Black Earth, Red Star*, 298; and Bush, "Europe Whole and Free."

37. Sarotte, *1989*, 105.

38. Charap, "Ukraine Crisis: Causes and Consequences."

39. Charap and Shapiro, "New European Security Order," 2.

40. Ibid., 5.

41. Shevtsova, "Post-Communist Russia," 901.

42. Charap and Shapiro, "New European Security Order," 3.

43. Åslund, *How Russia Became a Market Economy*, 152.

44. Darden, *Economic Liberalism and Its Rivals*, 56–57.

45. Ibid., 57.

46. Ibid., 98.

47. Chart, "Tariff Rate, Applied, Weighted Mean, All Products (%)," 1993–2016, World Bank data, https://data.worldbank.org/indicator/TM.TAX.MRCH.WM.AR.ZS?lo cations=RU&view=chart.

48. Darden, *Economic Liberalism and Its Rivals*, 53.

49. Roberts, "Russia's BRICs Diplomacy," 61.

50. Mankoff, *Russian Foreign Policy*, 274.

51. Momani, "Another Seat at the Board," 921. The USSR was originally granted a sole executive director seat but lost it when the country withdrew from the IMF soon after its founding. See ibid., 924.

52. Ibid., 923.

53. Gilman, *No Precedent, No Plan*, 28–29.

54. Ibid., 17.

55. Momani, "Another Seat at the Board," 927.

56. Ibid., 929.

57. Adomeit, "Russia as a 'Great Power' in World Affairs," 45.

58. Mankoff, *Russian Foreign Policy*, 37.

59. Gustafson, *Capitalism Russian-Style*, 171. This is not to argue that reformers faced an easy task or that they went about reform the wrong way. It is simply to note that the Russian population suffered and, rightly or wrongly, that suffering had consequences for Russia's relationship with the United States.

60. Shiraev and Zubok, *Anti-Americanism in Russia*, 55.

61. Hough, *Logic of Economic Reform in Russia*, 7; and Mankoff, *Russian Foreign Policy*, 37. As Shiraev and Zubok point out, the United States also made a useful scapegoat, regardless of the country's actual responsibility or culpability.

62. Dubin, "Myth of the 'Special Path,'" 36.

63. Kuchins and Zevelev, "Russia's Contested National Identity," 182.

64. Clunan, *Social Construction of Russia's Resurgence*, 72; and Mankoff, *Russian Foreign Policy*, 5.

65. Mankoff, *Russian Foreign Policy*, 6; and Tsygankov, "Preserving Influence in a Changing World," 31. It should be noted that Mankoff suggests the lack of challenge may be more due to Putin's repression of the media than genuine consensus.

66. Hopewell, *Breaking the WTO*, 14–15.

67. Zagorski, "Russian Approaches to Global Governance," 28.

68. See, for example, Lavrov, "Face to Face with America," 58.

69. EASI Working Group on Historical Reconciliation and Protracted Conflicts, "Historical Reconciliation and Protracted Conflicts," 4–5. The CSCE formally became the OSCE in January 1995.

70. As reproduced in Tsygankov, "Preserving Influence in a Changing World," 32.

71. Tsygankov, *Russia's Foreign Policy*, 79.

72. Darden, *Economic Liberalism and Its Rivals*, 59.

73. Naumkin, "Russian Policy toward Kazakhstan," 46.

74. Darden, *Economic Liberalism and Its Rivals*, 69–70.

75. Cooley, *Great Games, Local Rules*, 59.

76. Vinokurov, "Eurasian Economic Union: Current State and Preliminary Results," 56.

77. Cooley, *Great Games, Local Rules*, 61. See chapter 5 for a more detailed discussion of the Eurasian Union.

78. Ibid., 56.

79. Ibid.; and Sarotte, *1989*, 105.

80. Cooley, *Great Games, Local Rules*, 72.

81. Chung, "Shanghai Co-Operation Organization," 991.

82. Lo, *Axis of Convenience*, 106–9.

83. Norling and Swanström, "Shanghai Cooperation Organization," 431.

84. Standish, "China and Russia Lay Foundation."

85. Iran currently has observer status in the SCO, while Turkey is a dialogue partner. See "The Shanghai Cooperation Organisation," Shanghai Cooperation Organisation Secretariat, January 1, 2009, http://eng.sectsco.org/about$$ussco/.

86. Lo, *Russia and the New World Disorder*, 78.

87. Makarychev and Morozov, "Multilateralism, Multipolarity, and Beyond," 355.

88. Kuchins and Zevelev, "Russia's Contested National Identity," 188; and Pant, "Feasibility of the Russia-China-India 'Strategic Triangle,'" 52. See the third chapter for a more in-depth discussion of Primakov and the Russia-India-China (RIC) strategic triangle.

89. Panova, "Mesto Rossiia v BRIKS"; and Makarychev and Morozov, "Multilateralism, Multipolarity, and Beyond," 355.

90. Makarychev, *Russia and the EU*, 57.

91. Makarychev and Morozov, "Multilateralism, Multipolarity, and Beyond," 354, 361.

92. Legvold, "Role of Multilateralism," 27.

93. Zagorski, "Russian Approaches to Global Governance," 31. A more recent iteration of the idea of multipolarity is "polycentrism," but the underlying meaning is the same.

94. Silvius, "Embedding of Russian State-Sanctioned Multipolarity," 10.

95. Nikonov, "Ot Kontserta derzhav k Kontsertu tsivilizatsii."

96. Zagorski, "Russian Approaches to Global Governance," 32.

97. Ibid.

98. Ibid., 32–33.

99. Makarychev and Morozov, "Multilateralism, Multipolarity, and Beyond," 362.

100. On the primacy of international law, see Lavrov, "Face to Face with America," 46. The BRICS summit statements all stress the primacy of international law, suggesting that, at least from a rhetorical perspective, Russia finds common cause on this issue with its BRICS partners.

101. Tsygankov, "Preserving Influence in a Changing World," 29.

102. Wallander, "Russia," 141.

103. Tsygankov, "Preserving Influence in a Changing World," 31.

104. Stent, "Restoration and Revolution in Putin's Foreign Policy," 1089.

105. Gould-Davies, "Russia's Sovereign Globalization," 2.

106. Ibid., 11–12.

107. Smith, "Russia and Multipolarity since the End of the Cold War," 44. Emphasis original.

108. Lo, *Russia and the New World Disorder*, 50.

109. Ibid.

110. Krauthammer, "Unipolar Moment."

111. Ibid.

112. Fukuyama, *End of History and the Last Man*.

113. Ibid., 39–42.

114. On the role of ideas in the Cold War, see Nau, "Ideas Have Consequences," 460.

115. Pew Research Center, "Global Unease with Major World Powers," 5.

116. Ibid.

117. Ibid, 6. It is worth noting that although trust in the United States had declined, there was also deep skepticism of the challengers to US global leadership, such as Venezuela, and considerable fear of the rise of China.

118. George W. Bush is not the only cause of the decline of trust in the United States. A WIN/Gallup poll from 2013, a year into Obama's second term, had similar findings to the 2007 Pew survey. See Sarah Wolf, "A New Poll Says These Nations Are the Top 4 Threats to World Peace. Guess Who's Number One." *GlobalPost*, January 3, 2014, https://www.pri.org/stories/2014-01-03/new-poll-says-these-nations-are-top-4-threats-world-peace-guess-whos-number-one.

119. Andreev, "BRIKS," 127.

120. "World Economic Outlook Database," October 2007 edition, https://www.imf.org/external/pubs/ft/weo/2007/02/weodata/index.aspx.

121. Kenen, "Reform of the International Monetary Fund," fig. 1. In the portion of the quota formula that accounts for GDP, the IMF uses a weighted mix of GDP measured in PPP and GDP measured in market exchange rates (MER), with a bias toward the latter. This bias is its own source of friction between emerging markets and advanced economies because GDP (MER) tends to understate dramatically the weight of developing economies. For more, see Callen, "PPP versus the Market."

122. Woods, *Globalizers*, 192.

123. Ibid.

124. Kenen, "Reform of the International Monetary Fund," 12.

2

From BRIC to BRICS

An Institutional History

> Today, the BRICs have become essential players in major international
> decision-making. As such, we are acutely aware of our potential as agents of
> change in making global governance both more transparent and democratic.
> —Luiz Inácio Lula Da Silva, 2010

A COMPLETE AND UNINTERRUPTED HISTORY OF THE INSTITUTIONAL
development of BRICS is useful grounding for the deeper analysis of the term's
evolution in Russian discourse and evaluation of its impact. The goal in this
chapter, therefore, is to give a straightforward institutional history of BRICS and
an assessment of its accomplishments through its landmark 2014 summit, divorced
from the changing ways in which Russia approached the group over time. The
2015 and 2016 summits are dealt with separately in later chapters.

The chapter proceeds in two parts. The first part approaches BRICS development from a qualitative perspective. It begins with a brief account of how the
term "BRIC" jumped from the private sector to the public sphere, emphasizing
how the idea fit with other notions in the intellectual ether of the time. It then
looks at three institutional antecedents of BRICS: Evgenii Primakov's "Strategic
Triangle" of Russia, India, and China (RIC); the India-Brazil–South Africa Dialogue Forum (IBSA); and the Outreach 5 (O5) or the G8+5 process. The narrative then turns to BRICS itself, looking at the group's early years and its rapid rise
to prominence in the wake of the 2008 global financial crisis. The qualitative
analysis concludes with a consideration of achievements through the 2014 Fortaleza summit.

The second part of the chapter presents BRICS from a quantitative perspective. This quantitative snapshot of main economic indicators gives visual and
numerical representations of how the economic relationships among these countries have evolved from the initial BRICS appellation in 2001 to the present day.
The generally weak economic relationships also vividly underscore that politics
provides a stronger rationale for continued cooperation than economics. The

quantitative section concludes with a numerical summary of the institutionalization of BRICS through 2016.

One final note: the question of how to define BRICS remains an ongoing
concern for both the politicians engaged with it and the academics who study it.
The official Russian term is *obedinenie* (association). "Group" is another term
used frequently in both Russian and non-Russian literature and is arguably a more
neutral term than "association." Still others have spoken about BRICS as a "quasi-
organization," a term as cumbersome as it is unhelpful. I shall for the most part
speak just of "BRICS," with the understanding that these countries are coordinating in a way that makes it conceptually rational to speak of common goals and
activities but are not (yet) sufficiently institutionalized to merit a more formal
designation. However, for the sake of linguistic variety, throughout the text I
employ the terms "forum," "group," and "association" interchangeably.[1] On a more
technical note, other than discussions related specifically to pre-2011 cooperation
(before South Africa joined), I use the expanded group name (BRICS) to discuss
general achievements and goals.

BRICS Beginnings

The term "BRIC" first appeared in a 2001 analytical report called "Building Better Global Economic BRICs," authored by Jim O'Neill, then head of global economics research at Goldman Sachs.[2] The paper was inspired by O'Neill's
realization, spurred in part by the terrorist attacks of September 11, 2001, that in
the future, "globalization" would no longer be synonymous with "Americaniza-
tion."[3] The report's goal was to identify the likely future leaders of the global
economy, based on anticipated GDP growth rates, GDP per capita, and population size.[4] Using these parameters, O'Neill concluded that the expected share of
global GDP of Brazil, Russia, India, and China (BRIC) could be expected to grow
substantially over the coming years.[5]

O'Neill was not blind to the potential political implications of his analysis. In
his paper, he argued that based on the figures presented, "it seems quite clear that
the current G7 needs to be 'upgraded' and room made for the BRICs in order to
allow more effective global policymaking."[6] However, his emphasis was very much
on these four countries as large economies, not as global political actors, and his
immediate audience was his own firm's clients.[7]

Indeed, O'Neill's paper was so successful from the perspective of Goldman's
marketing department that in 2003 two of his colleagues released a follow-up
report entitled *Dreaming with BRICs: The Path to 2050.*[8] This report was if anything aimed more specifically at an investor audience than was its predecessor.
Even so, it was with this report that the idea of BRIC made the leap from the
private sector to the public sphere.[9] The idea of the rise of the non-Western world
was compelling because it capitalized on the simultaneous increase in economic

fortunes in the Global South and the growing discontent with American international leadership as a result of the beginning of the Iraq War.[10]

The 2003 report also had the good fortune to be released as the countries were themselves beginning to think about how increasing South-South cooperation would be to their benefit. For example, in December 2002 then president-elect of Brazil Luiz Inácio Lula da Silva announced that he would make improving ties with rising powers, especially China, India, and Russia, a priority for his administration's foreign policy; Celso Amorim, Lula's minister of external relations, added Mexico and South Africa to the list shortly thereafter.[11]

There was therefore some luck in how the "BRIC" term took hold. Goldman Sachs was not the only company thinking about the role of these countries in the coming century; O'Neill was not even the first to publish on the topic. On the business side, Deutsche Bank and PricewaterhouseCoopers both did work on which countries to watch.[12] On the academic side, authors including Ignacy Sachs, Jeffrey Garten, and Robert Chase were writing about the possible political economic and policy impact of rising states.[13] The BRIC acronym, however, had the virtue of coming from one of the world's most prominent investment banks, of being clever and catchy, and of being reinforced by external events not driven by Wall Street. While the BRICS group has come to be seen as an unexpected outgrowth of O'Neill's investment strategy, the groundwork for a network of these countries was already developing parallel to the succession of reports coming out of Goldman Sachs's analytical department.

BRICS Institutional Roots: RIC, IBSA, and the O5

Although no one expected the BRIC countries to organize into an independent political bloc and then add to their number, the idea of these countries coordinating with one another did not originate with the advent of the term "BRIC" itself. Instead, their coordination has three distinct institutional roots: Evgenii Primakov's "Strategic Triangle" of RIC; IBSA; and the Outreach 5 (O5), initiated by the Group of Eight (G8) at the 2005 Summit in Gleneagles, Scotland. All three groups—two initiated by the countries themselves and one by Western powers—have different origins and purposes, but each played an important part in fostering the development of BRICS.

The earliest antecedent to BRICS is RIC, initially proposed by Evgenii Primakov in 1998 while he was prime minister of Russia. RIC was an explicit effort to balance against the West by aligning with non-Western great powers. Fearing that the proposal was too antagonistic toward the United States, neither China nor India was enthused by it when it originally emerged. However, in the face of geopolitical shifts, growing Russo-Chinese ties, and the gradual normalization of Sino-Indian relations, interest in the idea grew in Beijing and Delhi.[14] Officials from the three countries began gathering on the sidelines of international meetings in 2003, and the first stand-alone meeting of RIC foreign ministers took place in Vladivostok, Russia, in 2005. The leaders first met in the RIC format at the sidelines of the 2006 G8 meeting in St. Petersburg.[15]

Although the leaders have met under RIC auspices, there has never been an independent RIC leaders' summit, and the RIC dialogue is coordinated primarily through the foreign ministries. The primary operational focus of RIC is increasing regional security in Eurasia. However, it also includes formal cooperation on agriculture, poverty, and health as well as some emphasis on nongovernmental contacts.[16] Despite an expanding official agenda, however, actual intra-RIC cooperation remains low. Scholars in all three countries remark on RIC's unfulfilled potential, and there are regular academic forums and diplomatic meetings, but the group has never attracted sustained attention from top political leadership.

From the perspective of RIC as an antecedent to BRICS, there are two significant points. It was the first somewhat formalized group that brought Russia, India, and China together. More importantly, the ideological basis of both RIC and BRICS, especially from the Russian perspective, is almost identical. Putin himself speaks of RIC primarily as the progenitor of BRICS.[17] In an examination of Russian policy toward BRICS, then, the antecedent of RIC is critical, even if RIC itself has been somewhat underwhelming.

The next forum to emerge was IBSA, which was formalized in the June 2003 Brasilia Declaration.[18] The decision to form the group was spurred in part by anger with the G8. In 2003 the leaders of India, Brazil, and South Africa were invited to attend the G8 summit in Evian, France, but the leaders left feeling as though their presence had been more ornamental than substantive.[19] The countries agreed to form IBSA three days later.[20]

IBSA describes itself as an informal group designed to promote cooperation among countries of the Global South. The group is in many ways a more logical and cohesive group than either RIC or BRICS. The countries all have democratic political systems, they all lack representation on the UNSC, and they all have similar challenges to overcome, including significant income inequality and a multiethnic and multilingual population.[21] Like RIC, IBSA never achieved the worldwide name recognition that BRICS enjoys, although IBSA too continues to meet as an independent forum. IBSA held annual independent leaders' summits but has not done so since the meeting set for 2014 was postponed and never rescheduled (though the IBSA foreign ministers met on the sidelines of the 2018 BRICS summit in Johannesburg).[22] Part of the problem is that while India still values IBSA as a separate grouping, both South Africa and Brazil seem to prefer BRICS.[23]

IBSA constitutes the second building block of BRICS for two main reasons. First, it is the forum that brought together the democratic members of BRICS for the first time. Second, and no less important, it is the origin of the BRICS mantle of representing the Global South, something the BRICS group claims but which the RIC great power premise could not support.[24]

The final piece of the institutional mosaic that formed the foundation for BRICS is the Outreach 5, also known as the G8+5 or (later) the Heiligendamm Process. Initiated by British prime minister Tony Blair for the 2005 G8 summit in Gleneagles, the O5 came about in large part as a result of increasing generalized anxiety about the legitimacy of the G8 on the part of both its membership and those who felt they were (wrongly) excluded.[25] The five countries invited to the summit as part of the initiative were China, India, Brazil, Mexico, and South Africa.[26] Since Russia was then a member of the G8, all the future BRICS were present. The O5 had a fairly limited mandate; it was initially convened to consider "issues of climate change, clean energy, and sustainable development."[27] That focus has broadened somewhat to include investment, development, and technology as the O5 has evolved into the Heiligendamm Process.[28]

With the rise of the Group of Twenty (G20) following the 2008 financial crisis, the inclusion of outside powers at G8/G7 meetings is less important, and the O5 is not consistently included in G8/G7 meetings.[29] At the time of its initiation, however, the O5 constituted an explicit recognition from traditional powers that global governance architecture was not sufficiently representative or inclusive. As the independent creation of RIC and IBSA demonstrate, those outside the G8 did not need to be told that they were underrepresented. What is conceptually important about the creation of the O5 is that it signified a point at which it was not just global malcontents who wished to change the system. Instead, all the major states seemed to be reaching the conclusion that the system that had persisted in various permutations since the end of World War II needed serious adjustment.

RIC, IBSA, and the O5 never made headline news. Although they all persist in some form, each is also weaker than BRICS itself, and none meet regularly. Together, though, they serve as important precedents for cooperation among traditionally peripheral powers with the specific aim of addressing global problems and revising the existing architecture of global governance.

BRIC Begins to Organize

In the midst of the institutional innovation of RIC, IBSA, and the O5, the idea began to take hold in Brazil and Russia of deploying the BRIC designation to achieve political aims.[30] Coordination among the countries began in 2005 with a meeting of the deputy foreign ministers.[31] The following year, at Russian president Vladimir Putin's initiative, the four foreign ministers met on the sidelines of the UN General Assembly. The first meeting of heads of state took place on the sidelines of the 2008 G8 in Hokkaido, Japan, again at Russia's behest.[32] At that meeting the leaders agreed to hold the first stand-alone BRIC summit in Ekaterinburg, Russia, the following year; the group has met annually at the heads of state level ever since. The transformation of the group from investment strategy to political forum was completed in 2011, when South Africa joined and BRIC became BRICS.

This initial period from 2005 to 2008 reveals two significant elements of BRIC's coalescence. First, it shows that the impetus for these early meetings came from the very top. For example, Vyacheslav Trubnikov, who served as ambassador to India from 2004 to 2009 and would have been a logical candidate for priming his Indian counterparts for a meeting, was not involved in arranging the 2006 meeting at the United Nations.[33] Although academic institutions were involved in refining the ideas at the beginning, BRICS began as a very top-down initiative.[34]

The second conceptual novelty of the early period is how little it involves anyone from an economic ministry. All of the initial gatherings, or at least those in the public record, were of representatives from the foreign ministry or, later, the leaders themselves. In Russia the idea originated in the policy planning section of the foreign ministry, and only later were economic ministries included in the process.[35] Further, the Russian foreign ministry has no formal authority over foreign economic policy. This suggests that the initial overtures from the Russian side were concerned with politics rather than economics. The other countries had more interest in geo-economics, as evidenced by the initial 2006 agreement to focus primarily on increasing cooperation with respect to trade and management of the international financial system.[36] However, other than sideline meetings at the semiannual World Bank and IMF meetings, coordination involved primarily the foreign ministers and their deputies until after the onset of the financial crisis.[37]

This early decoupling of "BRIC as a political entity" from "BRIC as an investment strategy" is exemplified in the ire that South Africa's initial exclusion from the group incurred in Pretoria.[38] From the very beginning of BRIC coordination on the international stage, South Africa lobbied for inclusion.[39] South African president Jacob Zuma wrote a letter to the group in 2009 seeking membership, and in 2010 he lobbied each of the original BRIC members individually, sometimes bringing large delegations of businessmen to highlight the trade opportunities that existed.[40] Although the lobbying focused on business, the goal was to project "South Africa as an emerging power and regional leader."[41] The South African leadership also saw significant convergence between South African and BRIC foreign policy goals.[42]

The implication is that South Africa was not unhappy that Jim O'Neill did not name it as one of the four emerging economies to watch in 2001. Instead, the problem was being excluded as BRIC began to cooperate as a political organism.[43] As Francis Kornegay Jr., an American-born scholar who lives and works in South Africa, writes: "As BRIC has become BRICS, the resulting quintet, in jazz-like fashion, has retuned itself in accordance with the rhythmic beat originally intended—one having nothing to do with the increasingly discordant notes in the global financial districts of an occupied Wall Street."[44] Note Kornegay's assumption that cooperation among the BRIC(S) countries was never governed by Goldman's parameters. South Africa from the beginning understood BRIC as a political initiative designed to challenge the global status quo. Attaining BRICS membership has helped South Africa solidify its regional role and could be considered one of the main policy achievements of the Zuma administration.[45]

South Africa is not alone in its understanding of BRICS. The BRICS group that now exists is entirely distinct from Jim O'Neill's "global economic BRICs."[46] According to Georgii Toloraya, CEO of the National Committee for BRICS Research in Russia, BRICS is first and foremost a political group.[47] Most of the coordination happens in international financial organizations, but the fight is over political control of the organs of global economic governance. Further, long-term goals are broader, including (on the part of the IBSA contingent) an expansion of the UNSC. The end goal, as Nandan Unnikrishnan put it, is "to redesign the world"; the BRICS countries wish to revise the current system to the point that they have more voice and agency.[48]

A Brief Digression: What Is Global Governance?

At this point it is necessary to consider more fully what the BRICS group and its antecedent organizations mean when they express a concern for increased legitimacy in organs of global governance. "Global governance" is a vague term that means many different things depending on context and audience. For BRICS, however, it has come to have a quite specific meaning that is worth parsing more explicitly. This section first offers a general definition of global governance. It then identifies the primary loci of BRICS's dissatisfaction.

Thomas Weiss and Ramesh Thakur define global governance as "the sum of laws, norms, policies, and institutions that define, constitute, and mediate relations among citizens, society, markets, and the state in the international arena."[49] Organs of global governance include international institutions such as the IMF and United Nations, international courts, and multinational companies as well as prevailing norms and expectations.[50] They also increasingly include informal constellations of countries, such as the G7 and the G20.

Although global governance itself is rather all encompassing, it can be broken down into discrete systems that manage different sectors.[51] For example, financial/economic global governance is composed of institutions such as the IMF and WTO, groups including the G7 and G20, and a host of regional organizations such as the Organization for Economic Cooperation and Development or the EU. Energy governance, by contrast, includes the International Atomic Energy Agency, the Energy Charter Treaty Organization, and the International Renewable Energy Agency, among others. These systems are crosscutting—for example, the EU deals with much more than economics, and the International Atomic Energy Agency is one of a number of agencies under the broader UN umbrella. Together these discrete systems of sectoral governance compose the global order.

As the broad definition by Ramesh and Thakur indicates, there is also an ideational aspect of global governance. These are the norms that underlie the different systems and organizations discussed above. Since the end World War II, international norms have been defined primarily by economic and political liberalism. On the economic side, the drive has been toward increasingly open markets and freer capital flows. While economic liberalism was mediated during the first three decades of the postwar era, it became increasingly unfettered after the collapse of the Bretton Woods system in the early 1970s. Especially since the end of the Cold War, the system has pushed for increased deregulation and more dependence on the "invisible hand" of the market.[52]

Political norms focus on issues such as governance and human rights. This area has also evolved substantially since the end of the Cold War. Most notable is the increased focus on democracy as the best form of government and the acceptance of intervention into domestic affairs in the event of state failure to protect its population (codified in 2005 as the Responsibility to Protect). Political norms are in some ways more controversial than economic norms, not because they sow more discontent but because they are tied more closely to who is considered a "legitimate actor" in the system. The main grievances of the RIC/IBSA countries, later standardized in BRICS statements, are primarily institutional and ideational. While most of the BRICS countries are still reasonably protectionist at home and argue for structural rather than neoliberal developmental models, they do not wish to overturn the global consensus on economic liberalism.[53]

The ideational objection is that Western hegemony is no longer appropriate in global governance. There has long been concern over Western dominance of international institutions, and nations outside the ideological West, particularly in the developing world, have long felt a lack of ownership in the American-dominated international order.[54] General concern and specific protests have crystallized in recent years, however, as a result of shifts in economic power and perceived Western violations of international law, in particular disregard for national sovereignty.[55] The BRICS countries seek a world order that allows for a multiplicity of values and domestic orders rather than the perceived imposition of a single set of norms and standards. The quarrel is not necessarily with democracy or protecting human rights per se but rather with what both democratic and autocratic members of BRICS see as the West's selective application of those principles for their own gain.[56]

The ideational objection can seem easier to dismiss, especially since the BRICS countries have not substituted an alternative normative framework. The institutional objections, however, have remained distinct and concrete since the initial BRIC meetings. The BRICS group's demands tend to center on two institutions: the IMF and the UNSC.[57] When BRICS summit documents speak of the need for more democratic international relations, they refer in particular to increased quota and voting weights in the IMF and expanding the UNSC to include India, Brazil, and South Africa. As discussed in the first chapter, voting weights in the

IMF do not represent the contemporary distribution of economic power. The same might be said of the UNSC regarding political power. The IBSA countries have long histories of seeking permanent UNSC seats with veto power. China and Russia, in the context of BRICS, rhetorically support these countries' goal to have a larger voice in the United Nations but have not explicitly endorsed UNSC expansion.[58]

Throughout the remainder of this study, the idea of reforming global governance is used in reference specifically to these concerns and demands: the general desire for the West to cede ideational control and the localized concerns about representation in the IMF and the UNSC. These also are some of the concerns that RIC, IBSA, and the O5 aimed to address, from different angles. The bases of these concerns and the extent to which they are linked to anti-Americanism or rooted in real grievances with the dominant system are addressed in more detail in chapter 5.

The Global Financial Crisis, the Rise to Prominence, and Nascent Institutionalization

Although the BRIC countries began meeting in 2005, they forged as a group only in the crucible of the 2008 global financial crisis. They quickly became an important subgroup in the newly prominent G20.[59] At Brazil's initiative, the finance ministers began meeting as a group following the 2008 G20 in São Paolo. In 2009 the finance ministers met twice to coordinate their positions for upcoming G20 meetings.[60] That coordination paid dividends. The high-water mark of BRIC visibility and success within the G20 came at the 2009 Pittsburgh summit, when the group was able to push through significant reforms on weights and quotas within the IMF. As a mark of their influence at the time, then–US treasury secretary Timothy Geithner met with the countries as a group, the only time a US official has met with BRIC(S).[61]

Since the 2009 G20, much BRICS coordination has focused on strengthening relations among members of the group rather than acting as a bloc to achieve ends in larger international arenas. This is in part because the IMF quota and governance reforms agreed to in 2010 remained stuck in the US Congress until December 2015, despite pressure from IMF leaders.[62] However, this may have been something of a blessing in disguise in the long term. While all five countries would have preferred to see the reforms go through more quickly, the forced focus on building the internal aspect of BRICS was not wasted effort.

The leaders' summits get most of the press, but they are only the tip of the iceberg when it comes to coordination and cooperation within the BRICS framework. The countries have slowly ramped up their cooperation; it now includes working groups on topics ranging from health to agriculture to education. Some of these working groups are ultimately more about photo ops than substance, but some do significant work. For example, in 2012 the countries established the

BRICS Think Tank Council (BTTC).[63] The BTTC comprises specific institutes in each country designated to act as BRICS research centers, and it supports the academic forums that have run annually (in various forms) since 2008. At the fifth summit in 2013 in Durban, South Africa, the group created the BRICS Business Forum. The BRICS Business Forum is an analog to the B20 (a forum through which international business leaders provide policy recommendations to the G20); it formalizes the business meetings that began during the 2011 summit in Sanya, China.[64]

These are not just empty statements and institutions. The national think tanks that are part of the BTTC, and the yearly academic forums they support, have produced a wide variety of reports. Shortly after its formation, the BTTC began work on a strategic concept for BRICS, spurred in part by a paper authored by several Indian experts from the Observer Research Foundation, the Indian arm of the BTTC; these reports were followed by a more comprehensive report on BRICS principles in 2017.[65] In 2017, in preparation for its BRICS presidency, China formed a BRICS Think Tank Network to coordinate the work of all Chinese think tanks that focus on BRICS and related issues. The Russian arm, the National Committee for BRICS Research, is also active. It has produced several monographs and edited volumes, hosts large international conferences on a regular basis, and circulates semiregular bulletins summarizing recent BRICS research.[66]

On a more concrete level, the BTTC has supported socialization among academics from the different countries, bringing what began as a very leader-led initiative further down into the respective societies. The feedback loop is not (yet) reciprocal: the ideas from the academic forums tend not to make it into the final summit statements. However, their persistence and the substantive research presented at the forums are signs of BRICS making it down to another level of local elites. More broadly, the cross-pollination of ideas among scholars from the Global South is an indication of how BRICS has facilitated the multipolarization of ideas about international relations and global governance away from Western-centric discourse.[67]

The most significant BRICS achievements to date happened during the 2014 summit in Fortaleza, Brazil. The Fortaleza summit is important for two reasons: one about optics and one about actions. The 2014 summit was the sixth BRICS summit. It marked the beginning of the second summit rotation. All the member countries have now hosted at least once. Further, every member other than South Africa (at the time) had retained its interest in the group through a change in leadership, and no leader has ever missed a summit. The group can therefore point to an institutional track record of convening on an annual basis that has survived to repeat hosting and new administrations in both its democratic and nondemocratic members. This shows that the group has staying power.

More important are the deliverables from the sixth summit. In Fortaleza, the leaders agreed to establish a BRICS development bank (the New Development

Bank, NDB) and a currency pool, the Contingency Reserve Arrangement (CRA).[68] It is too soon to judge how well these institutions will function, but they are significant not just because they are the first concrete BRICS institutions but also because they represent the first time that BRICS membership has imposed a cost on its members. Until Fortaleza, one of the main benefits of BRICS was that it offered members some level of extra clout within international forums without also imposing costs for membership.[69] The NDB and the CRA are modest by international standards: the NDB has initial authorized capital of $50 billion, and the CRA has committed funds of $100 billion.[70] The initial sums notwithstanding, the creation of these institutions indicates a growing willingness among members to devote more than just their voices to the BRICS cause. The NDB officially launched in July 2015 in Shanghai and has a full slate of projects working on green development across the five BRICS countries.[71]

There is another element of this institutional creation that bears mention. Much of the criticism of BRICS's viability focuses on the many divisions among the member countries, particularly on the animosity between India and China. That these five countries were able to agree on who hosted the bank (China), who would be the first president (India), and that the bank would operate on a "one country, one vote" basis despite China's economic preeminence suggests that the five are learning to cooperate as a group.[72] The significance of that agreement should not be overblown, but it is also a step forward in BRICS cooperation and cohesion.

China (officially) sees the NDB as supportive of its Asian International Infrastructure Bank (AIIB), although the AIIB is a much larger and more multilateral undertaking with double the initial capitalization.[73] Kundapur Vaman Kamath, the first NDB president, stated that the two institutions would closely cooperate.[74] While their missions are somewhat iterative of each other, they have different geographic scopes. The AIIB focuses specifically on development financing in Asia whereas the NDB has a global remit and an office in South Africa.[75] Together the two institutions represent China's effort to make its mark in development financing as well as the lessening of the dominance of the Bretton Woods institutions in international financial architecture.[76] The extent to which other BRICS countries, and China since the NDB's creation, see the AIIB and NDB as complementary as opposed to contradictory is discussed in further detail in chapter 6.

The question of how new institutions interact with one another leads to the larger question of whether these new institutions are supportive of or destructive to the current global economic order. The answer goes both ways. If lending from the NDB comes without the governance and other requirements that are hallmarks of World Bank and IMF programs, the NDB will do damage to the political side of the current economic order. If, by contrast, the NDB follows through on its pledge to work with existing banks including not only the AIIB but also World Bank Group institutions such as the Asian Development Bank, then it could

presumably help to fill real gaps in global infrastructure funding without destroy-
ing the fabric of global economic norms. However, the mere existence of the
plethora of new organs of global economic governance, including but not limited
to the NDB and the AIIB, will give countries the option of working through a
primary partner less likely to impose rules about domestic political or economic
order as part of loan conditionality. That could have consequences.[77]

Kristen Hopewell, in her book *Breaking the WTO*, suggests a distinction between
antisystemic intent and antisystemic effect.[78] Her basic argument is that countries
including Brazil, India, and China have largely accepted the principles of neolib-
eralism in their foreign economic policy (domestic economics is another story),
particularly regarding international trade. The problem is that in demanding
equal treatment in organizations such as the WTO (for example, by pressing for
open agricultural markets in developed economies), these rising powers have
rendered the system nonfunctional. Neither developed nor developing countries
wield enough power to break the deadlock in negotiations, leading to institutional paralysis.[79] While not all organs of economic governance have faced the
same travails as the WTO, the broader point applies. The proliferation of alternative institutional options beyond those tied to the postwar liberal order have the
potential to have detrimental second-order effects even if they were founded to
fill gaps rather than to punch holes.

BRICS is still in its early days, and it would be unwise to make predictions
about its prospects. Indeed, since the flurry of measurable activity at the Fortaleza
summit, BRICS activity has generated more light than heat, despite (or perhaps
because of) the increasing number of annual BRICS events and paragraphs in
summit declarations. What does seem clear, however, is that the group now operates like an international club, with privileges for its members and mechanisms
for observers and dialogue partners.[80] It also has a policy outlook and, if implemented, an ambitious agenda that pushes both intragroup and lobbying cooperation forward.[81] Furthermore, its track record indicates that it continues to be a
group in which its members find value and to which its members are willing to
devote not only time but financial resources as well. This suggests that BRICS,
even if just at the leaders' level, is likely to remain a permanent feature of the
global governance landscape.

BRICS by the Numbers

The previous sections have detailed BRICS's institutional development from a
qualitative perspective. This section considers BRICS from a quantitative angle,
looking specifically at the following indicators: GDP growth, share of global GDP,
GDP per capita, major trade partners of each BRICS country, and institutional
trends.

The purpose of this analysis is not to provide a quantitative picture that mirrors the qualitative picture. Instead, it is to show that economic relations are not sufficient to explain overall BRICS institutionalization. In addition, and somewhat in contrast to the previous point, much of the motivation for intra-BRICS cooperation is to promote economic development in each country. Although my focus is the political aspect of the group and its development as a cohesive international organization, internal cooperation composes the majority of BRICS activities at this point. It is therefore important to explore, however briefly, the extent to which these countries invest in economic relations with their BRICS partners.

BRICS and the World Economy

The general economic picture is unsurprising. First and foremost, China is the economic giant of the BRICS countries on all metrics. Second, and also important, over the last decade all the BRICS countries generally grew at a faster pace than either the G7 as a group or most individual G7 member (figures 2.1 and 2.2). Growth has been slowing overall for several years, but it was not until the 2014 crises in Brazil, Russia, and South Africa, and the uptick in growth in the United States, that any G7 economy showed stronger growth than the BRICS countries. Indian and Chinese growth—the strongest in BRICS for most of the group's history—remains well above average G7 growth, even accounting for both countries' recent economic troubles.

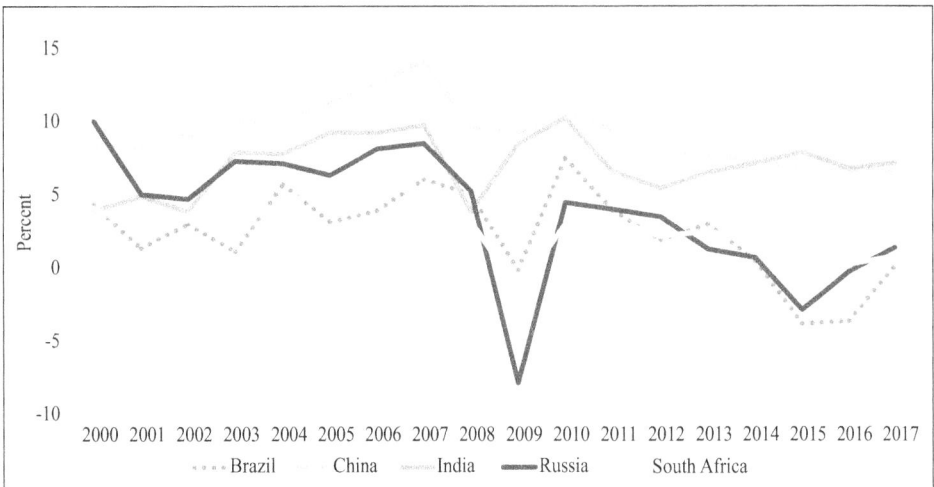

Figure 2.1 BRICS GDP Growth (estimated after 2016)

Data Source: International Monetary Fund World Economic Outlook Database, April 2017.

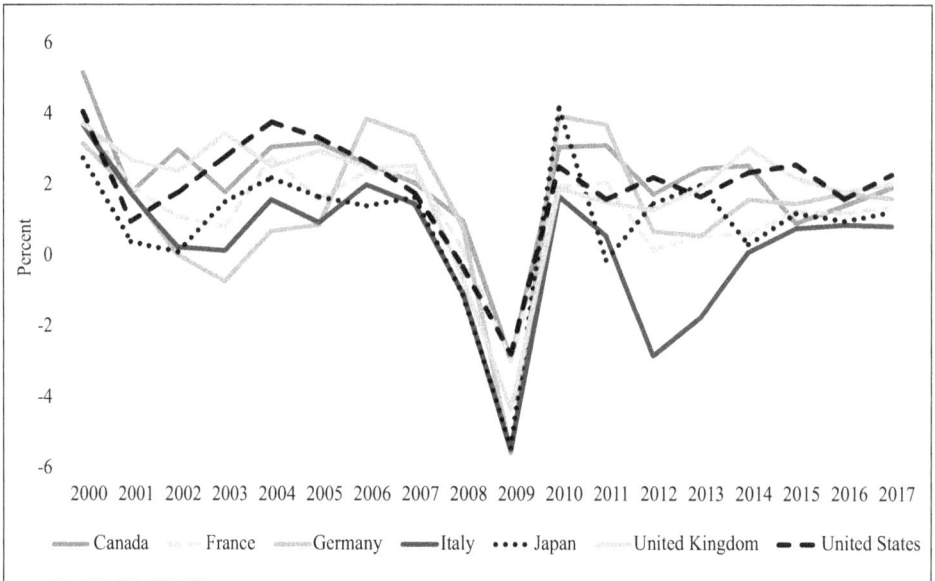

Figure 2.2 G7 GDP Growth 2000–2017 (estimated after 2016)

Data Source: International Monetary Fund World Economic Outlook Database, April 2017.

A comparison of BRICS versus G7 share of global GDP tells a similar story. Overall, although the global economic position of the BRICS countries is not as strong as it was (either factually or in terms of perception), they still collectively hold a large and growing share of world GDP, especially when measured using purchasing power parity. Their share of GDP has also been steadily increasing, whereas the G7 share of global GDP has been on a steady downward trend. This is important because even though the official position is that BRICS is a political group no longer united just by strong economic performance, the countries' growth rates continue to be an important prism through which observers perceive the strength and longevity of the group.

A second word about China is warranted. The discussion of BRICS's share of global GDP is effectively synonymous with speaking about China's share of global GDP. India makes some contribution, but Brazil, Russia, and South Africa are clear laggards, even in years when their growth rates were impressive. This raises the question of whether it is misleading to speak in aggregate about BRICS's share of global GDP, and thereby bestow on the other BRICS the reflected glory of China's economic success. It is likely that if China were to find BRICS cooperation against its interest and publicly disavow membership, interest in BRICS would plummet. On the other hand, despite China's primary interest in using the group toward geo-economic goals, Chinese leadership understands that effecting

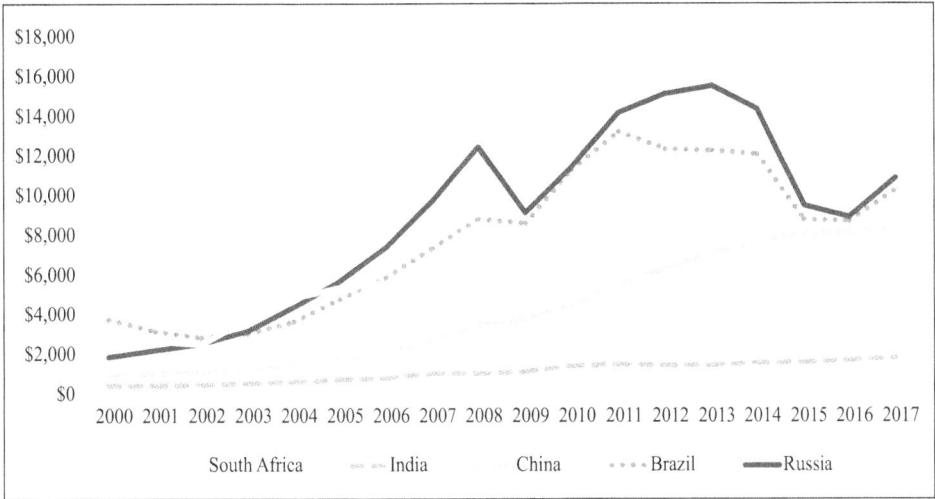

Figure 2.3 BRICS GDP Per Capita, USD Current Prices

Data Source: International Monetary Fund World Economic Outlook Database, April 2017.

change in international institutions is ultimately a question of politics. The country is therefore unlikely to renounce the group even as it falls down the list of priorities. This further underscores the fundamental argument that there is more to the BRICS story than macroeconomics.

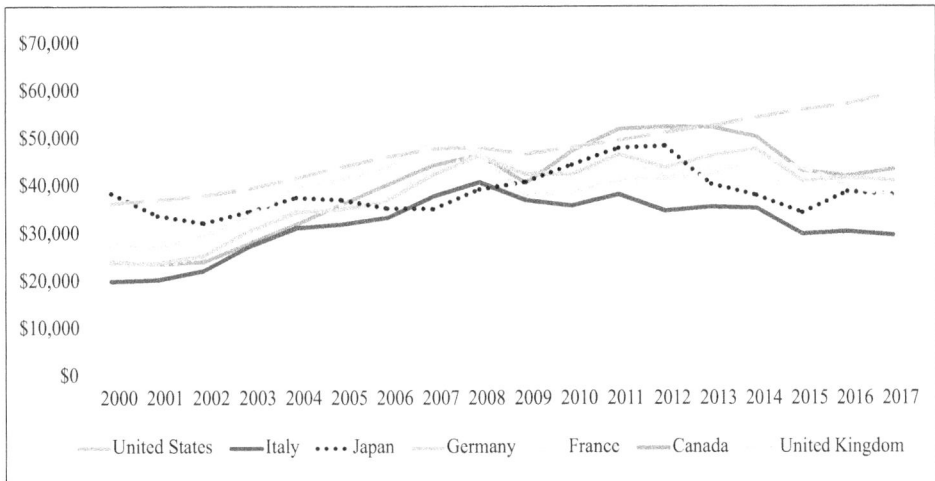

Figure 2.4 G7 GDP Per Capita, USD Current Prices

Data Source: International Monetary Fund World Economic Outlook Database, April 2017.

Finally, one word of caution: as impressive as GDP is in China, GDP is a less useful measure of development than is per capita income. On this measure, BRICS has a long way to go (figure 2.3). The G7 country with the lowest GDP per capita, Italy (figure 2.4), has per capita income more than twice as high as the BRICS country with the highest GDP per capita (Russia). China's GDP per capita in 2016 was nearly three times smaller than Italian GDP per capita. In part, this is a story of demographics: both China and India have well over 1 billion people. Both countries face formidable hurdles in reaching developed country levels of GDP per capita. More broadly, however, the disparity between the story of GDP growth and the story of GDP per capita illustrates a prime tension in BRICS. These are countries that in the aggregate look strong, but the aggregate number hides the challenges beneath the surface. While BRICS economic growth has been impressive over the past decade, it would be foolish to translate that success into readiness for stepping into all the global roles that developed countries now hold.

Intra-BRICS Economic Relations

The main story of intra-BRICS economics is that cross-national economic relations, with the singular exception of each country's relationship with China, are very weak. According to data on the World Bank Group's World Integrated Trade Solution portal, nearly ten years of cooperation has had little impact on trade patterns beyond each country's individual growth over that time. Even major economic upheavals, such as the US and EU sanctions levied on Russia since 2014, have not spurred trade with BRICS partners. There is no single significant intra-BRICS trade relationship other than China's outsize presence in each country's trade. Further, none of the BRICS countries feature among China's main trade partners.

The trade data also point to another interesting angle: with few exceptions, the top five trading partners (other than China) of each of the BRICS countries are all developed economies. Again, that has not really shifted over the last decade, despite the weaker growth in the United States and Europe compared with the developing world. This is important because it illustrates the gap between the rhetoric about BRICS as a paradigm for South-South cooperation and the reality that the countries remain much more economically tied to Western countries than to any country in the developing world.

Trade is not the only area in which intra-BRICS economic relations are fundamentally weak. The story is much the same regarding inward and outward foreign direct investment: cross-BRICS foreign direct investment is very weak. China is a player in all the markets, and Russia a marginal player in China, but all are far down the list of sources and destinations for foreign direct investment.[82] Ultimately, there may be no better proof that BRICS is a political rather than economic group than the relative paucity of economic relations among its members.

Indeed, those who dismiss BRICS as unimportant based on both weak economic performance and weak intragroup economic ties miss the point. The BRICS countries have different regime types, differently structured domestic economies, and different economic bases, not to mention their geographic dispersion. All of these make the group a poor candidate for either a free trade zone or anything resembling an optimum currency area. These differences, though, need not hinder political cooperation. As argued in the preceding sections, BRICS cooperation is primarily concerned with a reallocation of power within global economic governance. Accomplishing that goal requires alignment on a discrete set of political concerns. The group would be stronger and more balanced with increased intra-BRICS trade rather than a mini hub-and-spoke model around China, but the lack of crosscutting trade does not spell the end of cooperation.

The Numbers of BRICS Institutionalization

Unlike the weak economic relationships, the level of BRICS institutionalization as measured by number of meetings has increased substantially since the group's inception. In 2008, the year of the first leaders' sideline meeting, the group held five meetings, all at the ministerial level or above. In 2017 China oversaw 98 BRICS-related events, of which 31 were at the ministerial level.[83] The record through 2017 was India's 2016 chairmanship, which saw 125 BRICS-related events over the course of the year; 33 of those were at the level of senior officials or above.[84]

The increase in meeting intensity can be read in two ways. From one perspective, it shows both a growing commitment to increase contacts across multiple vectors at high levels and the gradual penetration of those contacts down to staff-level meetings. An increase in staff-level meetings may be positive in the long term: while the photo ops are better at events with senior officials, the real work happens lower down. From another perspective, the recent proliferation of meetings may be a sign of lost focus. BRICS is most effective when it cooperates on areas in which all five countries have common aims, even if the commonality exists only at a high level of abstraction. The more in the weeds the topics and meetings are, the less likely it is they will produce operable outcomes for all concerned. Questions of development, health, and education are common to all members, but the differences in domestic situations make cooperation more difficult on these topics. (Coordination on issues of, for example, health, in international organizations is a slightly different question.) These meetings also draw attention away from the core focus of reforming global economic governance.

The BRICS group is not alone in its continuous creation of subgroups and crosscutting contacts. The G7 and the G20 both host a plethora of technical working groups throughout the year in addition to the annual leaders' summits. To some extent, this is both in the nature of plurilateral organizations and a question of each host wishing to outdo the previous host.[85] Leaving aside diplomatic competition and the danger of trying to do too much too soon, though, the most important takeaway from the increasing number of contacts is the group's ongoing effort to find new areas of cooperation. Some efforts do not bear fruit, and some are just for show. That the group remains committed to trying new formats and building new working groups, however, suggests that at a basic level the countries find it useful to coordinate within BRICS on a range of issues and are not leaving the group to languish as the momentum from the acute phase of the global financial crisis subsides.

Conclusion

BRICS has come a long way since 2001. Building on three previous configurations of developing countries, the group has matured into a forum that holds multiple independent meetings annually, including one among its leaders. The leaders also always convene on the sidelines of other global forums and often coordinate the group's position on questions of interest. Cooperation encompasses everything from finance to health and includes academic and business councils that supplement the contacts between officials. In barely a decade, BRICS has transformed itself into a persistent feature of the landscape of global governance.

Economic cooperation, however, remains anemic. There is no strong economic network among the BRICS countries. Instead, each has strong bilateral ties with China, with the West, and within its own region. This reinforces the position that BRICS is at this point primarily political. It poses a problem, however, in that much of intra-BRICS cooperation is theoretically aimed toward addressing common socioeconomic challenges that hinder economic development in emerging powers. For that goal to come to fruition, the group will need a much denser web of economic ties.

The idea of BRICS as a political organism brings the narrative back to Russia. The next chapter presents an analysis of Russian elite political discourse during Vladimir Putin's first two presidential terms. Most of this period predates the coalescence of BRICS into a political group. Instead, the emphasis is on how changing rhetoric from Russian leadership about the concepts of sovereignty and national identity laid the foundations for the role BRICS would come to play in Russian foreign policy before the onset of the crisis in Ukraine.

Notes

Epigraph: Lula Da Silva, "BRICS Come of Global Age."

1. This paragraph appears in slightly different form in Salzman, "From Bridge to Bulwark," 3.

2. O'Neill, "Building Better Global Economic BRICs."

3. O'Neill, *Growth Map*, 12; and Gillian Tett, "The Story of the Brics," *Financial Times*, January 15, 2010, https://www.ft.com/content/112ca932–00ab-11df-ae8d-00144 feabdc0.

4. Stuenkel, "Financial Crisis," 613.

5. O'Neill, "Building Better Global Economic BRICs," S.03.

6. Ibid., S.10. Although Russia was a member of the G8 at this point, the finance ministers continued to meet separately at the G7 level.

7. Tett, "Story of the Brics."

8. Wilson and Purushothaman, "Dreaming with BRICs."

9. Stuenkel, "Financial Crisis," 613–14.

10. Laidi, "BRICS against the West?," 2.

11. Martynov, "BRIK i degradiruiushchii miroporiadok," 7.

12. Davydov and Bobrovnikov, *Rol voskhodiashchikh gigantov*, 13.

13. Stuenkel, *BRICS and the Future of Global Order*, 4nn29–31.

14. Lukin, "Rossiia i Kitai v RIK i BRIKS," 275.

15. Ibid.

16. Ibid., 275–76.

17. Lo, "New Order for Old Triangles?," 23.

18. Stuenkel, "Uncertain Future of IBSA."

19. Stuenkel, *BRICS and the Future of Global Order*, 5.

20. Ibid., 6.

21. Emerson, "Do the BRICS Make a Bloc?," 2.

22. Stuenkel, "Uncertain Future of IBSA"; and Mishra, "IBSA and South-South Cooperation."

23. Saran, "India's Contemporary Plurilateralism," 629.

24. Stuenkel, "Uncertain Future of IBSA."

25. Cooper and Jackson, "Incremental Transformation of the G8," 79–80; and Payne, "G8 in a Changing Global Economic Order," 520.

26. Russia was not happy at the inclusion of these five countries in the summit.

27. Payne, "G8 in a Changing Global Economic Order," 530.

28. Ibid., 531.

29. Stuenkel, *BRICS and the Future of Global Order*, 11.

30. Borisoglebskaia and Chetverikov, *Razvitie stran BRIKS v globalnom prostranstve*, 74; and Vladimir Davydov, interview with author, Moscow, Russia, September 22, 2014.

31. Andreev, "BRIKS," 127.

32. Stuenkel, "Emerging Powers and Status," 91.

33. Vyacheslav Trubnikov, interview with author, December 18, 2014, Moscow.

34. On the role of academic institutions, see Davydov, interview (2014); and Davydov and Bobrovnikov, *Rol voskhodiashchikh gigantov*, 13. Lula's 2002 speech and Putin's role in initiating the 2006 meeting also support the contention that BRICS has flowed from the top.

35. Georgii Toloraya, interview with author, May 14, 2014, Moscow.

36. Titarenko and Ulianaev, "Perspektivy formata BRIK."

37. On IMF and World Bank sidelines, see Armijo and Roberts, "Emerging Powers and Global Governance," 504.

38. Kornegay, "South Africa, the Indian Ocean," 4.

39. Stuenkel, *BRICS and the Future of Global Order*, 41.

40. Ibid., 42.

41. Ibid.

42. Shubin, "Ot BRIK k BRIKS," 198.

43. Kornegay, "South Africa, the Indian Ocean," 4.

44. Ibid., 3. Part of that anger was based on a feeling of being "deserted" by IBSA partners India and Brazil. See ibid.

45. Stuenkel, *BRICS and the Future of Global Order*, 51. O'Neill disagrees with the inclusion of South Africa. See Sharda Naidoo, "South Africa's Presence 'Drags down Brics,'" *Mail & Guardian*, March 23, 2012, http://mg.co.za/article/2012–03–23-sa-presence -drags-down-brics/.

46. This distinction is reinforced by the fact that those writing for a business audience often continue to write about BRIC rather than BRICS. Wikipedia has the two terms as separate entries.

47. Toloraya, interview.

48. Nandan Unnikrishnan, interview with author, September 22, 2014, Moscow.

49. Weiss and Thakur, *Global Governance and the UN*, 6.

50. Ruggie, foreword to *Global Governance and the UN*, xv.

51. Biermann et al., "Fragmentation of Global Governance Architectures," 14.

52. Kirshner, *American Power after the Financial Crisis*, 7.

53. Hopewell, *Breaking the WTO*, 11.

54. Acharya, *End of American World Order*, 39.

55. Laidi, "BRICS against the West?"; and Lukyanov, "What Holds the BRICS Together?"

56. Stuenkel, *Post-Western World*, 61.

57. Larionova, "BRICS: A Rising Global Governance Actor."

58. In August 2015 Russian foreign minister Sergei Lavrov indicated that Russia supports India's bid for a permanent seat on the UNSC. See Smriti Kak Ramachandran, "Russia Backs India's Bid for a Permanent UNSC Seat," *Hindu*, March 29, 2016, https:// www.thehindu.com/news/national/russia-backs-indias-bid-for-a-permanent-unsc-seat /article7551058.ece#!.

59. Stuenkel, "Financial Crisis," 612.

60. Larionova, "BRIKS v sisteme globalnogo upravleniia," 2.

61. Panova, "BRIKS: Mesto Rossii v Gruppe," 51.

62. IMF, "Press Release: IMF Managing Director Christine Lagarde"; and IMF, "Press Release: Statement by IMF Managing Director."

63. Baumann das Neves and Gregol de Farias, *VI BRICS Academic Forum*, 14.

64. See "BRICS Information Centre," University of Toronto website, n.d., http:// www.brics.utoronto.ca/docs/index.html.

65. Toloraya, interview; Saran, Singh, and Sharan, "Long-Term Vision for BRICS"; and BRICS Think Tank Council, "Realising the BRICS Long-Term Goals."

66. See Natsionalnyi Komitet po issledovaniiu BRIKS, Rossiia (The National Committee on BRICS Research, Russia), www.nkibrics.ru (in Russian).

67. Stuenkel, "Connecting the Global South."

68. David Pilling, "The BRICS Bank Is a Glimpse of the Future," *Financial Times*, July 30, 2014, https://www.ft.com/content/f7b876a0–170e-11e4-b0d7–00144feabdc0.

69. Oliver Stuenkel, interview with author, December 4, 2014, Skype.

70. BRICS Leaders, "Agreement on the New Development Bank"; BRICS Leaders, "Treaty for the Establishment of a BRICS Contingent Reserve Arrangement"; and Toloraya and Chukov, "BRICS to Be Considered?," 74.

71. Mboweni, "Brics Bank to Balance Global Order."

72. "Agreement on the New Development Bank."

73. Saran, "From Cold War to Hot Peace"; Ye, "BRICS New Development Bank Moves Ahead Quietly"; Panda, "Asian Infrastructure Investment Bank Is Open for Business."

74. Brenda Goh, "'BRICS' Bank Launches in Shanghai, to Work with AIIB," Reuters, July 20, 2015, https://in.reuters.com/article/emerging-brics-bank/brics-bank-launches-in -shanghai-to-work-with-aiib-idINKCN0PV07Z20150721.

75. Biswas, "How China Is Reshaping Global Development"; and Mboweni, "Brics Bank to Balance Global Order."

76. "How China Is Reshaping Global Development."

77. In addition, it is worth noting that much of Chinese lending for infrastructure projects such as the Belt and Road Initiative comes through nontransparent bilateral deals between partner countries and Chinese banks. The AIIB gives China a patina of playing by the rules, but the facts on the ground are somewhat different.

78. Hopewell, *Breaking the WTO*, 3.

79. Ibid., 11–12.

80. Armijo and Roberts, "Emerging Powers and Global Governance."

81. Kirton, "Explaining the BRICS Summit," 6.

82. "BRICS Joint Statistical Publication," 172–74.

83. BRICS 2017 China, "Meetings Calendar for China's 2017 BRICS Chairmanship," https://www.brics2017.org/English/China2017/BRICSCalendar/.

84. BRICS India 2016, "Calendar," http://brics2016.gov.in/content/calender.php.

85. H.H.S Viswanathan, Distinguished Fellow, Observer Research Foundation, interview with author, January 17, 2017, Delhi, India.

3

Laying the Rhetorical Foundation for BRICS

The Evolution of the Concepts of Sovereignty and National Identity, 2000–2007

> Do you believe that if [Peter I] had found a rich and fertile history . . . he would not have hesitated to cast the nation into a new world, to divest it of its nationality? On the contrary, would he not have sought the means of regenerating the nation in this nationality itself? And as for the nation, would it have put up with the fact that its past was ravaged, that Europe's was, as it were, imposed upon it?
>
> —Peter Chaadaev, *Apologia of a Madman*, 1837

> No doubt, messianism is of no use to us now, but the mission of the Russian nation needs to be specified. Without establishing Russia's role among other countries . . . , without understanding who we are and why we are here, our national life will not be full-fledged.
>
> —Vladislav Surkov, 2007

BEING NAMED A BRIC COUNTRY BY GOLDMAN SACHS IN 2001 COULD NOT have come at a timelier moment for Russia. The country was beginning to recover from nearly a decade of economic instability that culminated in the August 1998 default. Being included in the list of likely future leaders of the global economy by one of the world's premier investment banks provided external validation that others had noticed Russia's revival.

However, there was no immediate move to begin bringing BRIC together as a political group. The notion of the rise of the non-Western world appealed to existing strains within Russian foreign policy, particularly with Pragmatic Nationalists who gained power in the latter years of the Yeltsin presidency. Nevertheless, the focus, especially during Putin's first presidential term, was on consolidating domestic economic growth and political stability. In addition, Putin's early political rhetoric lacked the bluster and wounded pride that marked many of the statements from the Yeltsin era.[1] Therefore, although it was evident from the outset that Putin would not pursue a strictly pro-Western foreign policy, neither did he immediately begin building alternative coalitions (rhetorical or otherwise).

Further, the BRIC appellation hit Russia at the core of its internal debate over national identity. Being a "BRIC" also meant being separate from Europe and the West, if the idea were taken to a political connotation. The debates over identity and civilizational association (European or specifically Russian) had hamstrung foreign policy under Yeltsin.[2] Putin, because of his ties to both the liberal Anatoly Sobchak and the more conservative security forces, was acceptable across the identity spectrum. He also had sufficient political acumen to understand that reviving the national identity debate would undermine his efforts to put Russia on a more stable path both domestically and internationally.[3] Therefore, although much of Putin's early rhetoric placed Russia more in European than Eurasian civilization, civilizational discourse in general was a minor feature of his early speeches.

This approach shifted over the course of Putin's first two terms as president. As a result of changes in both the domestic and international environments, Putin's political rhetoric became more strident and more anti-Western during his first eight years in office. This chapter examines how that shift laid the groundwork for incorporating BRICS into Russian foreign policy. The aim is to trace the evolution of two concepts critical for understanding Russia's relationship to BRICS: sovereignty and national identity. Identifying how the rhetorical framing of these ideas showcased an increasingly antagonistic view of the West sets the stage for understanding the role BRICS would play in Russian foreign policy.

Sovereignty and Independence

One of the persistent themes in official rhetoric about foreign policy in Russia is the degree of policy "independence"—the extent to which Russia is able to conduct the foreign policy it wishes without concern for international influences or repercussions. The idea of policy independence is closely linked with the broader concept of national sovereignty. As explained in the first chapter, sovereignty in the Russian lexicon means complete control over domestic affairs without external meddling or any devolution of control to supranational or international bodies.[4] Sovereignty, in turn, is tied to the overall goal of multipolarity, a world system wherein no single country has the power to bend other great powers to its will.

The tone in the National Security Concept and the Foreign Policy Concept that Putin approved in his first months in office bears out this point. The National Security Concept avows that "Russia will help shape the ideology behind the rise of a multipolar world."[5] Similarly, the Foreign Policy Concept notes the importance of Russia's balanced and multivector policy and lists the creation of a new world order based on multipolarity as the top international priority.[6] However, while the fundamental assumption of sovereignty and independence was present from the beginning, the way the ideas were framed and presented changed from 2000 to 2008.

During the 2000 address to the Federal Assembly, Vladimir Putin declared unequivocally, "The independence of our foreign policy is not in doubt."[7] The tone, however, was not confrontational. Instead, it reads almost as a required nod to a long-standing Russian policy in the midst of a speech much more consumed with overcoming Russian domestic struggles. This is not to argue that Putin did not believe in the importance of Russian foreign policy independence. Rather, his primary focus was on domestic issues. Similarly, in an article published shortly before he assumed office as acting president, Putin carefully framed Russia's development within the context of a larger universal narrative and process.[8] Further, the absence of mention of foreign policy independence in the annual addresses from 2001, 2002, and 2003 suggest that in the early years, emphasis on sovereignty was lower on the priority list and less important for the domestic political audience.[9]

In part, this is because the early years of Putin's tenure were devoted to stabilizing Russia both politically and economically. Putin and his first prime minister, Mikhail Kasyanov, "were waging a two-front war for legitimacy: one a battle for Chechnya and the other a struggle to push through economic reforms that had stalled in the late 1990s."[10] The problem was not only one of discrete issues, such as tax reform and instability in the North Caucasus. Instead, part of Putin's task was to restore faith in the government after the erratic final years of his predecessor. This was also important for foreign policy: Putin had to stabilize the situation so that foreign policy became more consistent and less apt to fall victim to party politics.[11] In practice, this involved bringing domestic constituencies in line by building a broad base of support and gaining the support of both the elite and the general public as well as reigning in the oligarchs who had dominated politics in the late Yeltsin era.[12] Part of gaining that confidence was stabilizing the economy, returning the country to a balanced budget, and showing that Putin was a leader who followed through on his commitments.[13]

By 2004 this had been accomplished. Between 2000 and 2003 (inclusive), Russia's GDP grew at an average rate of 6.8 percent per year.[14] In addition, in 2004 Russia went through a stable election cycle, with Putin elected to another four-year term. The 2004 elections were less competitive than previous presidential elections.[15] However, this is evidence of less democracy, not less stability; in Putin's mind, these may be two sides of the same coin. By these metrics and many others, Russia was a dramatically more stable country in 2004 than it had been when Putin inherited control four years prior. Putin touted these accomplishments in his 2004 address to the Federal Assembly. How he did so matters, however, and indicates that 2004 was a turning point in how Putin discussed the twin concepts of independence and sovereignty.

During the 2004 address Putin announced that, in the previous year, "for the first time in a long period Russia became a politically and economically stable and independent country in financial relations and in international affairs."[16] Had he simply left it at that, it would be reasonable to interpret the declaration as simply an acknowledgment of the improvement in the national economy and increased domestic political stability. However, Putin combined his praise for Russia's newly stable situation with a warning that Russia's resurgence would engender discontent in other corners of the world. He stated, "Far from everyone in the world wishes to deal with an independent, strong, and self-assured Russia. Now in the global competitive fight, which actively uses political, economic and information pressure, the strengthening of our statehood [*gosudarstvennosti*] is sometimes consciously construed as authoritarianism."[17] The warning that Russia's resurgence would provoke negative reactions in other countries shows the beginning of the return of the "fortress Russia" mentality. It also points to a link between a Russia that pursues an independent policy and one that is alone in its fight for its place in the global order.

There are two other important pieces here. The first is the reference to *gosudarstvennost*. Jeffrey Mankoff translates this as *etatism* (statism) and defines it as "the idea that the state should play a leading role in the economic and political life of the country, and that the national interest in foreign policy should be defined in reference to the well-being of the state itself."[18] As noted elsewhere, the centrality of the well-being of the state, rather than the emphasis on the well-being of the citizens of that state, marks one of the key differences in how Russia defines sovereignty from how it is defined in the West. While this was not a new idea to Russian discourse in 2004, it is significant that it is this specific definition, rather than the more generic "sovereignty" (used earlier in the quotation), that Putin brings in as he revives his discussion about Russia's political independence.

The second element of note is linked to the idea of sovereignty, especially control over domestic affairs. In his reference that some countries equate the strengthening of the Russian state with authoritarianism, Putin underscores the fact that some of the discomfort other countries may have with Russia's rise was about the Russian domestic order rather than its increased assertiveness in foreign policy. Much of the BRICS argument with the current global order hinges on disagreement with the perceived interference in the domestic affairs of sovereign states. It is therefore worth highlighting the reemergence of this argument in Russian political discourse in the year before the BRIC countries held their first informal meeting.

Although improved domestic conditions and increased national confidence compose part of the basis for this newly assertive tone, it is also a product of changes in Russia's international relationships. By 2004 what had begun as good relations between Putin and US president George W. Bush, bolstered by close cooperation following the terrorist attacks of September 11, 2001, had deteriorated considerably. The decline began in May 2002, when Bush withdrew the United States from the 1972 Anti-Ballistic Missile Treaty and began pursuing missile defense initiatives.[19] Other than calling the decision a "mistake," Putin reacted coolly to the announcement.[20] He averred that an American missile defense program would not threaten the Russian deterrent, and cooperation on issues of mutual interest continued.[21] Although the specific issue of missile defense would not become the main irritant in the relationship until later, the US abrogation of the Anti-Ballistic Missile Treaty marked the end of the "honeymoon in U.S.-Russian relations" that followed 9/11.[22]

In 2004 the primary causes of strain in US-Russian relations were the Iraq War, the recent spate of color revolutions in the post-Soviet space (especially the 2004 Orange Revolution in Ukraine), and Russia's domestic politics.[23] In 2003, when the United States invaded Iraq without UNSC authorization, Russia joined with France and Germany to condemn the invasion.[24] The initial US reaction was summed up as "punish France, ignore Germany, forgive Russia," attributed to National Security Advisor Condoleezza Rice.[25] That attitude did not last long. The repercussions of the US invasion of Iraq, particularly the operational beginnings of the Bush "Freedom Agenda" (later formalized in 2005) and its implications for democratization efforts in former Soviet republics, further soured already troubled US-Russian relations.

Russia's domestic situation compounded the problem. The core of the disagreement between the United States and Russia over both the invasion of Iraq as well as the broader Freedom Agenda was the problem of interference in the domestic affairs of sovereign states in contravention of international law. The Freedom Agenda became central to American foreign policy at the same time that tainted presidential elections signaled Russia's domestic trajectory away from democracy and the seizure of the Yukos oil company indicated a shift from liberal economic reform and global economic integration.[26] This disagreement is the root of Putin's statement about increasing state capacity being "consciously construed as authoritarianism." Putin is arguing that, by the precepts of US policy, intentionally misconstruing a strong, independent Russia as authoritarian would give the United States pretense to work toward regime change in Russia itself and not just on its borders.

The strain in relations with the United States affected how Putin described Russia's international partnerships in the 2004 address. In listing important international partners, Putin equated the importance of Russia's relations with the United States with that of its relations with China and India.[27] This is not a serious equation. Putin did actively pursue partnerships with countries and organizations in the Asia Pacific from the beginning of his first presidential term.[28] However, Russia did not begin really designing a coherent policy toward Asia until after the 2008 financial crisis, and the relationship remained quite shallow even after the beginning of the crisis in Ukraine.[29] The emphasis on relations with China and India was instead a signal of the renewed attention to Primakov's "strategic triangle" (RIC) in Russian strategy after lying fallow since its inception in 1998.[30] Further, it indicated the beginning of the rhetorical deployment of

Russia's relations with these countries as an alternative to its relationship with its Western partners.

The shift in rhetorical framing of sovereignty and independence between 2000 and 2006 was overall fairly mild. However, 2007 marked a seismic change in the development of these concepts and, concurrently, of the incorporation of BRIC into Russian foreign policy strategy and discourse. Two documents exemplify this change: internationally, Putin's speech at the annual Munich Security Conference signaled his administration's change in perspective.[31] Domestically, the 2007 Survey of Russian Foreign Policy, the first major review of foreign policy since Putin assumed office in 2000, laid out the extent of the changes and their implications for foreign policy objectives.[32]

In truth, Putin's Munich speech was something of a coming-out party for views that had been in development for some time. In a 2006 speech to members of the United Russia party, first deputy chief of the Russian presidential administration Vladislav Surkov said that the former members of the Eastern Bloc who joined the European Union were simply trading one type of diminished sovereignty for another, an overt denigration of Western integration.[33] In the same speech, Surkov declared that sovereignty was the "political synonym of [Russian] competitiveness."[34] By 2007, four years after the invasion of Iraq and three years after the Yukos affair, Putin's dissatisfaction with US foreign policy, and the West more broadly, was already well documented. That dissatisfaction was also being stoked anew by the announcement about planned US missile defense sites in Poland and the Czech Republic.[35]

The Munich speech is therefore not distinctive because of its general content. Instead, its import derives from the following three elements: its tone, its specificity, and its foreshadowing of future policies. On tone, this was no gentle chiding of the keepers of the global status quo; it was a forceful and even vitriolic recrimination against nearly two decades of (perceived) ill treatment. Putin condemned what he saw as the hypocrisies of the United States regarding democracy, arguing "Russia—we—are constantly being taught about democracy. But for some reason those who teach us do not want to learn themselves."[36] Here Putin conflates democracy at the domestic level (the US concern) with democracy in international relations (the Russian concern). The implicit message is unequivocal: the United States expects other countries to operate by one set of standards while it remains unbound by those same standards.

Putin then made that message explicit: "One state and, of course, first and foremost the United States, has overstepped its national borders in every way. This is visible in the economic, political, cultural and educational policies it imposes on other nations."[37] This was not a new criticism, but it was more forceful than its previous iterations. If Western policymakers had before been able to brush Russian concerns aside, Munich made clear that further inattention was ill-advised.

Second, the speech represented the first formal announcement of Russia's "nonalignment" and search for new partners and a new system. At the conclusion of his remarks, Putin stated:

> Russia is a country with a history that spans more than a thousand years and has practically always used the privilege to carry out an independent foreign policy.
>
> We are not going to change this tradition today. At the same time, we are well aware of how the world has changed and we have a realistic sense of our own opportunities and potential. And of course we would like to interact with responsible and independent partners with whom we could work together in constructing a fair and democratic world order that would ensure security and prosperity not only for a select few, but for all.[38]

There are two important elements here: the stress on Russia as an independent actor on the international stage, and the call to build a new world order that does not privilege the interests of certain members of the international community over those of others. The former is a public declaration that Russia is a country out to protect its own interests and does not consider itself bound by the preferences of the Euro-Atlantic community. The latter is a verbatim foreshadowing of the overall goal that would soon be incorporated in every BRICS summit declaration.

This foreshadowing of BRICS concerns is the third symbolism in the Munich speech. During the speech, after highlighting the impressive growth rates of Brazil, Russia, India, and China, Putin declared that "there is no reason to doubt that the economic potential of the new centres of global economic growth will inevitably be converted into political influence and will strengthen multipolarity."[39] The quick connection between the economic rise of the BRIC countries and the assumption of their future political prowess is evidence that, less than five months after the first meeting of the BRIC foreign ministers at the 2006 UN General Assembly, Putin was already considering the potential for BRIC to be mobilized as a political force.

These public pronouncements are reinforced by the findings and recommendations in the 2007 Survey on Russian Foreign Policy, an internal document produced by the Ministry of Foreign Affairs. The survey hails the "newly acquired foreign policy independence of Russia" and argues that the time is ripe for Russia to take a more active role as a subject rather than an object of international affairs.[40] As the introduction to the document explains, "Russia is firmly entering the mainstream of international life, and therefore the supertask [*sverkhzadacha*] of the Survey is intellectually and psychologically to get accustomed to this new position for us. The qualitatively new situation in international relations creates favorable opportunities for our intellectual leadership in a number of areas of world politics. In other words, it is about Russia's active participation not only in carrying out the international agenda, but also in shaping it."[41]

The "qualitatively new situation" to which the document refers is the effects of globalization. The survey opens with the following observation: "Substantial changes have taken place on the world scene in recent years. The growing processes of globalization, despite their contradictory consequences, lead to a more even distribution of resources of influence and economic growth, thus laying the objective basis for a multipolar construct of international relations."[42] The rest of the document details a plan for how best to capitalize on those developments to increase Russian weight in the international system. BRIC is explicitly part of that plan. Although the group is mentioned only once, in the section on economic diplomacy, the survey recommends that Russia "continue developing cooperation in [the BRIC] format."[43] More significantly, it also recommends that cooperation move beyond economics and onto other issues of mutual concern, including counterterrorism.[44] This is an indication that in 2007 the Russian foreign policy apparatus already saw in BRIC a political platform. The overriding message of the 2007 survey is of a coming change in the international order. It is also of a resurgent Russia, one with the capacity to influence this change and to do so from an independent foreign policy position.

Russia's Evolving National Identity and the Rise of "Civilizationalism" in Foreign Policy Discourse

The preceding section explores the development of the concepts of sovereignty and independence in Russian foreign policy discourse. This section considers the evolution of the rhetorical framing of Russian national identity during Putin's first two terms in office, with particular emphasis on two issues: the question of Russia's developmental path and how that question morphs into the related but broader idea of a "dialogue of civilizations." Putin's rhetorical construction of Russia as a distinct civilization builds on long traditions within Russian intellectual history, especially the nineteenth-century Slavophiles and the Eurasianists of both the early Soviet period and the early post-Soviet period. The argument here is therefore not that Putin was presenting a novel conception of Russian national identity. Instead, the point is that he redirected national identity to these more exclusionary definitions away from the idea of Russia as part of European civilization in an intentional and conscious manner.

Two main questions animate the exploration. First is the extent to which Russia's European identity is stressed over a unique Russian identity. Second, and related, is the broader question of how the idea of "civilization" is framed, particularly whether it is singular or multiple, and how it is connected to economic and political development.

In "Russia at the Turn of the Millennium," Putin makes clear his views on Russia's place in the world and its future development. He argues: "Russia is completing the first, transition stage of economic and political reforms. Despite problems and mistakes, it has entered the highway by which the whole of humanity is traveling. Only this way offers the possibility of dynamic economic growth and higher living standards, as the world experience convincingly shows. There is no alternative to it."[45] To underscore the message of joining the universal path to development, Putin stated that communism "was a road to a blind alley, which is far away from the mainstream of civilization."[46] Indeed, much of the first section of the Millennium Manifesto details the negative legacies the Soviet economic structure bequeathed to Russia, including the emphasis on natural resources and the lack of competition. In his analysis of the current situation in Russia, Putin declared, "Today we are reaping the bitter fruit, both material and mental, of the past decades."[47] The desire to leave behind the previous model of development and its crippling effects on Russia's global competitiveness are clear.

Putin is not arguing that all countries and peoples are the same. He writes about the specificities of Russian national identity and how those specificities fit with more universal values. He speaks of the dangers of simply applying foreign models whole cloth. The emphasis on a strong and stable state as a prerequisite for Russian success that would become sharper over the course of his first term in office also comes through clearly in the Millennium Manifesto. He decries all extreme reform models, including those pursued in the early 1990s. However, Putin's argument is primarily that the principles of a model must fit the realities on the ground. He is not arguing that having a distinct national identity implies being a member of a distinct civilization requiring an entirely different development path.

Equally significant is the abandonment of the long-standing tradition of Russia as the vanguard of a countermovement in the global marketplace of ideas. This marks a decisive turn from (late) tsarist and Soviet iterations of Russian foreign policy, in which leadership of a global counterculture—whether Moscow as the "Third Rome" or, as in the previous example, communism—was a bedrock principle. Russia (like the United States) has a long history of believing it has a global mission. Putin's call to join the path of the rest of civilization and his disavowal of communism and all it represented developmentally thus marked a major change.

This is not to argue that Russia professed no global ambition during Putin's early years in office. As noted in the previous section, the 2000 National Security Concept underlines the importance of promoting a multipolar world with Russia as "one of [its] influential centres."[48] The 2000 Foreign Policy Concept, like all its successors, identifies the formation of a new world order as the top Russian priority in "resolving global problems."[49] The difference is that in the earlier documents, Russia's conflicts with Western policies are framed in political rather than civilizational or identity terms.

The annual addresses to the Federal Assembly from 2000 to 2003 bear out this interpretation. In these speeches, Putin expressed frustration with humanitarian intervention and NATO expansion, but he also repeatedly stressed that relations with the European Union and the United States were Russia's top foreign policy priorities after relations with the countries in the Commonwealth of Independent States. Throughout this period, the refrain was of Russia reclaiming its rightful place as a European great power and a member of the top echelon of developed nations.[50]

This approach is best exemplified in the 2003 address, in which Putin touted the achievement of the full membership in the G8 as the best indication of Russia's international integration: "Above everything else, in June of last year Russia was invited to become a full member of the club of eight most developed states in the world. In it, together with our partners, we are working on providing for our national interests and in resolving general problems that stand before modern civilization."[51] Here is a clear statement of both international priorities and, less directly, Russian identity. Russia is identified as a country of the Global North, a developed country cooperating with its rightful partners, the other most developed countries. Further, Putin speaks of the idea of confronting common problems of "modern civilization." Although elsewhere in the speech Putin speaks of Russia as "unique community," and there is the reference to protecting Russian national interests, there is no indication of the existence of a multiplicity of civilizations or alternative paths of national development.

As with the discourse about sovereignty and independence, the approach to identity began shifting noticeably in 2004. However, the change was not immediately apparent as an adjustment in the framing of national identity. Instead, the change is visible in two smaller rhetorical stresses and innovations that began appearing in the annual addresses after 2004. The first is the renewed emphasis on the Great Patriotic War (Russia's name for the portion of World War II following the German invasion of the Soviet Union in June 1941) as a cornerstone of contemporary Russian national identity. The second is the revival of the idea of responsibility for ethnic Russians living beyond Russia's borders.

The Narrative of the Great Patriotic War

It is hard to overstate the impact of World War II on the Soviet Union. The USSR suffered the greatest losses among the combatant powers during the war and also made the greatest contribution to the Allied victory.[52] The number of Soviet casualties was five times that of German casualties.[53] Despite these unimaginable losses, or perhaps because of the collective experience of surviving and ultimately defeating the enemy, "the war strengthened Communist rule, especially by creating a sense of besieged national unity and providing the government with a source of legitimacy as defender of the homeland."[54] It is the idea of the war as a source of unity in a hostile world that became most important when Putin began invoking the memory of the war in 2005.

During his 2005 address (the sixtieth anniversary of the victory), Putin argued that "victory was achieved not just through the strength of weapons, but through the fortitude of all the peoples [*narodov*] united at the time in the union state."[55] The important element here is the emphasis on the spiritual aspect of victory, reinforced later in the speech with the statement that "the soldiers of the Great Patriotic War should by rights be called soldiers of freedom."[56] The reference to freedom has more to do with the role of the Soviet army in liberating Russia and other Soviet republics from occupation, and in that sense it fits with the previous discussion about the importance of national sovereignty. However, whatever its context, such a characterization explicitly ignores the Molotov–Ribbentrop Pact and its implications for countries across Eastern Europe, the atrocities of the Soviet army on its march to Berlin, and NKVD (the People's Commissariat for Internal Affairs) crimes across Eastern Europe, including the Katyn massacre in Poland. Glossing over these more uncomfortable sides of the Soviet war experience, Putin's arguments are consciously linked with statements about contemporary Russia's freedom as a sovereign nation to define its own path to and variant of democracy.[57] The pageantry and veneration of victory on May 9 (*den Pobedy*, Victory Day) have become critical elements in the Putin government's efforts to construct a modern Russian national identity.

Given the horrors of the Soviet wartime experience, it makes sense that it would be incorporated into later constructions of the national sense of self. Putin is also not the first leader to use the memory of the Great Patriotic War for his own purpose. Indeed, it recalls the Brezhnev policy of lionizing the role of the Communist Party in the World War II victory as part of its own regime legitimation strategy following Nikita Khrushchev's ouster.[58] The problem is that the emphasis on the Soviet achievements during World War II without mention of Soviet crimes, and especially the seizure of the Baltic states and the atrocities committed in Poland, drives a wedge between Russia and its closest European neighbors.

This leads to the broader problem of the emphasis on the memory of the Great Patriotic War: the man who led the country at the time. Analysis of Putin's appeal to the (selective) memory of World War II would be incomplete without discussion of Joseph Stalin and Stalinism. Robert Legvold writes of Stalin: "Never before or since has a Russian ruler so ravaged existing political, economic, and social structure. Not a single institution, from the family to the inner sanctum of political power . . . escaped wholesale transmogrification. More than that, of course, the collectivization of agriculture, the forced-draft industrialization, and the purge of the party and military thoroughly rescripted the very underpinnings of society."[59] Stalin and the system he created were responsible for millions of civilian deaths across the Soviet Union as a result of direct execution, state-sponsored famine, and slave labor in the gulag system. Furthermore, Stalin's faith that Adolf Hitler would honor the Molotov–Ribbentrop Non-Aggression Pact of 1939 along with his purge of the Red Army left the USSR unprepared for war and increased the number of Soviet casualties among both soldiers and civilians.

Despite these crimes, Stalin has a complicated place in post-Soviet historical narratives. According to a poll commissioned by the Carnegie Endowment for International Peace and conducted by the Levada Center in 2012, "Almost half of Russians surveyed believe 'Stalin was a wise leader who brought the Soviet Union to might and prosperity.' But over half of the Russians surveyed believe that Stalin's acts of repression constituted 'a political crime that cannot be justified.' And about two-thirds agree that 'for all Stalin's mistakes and misdeeds, the most important thing is that under his leadership the Soviet people won the Great Patriotic War.'"[60] As the survey results show, it is precisely Stalin's links to World War II that make his legacy so complicated. If Stalin's crimes are fully acknowledged, then this taints his biggest achievement: the Soviet victory in World War II.[61] It also formally implicates him and Soviet leadership for responsibility for excess war casualties. Therefore, while his image has been erased from public life and street signs, he remains "a hidden hero" whose presence continues to influence both Russian politics and the relationship between state and society.[62]

Putin's approach to Stalin during his first two terms in office reflected the ambiguity of Stalin's place in the Russian consciousness. The strong state Putin established, with its dependence on the security ministries, is a Soviet vision of the state, and Stalin is closely associated with that model.[63] Putin oversaw a system in which school textbooks were changed to extoll Stalin as "an efficient manager" while simultaneously including *Gulag Archipelago* on the reading list.[64] In October 2007 Putin visited one of the places where mass executions took place during the Great Terror (the period between 1936 and 1938 when Stalin and the NKVD purged huge numbers of officials, Red Army leadership, and intellectuals, among others classes of citizens) and was apparently moved and shocked by the experience.[65] Nevertheless, his regime has also prevented the establishment of an official memorial center for Stalin's victims, and Memorial, the Russian organization devoted to rehabilitating Stalin's victims, is under frequent threat of closure.[66] Ultimately, the approach from 2000 to 2008 was one of a careful balance. Putin acknowledged some level of wrongdoing on the part of Stalin and his system, but he did not allow criticism to progress to a point that it threatened the narrative of the Great Patriotic War, especially when that narrative became more important to Putin's construction of national identity.[67]

The "Russian World" and Civilizational Discourse

The other shift that happened with Putin's second term in office was the revival of the idea of the broader Russian community beyond Russia's geographical borders. Mentions of Russia's responsibility to protect compatriots abroad are long-standing features of official Russian policy documents, but after 2004 the tone began to change. Indeed, the famous line of the collapse of the USSR as the "biggest geopolitical catastrophe of the [twentieth] century," which appeared in

Putin's 2005 annual address, is nested within a paragraph about Russians finding themselves on the wrong side of the border.[68]

The emphasis on the existence of a "Russian world," to be strengthened through the promulgation of Russian language and culture, is in some ways an example of Russia experimenting with soft power, just as Germany does with the Goethe-Institut and China with the Confucius Institute. It has also been interpreted as a renewal of historical Russian imperialism. Both of these interpretations have merit. In this analysis, however, what is important is the reintroduction of the idea that Russians are a distinct and unique civilization. Although not fully articulated in the annual speeches until later, these quiet nods to the idea laid the groundwork for the major innovations on this topic introduced in the 2007 foreign policy survey.

As with the discourse on independence and national sovereignty, 2007 marked a turning point in the discourse on civilization. The section on multilateral diplomacy of the 2007 survey prepared by the Russian Ministry of Foreign Affairs (Ministerstvo innostranykh del, or MID) includes an entire subsection entitled "Dialogue among Civilizations." The subsection opens with a statement about the dangers of globalization erasing "national distinctiveness," and goes on to argue,

> The promotion of the dialogue among civilizations in these circumstances is becoming one of the most important elements of our foreign policy strategy. There are grounds to make this theme the thread running through our international contacts and secure it as the "big idea" of Russian diplomacy for the foreseeable future. This is already becoming an effective means for asserting the intellectual leadership of Russia in world politics, upholding our foreign policy independence and advancing national interests in particular situations and questions of international life.[69]

This paragraph points to two major deviations from the Millennium Manifesto that was issued under Putin's name seven years prior. First is the idea of multiple civilizations, as opposed to (as in the Millennium address) joining the path that all civilization joins. This is particularly notable because the notion of a dialogue of civilizations is standard language in BRICS statements and declarations.

The second deviation is more striking and, from the perspective of how BRICS fits into Russian foreign policy, more important. Here is the reintroduction of the search for the next "great idea" that will reinstate Russia as the leader of a global counterculture. This is quite different from the assertion in the Millennium article that the Bolshevist experiment was a "historic futility."[70] It also suggests that part of the goal in bringing BRICS together was to create a forum in which Russia could offer "big ideas."[71] The phrase "intellectual leadership" is especially significant as it is the same phrase the chief executive officer of the National Committee for BRICS Research used to describe Russia's role in the group in 2014.[72]

The 2007 survey also explicitly identifies the aim of establishing Russia—and Russians—as a distinct civilization. In the subsection "Protecting the Interests of Compatriots Abroad," which appears in the chapter "The Humanitarian Direction of Foreign Policy," the report states: "For the new Russia, especially as tens of millions of our people as a result of the breakup of the USSR have found themselves outside of the country, defending compatriots' interests is a natural foreign policy priority, whose significance will only grow. There is a need for continuous all-round assistance to the strengthening of the compatriots' links with the historical Homeland and the creation of a 'Russian world' as a unique element of human civilization."[73] There are several notable ideas in this paragraph. First, it recalls the phraseology of the paragraph from the 2005 annual address about the context of the collapse of the Soviet Union as a great geopolitical catastrophe, suggesting that the message of that speech has been internalized into policy direction. Second, in recommending that resources be devoted to "creating" Russia and Russians as a distinct civilization, the survey implicitly indicates that the proposal represents a shift in policy. The recommendation builds on previously adopted documents related to language and resettlement assistance programs for Russians living abroad, but this shows a unification of these disparate attempts into a higher-level, conceptual push toward public unification of Russia as a separate civilization.[74]

Restoring Balance to Putin's Rhetorical Balancing

It is important to remember that even as Putin's rhetoric on issues of sovereignty and civilization became more strident, it never progressed to the point of a wholesale rejection of the West in terms of either identity or policy during his first two presidential terms. Neither was it an uncomplicated process of separation. Even in speeches delineating Russia from its European neighbors, Putin also declared that the country was a "great European nation."[75] The 2007 foreign policy survey touts Russia's inclusion in the G8 as proof that the group is becoming more representative and is no longer simply "an exclusive 'club of Western powers,'" while at the same time Russia balked at the idea of inviting the O5 countries to the 2006 G8 summit in St. Petersburg, the first (and only) hosted by Russia.[76] Russia was also initially opposed to the G20 financial group, worried that including other countries would minimize its own power even though it was already excluded from the G7 finance minister meetings.[77]

There are several interrelated issues here. First, regardless of the change in rhetoric, the political elite, including Putin, remained firmly Western oriented.[78] In addition, the overriding goal has always been maintaining Russia's preeminence in the world's most powerful (or most exclusive) clubs. Up until the beginning of the financial crisis, those clubs were almost entirely Western. The rhetoric therefore indicated possible changes in policy direction; it did not represent a real sea change in the core political perspective. In that sense, the combative and separatist rhetoric that emerged over Putin's first two terms in office is better understood as a warning shot against Western countries to prevent them from encroaching on Russian national interests rather than an intention to leave the Western sphere entirely.

This leads to the second issue: balancing. BRIC was in no way capable of being an actual balance against the West between 2000 and 2007. Although the countries' growth and future potential were recognized very early in Putin's first term, meetings did not begin until 2005. Indeed, as the brief partnership with France and Germany in the wake of the onset of the Iraq War demonstrates, early balancing efforts were more about dividing the United States and Europe rather than forming new coalitions. Finally, public efforts to coordinate against Western influence before the onset of the crisis, notably Russia's nomination of an alternative candidate for the position of managing director of the IMF in 2007, were unsuccessful.[79] The best Putin could do, therefore, was establish Russia's status as an independent actor rhetorically, deploying the BRIC moniker as a buttress when possible while slowly building up the group behind the scenes.

Finally, there is the question of economics. While it is tempting to read Russia's BRICS engagement, and the idea of a "multivector" policy more broadly, as strictly anti-Western, this would be an oversimplification, especially in the early years. The one absolute constant in all of Putin's speeches in his first two terms, and a constant that held in the official concepts produced by the ministries, was that the primary foreign and domestic policy goal was economic development. This necessitated both a diversification of the economy away from natural resources (which Putin did not achieve) and a diversification of economic partners (which he did). During his time as president, Russian trade with non-European partners did increase somewhat, even if not to the extent desired. Therefore, although BRICS was and is more about politics than economics for Russia, it is worth remembering that it also served economic objectives.

Understanding the role BRICS would play in Russian foreign policy once the group debuted on the international scene therefore requires accepting several competing truths simultaneously. Rhetoric about Russia as its own civilization distinct from Europe and the country's right to define its own development path increased between 2000 and 2007; this was both cause and consequence of deteriorating relations with the West. At the same time, the preference for remaining in the top echelon of international clubs mandated continued prioritization of groups like the G8 over fledgling associations with other powers. Finally, economic logic offered a veneer for emphasizing relations beyond the West, and a changing distribution of global economic power supported those efforts.

Conclusion

There is no official record of the first meetings of BRIC representatives. Major newspapers (Russian or otherwise) did not cover them, and it was not until the first leaders' meeting at the 2008 Hokkaido G8 that the Kremlin even published a press release about BRIC.[80] Neither was BRIC mentioned in any of the annual addresses during Putin's first two terms in office. In terms of documentary evidence, the very early years of BRIC in Russian political discourse are visible almost exclusively in how attendant concepts were framed.

This may be a result of the lack of an initial vision for what BRIC could become. Cynthia Roberts argues that Russia's initiation of BRIC meetings was more a tactical move than a strategic one.[81] From a procedural perspective, this is probably true. Certainly, it made little sense to advertise the group until its potential was evident. As soon as it became clear that the group had long-term prospects, Russia was at the forefront of publicly touting its importance.[82]

There is also evidence that BRIC was beginning to feature in Russian foreign policy planning before the 2008 financial crisis. This is evident in Putin's 2007 speech at the Munich Security Conference, where he suggested that new economic centers would become the new global political leaders. BRIC also features in the 2007 Foreign Policy Survey. Though the group is mentioned only in the context of economic diplomacy, the report stresses the importance of continuing to develop it as a dialogue forum. By 2007 BRIC had penetrated into MID strategic planning as a useful vector for Russian foreign policy, beyond the use of each individual BRIC country as an economic partner.

What is more important, however, is the extent to which the evolution of rhetoric during Putin's first two terms in office created a space for BRIC to be incorporated into Russian foreign policy. This is primarily a result of the twin phenomena of increasing frustration with the West and economic growth that made Russia a more self-assured actor on the international stage. By the time of the onset of the financial crisis in 2008, Putin had publicly redefined Russia's international orientation sufficiently to support a credible belief that the country was no longer interested in joining the Western-led international system but would instead forge an alternate path. That this was in some ways a rhetorical feint is both critical and incidental. Critical because that is very much the role BRIC played for Russia between 2008 and 2013: that of a theoretical alternative option deployed as a bargaining chip in other forums. It is incidental, though, because maintaining the fiction of BRIC as a real alternative led to an ongoing push for actual institutionalization.

In a twist of fate, even as Putin had primed the foreign policy machine to promote BRIC as a political group with the principal aim of balancing against Western hegemony, he also installed a successor whose rhetoric was markedly more conciliatory toward Russia's erstwhile partners in the West. Political BRIC thus began to flourish contemporaneously with the US-Russia Reset and better Russia-NATO relations than had existed since the early 1990s. The evolution of BRIC under Medvedev, and how it was incorporated into his approach to foreign policy, is the topic of the next chapter.

Notes

Epigraphs: Chaadaev, *Major Works of Peter Chaadaev*, 204; and Vladislav Surkov, as cited in Lukyanov, "Putin's Russia," 141.

1. Lo, *Vladimir Putin*, 4.
2. Ibid., 14–15.
3. Ibid., 15–16.
4. Makarychev and Morozov, "Multilateralism, Multipolarity, and Beyond," 362.
5. Ministry of Foreign Affairs of the Russian Federation, "National Security Concept of the Russian Federation," January 24, 2000.
6. Ministry of Foreign Affairs of the Russian Federation, "Foreign Policy Concept of the Russian Federation," June 28, 2000.
7. Putin, "Poslanie k Federalnomu Sobraniiu Rossiiskoi Federatsii," July 8, 2000.
8. Putin, "Russia at the Turn of the Millennium."
9. Putin, "Poslanie k Federalnomu Sobraniiu Rossiiskoi Federatsii," April 3, 2001; Putin, "Poslanie k Federalnomu Sobraniiu Rossiiskoi Federatsii," April 18, 2002; and Putin, "Poslanie k Federalnomu Sobraniiu Rossiiskoi Federatsii," May 16, 2003.
10. Judah, *Fragile Empire*, 39.
11. Lo, *Vladimir Putin*, 19–20.
12. Ibid., 20.
13. Judah, *Fragile Empire*, 41.
14. Data from the International Monetary Fund World Economic Outlook Database October 2014, https://www.imf.org/external/pubs/ft/weo/2014/02/weodata/index.aspx.
15. Colton, "Putin and the Attenuation of Russian Democracy," 39.
16. Putin, "Poslanie k Federalnomu Sobraniiu Rossiiskoi Federatsii," May 26, 2004.
17. Ibid.
18. Mankoff, *Russian Foreign Policy*, 63.
19. Stent, *Limits of Partnership*, 68–69.
20. Lo, *Vladimir Putin*, 18.
21. Ibid., 18.
22. Stent, *Limits of Partnership*, 66.
23. It was also in 2004 that the "big bang" enlargement occurred, when Warsaw Pact members, including the three Baltic states, joined NATO and the EU. This brought NATO directly to Russian borders.
24. John Tagliabue, "France and Russia Ready to Veto against Iraq War," *New York Times*, March 6, 2003, https://www.nytimes.com/2003/03/06/international/europe/france -and-russia-ready-to-use-veto-against-iraq-war.html.
25. "France Will Be Punished," *Telegraph*, June 2, 2003, https://www.telegraph.co.uk /comment/telegraph-view/3592078/France-will-be-punished.html.
26. Gould-Davies, "Russia's Sovereign Globalization," 10–11.

27. Putin, "Poslanie k Federalnomu Sobraniiu Rossiiskoi Federatsii," May 26, 2004.

28. Lo, *Vladimir Putin*, 17.

29. Alexander Gabuev, interview with author, December 5, 2014, Moscow; and Lo, *Russia and the New World Disorder*, xxi.

30. Putin, "Poslanie k Federalnomu Sobraniiu Rossiiskoi Federatsii," May 26, 2004.

31. "Putin's Prepared Remarks at 43rd Munich Conference on Security Policy," *Washington Post*, February 12, 2007, http://www.washingtonpost.com/wp-dyn/content/article/2007/02/12/AR2007021200555.html.

32. Ministry of Foreign Affairs of the Russian Federation, "A Survey of Russian Foreign Policy."

33. Cited in Pant and Joshi, "Russia: European or Not?," 212–13.

34. "Pervy zamestitl glavy kremlevskoi administratsii Vladislav Surkov: Suverenitet—eto politicheskii sinonim nashei konkurentosposobnosti," *Komsomolskaia Pravda*, March 7, 2006.

35. Michael R. Gordon, "U.S. Is Proposing European Shield for Iran Missiles," *New York Times*, May 22, 2006, https://www.nytimes.com/2006/05/22/world/middleeast/22missiles.html.

36. Putin, "Putin's Prepared Remarks at 43rd Munich Conference on Security Policy."

37. Ibid.

38. Ibid.

39. Ibid.

40. Ministry of Foreign Affairs of the Russian Federation, "Survey of Russian Foreign Policy."

41. Ibid.; and Ministry of Foreign Affairs of the Russian Federation, "Obzor vneshnei politiki Rossiiskoi Federatsii."

42. Ministry of Foreign Affairs of the Russian Federation, "Survey of Russian Foreign Policy."

43. Ibid.

44. Ibid.

45. Putin, "Russia at the Turn of the Millennium."

46. Ibid.

47. Ibid.

48. "National Security Concept of the Russian Federation."

49. Ministry of Foreign Affairs of the Russian Federation, "Foreign Policy Concept of the Russian Federation," June 28, 2000.

50. Putin, "Poslanie k Federalnomu Sobraniiu Rossiiskoi Federatsii," July 8, 2000; Putin, "Poslanie k Federalnomu Sobraniiu Rossiiskoi Federatsii," April 3, 2001; Putin, "Poslanie k Federalnomu Sobraniiu Rossiiskoi Federatsii," April 18, 2002; and Putin, "Poslanie k Federalnomu Sobraniiu Rossiiskoi Federatsii," May 16, 2003.

51. Putin, "Poslanie k Federalnomu Sobraniiu Rossiiskoi Federatsii," May 16, 2003.

52. Brown, *Rise and Fall of Communism*, 135.

53. Ibid., 138.

54. Riasanovsky and Steinberg, *History of Russia since 1855*, 544.

55. Putin, "Poslanie k Federalnomu Sobraniiu Rossiiskoi Federatsii," April 25, 2005.

56. Ibid.

57. Ibid.

58. Hough and Fainsod, *How the Soviet Union Is Governed*, 255.

59. Legvold, "Russian Foreign Policy," 85.

60. Lipman, Gudkov, and Bakradze, *Stalin Puzzle*, 16. Although the poll was conducted outside the timeframe addressed in this chapter, there is no reason to think that it would have yielded significantly different results in 2005, since the big change in veneration of World War II came with Putin's accession. See Satter, *It Was a Long Time Ago*, 105.

61. Lo, *Russia and the New World Disorder*, 22.

62. Lipman, Gudkov, and Bakradze, *Stalin Puzzle*, 16.

63. Ibid., 18. Putin is not Stalin, but Stalin did originate the strong state model so associated with the Soviet Union, and some elements of Putin's management recall that model.

64. Judah, *Fragile Empire*, 112.

65. Lipman, Gudkov, and Bakradze, *Stalin Puzzle*, 19.

66. Ibid., 20; and Lo, *Russia and the New World Disorder*, 22.

67. Aron, *Roads to the Temple*, 299.

68. Putin, "Poslanie k Federalnomu Sobraniiu Rossiiskoi Federatsii," April 25, 2005.

69. Ministry of Foreign Affairs of the Russian Federation, "Survey of Russian Foreign Policy."

70. Putin, "Russia at the Turn of the Millennium."

71. Fyodor Lukyanov, interview with the author, December 13, 2014, Moscow.

72. Georgii Toloraya, interview with the author, May 14, 2014, Moscow.

73. Ministry of Foreign Affairs of the Russian Federation, "Survey of Russian Foreign Policy"; and Ministry of Foreign Affairs of the Russian Federation, "Obzor vneshnei politiki Rossiiskoi Federatsii."

74. Ministry of Foreign Affairs of the Russian Federation, "Survey of Russian Foreign Policy."

75. Putin, "Poslanie k Federalnomu Sobraniiu Rossiiskoi Federatsii," April 25, 2005.

76. Payne, "G8 in a Changing Global Economic Order," 530.

77. Baev, "Leading in the Concert of Great Powers," 60. This is not the same G20 that materialized after the beginning of the 2008 global financial crisis.

78. Gabuev, interview; Lukyanov, interview; and Viktoria Panova, interview, September 19, 2014, Moscow.

79. Peter Finn, "Russia Challenges West with Nomination to IMF," *Washington Post*, August 23, 2007, http://www.washingtonpost.com/wp-dyn/content/article/2007/08/22/AR2007082202487.html.

80. BRICS Leaders, "Leaders of the BRIC Countries (Brazil, Russia, India and China) Met during the G8 Summit in Japan."

81. Roberts, "Building the New World Order," 4.

82. Ibid., 5.

4

Potemkin Villages and Rhetorical Bridges

BRICS in Russian Policy, 2008–13

> The Lisbon summit has made decisions related to the forming of a modern partnership, one based on the indivisibility of security, mutual trust, transparency and predictability. We have decided on how we will work on the creation of a common space of peace and security in the Euro-Atlantic region. This makes us moderately optimistic when we evaluate the prospects of our work on Russia's initiative on a new European security treaty.
> —Dmitry Medvedev, 2010

> Cooperation in the BRICS format is one of the key long-term priorities in foreign policy for the Russian Federation.
> —Sergei Lavrov, 2012

THE RUSSIAN APPROACH TO BRICS BETWEEN 2008 AND 2013 SHOULD HAVE become progressively deeper, wider, and more nuanced. Over the preceding seven years, Vladimir Putin's rhetorical constructions of sovereignty and national identity had prepared the foreign policy establishment to embrace BRIC as an alternative to the Western-led international system. When BRIC burst forth in the wake of the global financial crisis, it could have become a centerpiece of a new Russian foreign policy.

Instead, the approach to BRICS in this era remained largely static. The Russian leadership maintained it as a rhetorical alternative but never invested in it as a real policy priority. What's more, Putin's anointment of Dmitry Medvedev as his successor almost guaranteed that Russian political rhetoric and policy choices would reorient toward the West. Why Putin chose a successor who was so palatable to the West after years of increasingly anti-American rhetoric and how much agency Medvedev had over his foreign and domestic policy remain unknowns. This complicates the analysis of Russian policy and political rhetoric during his tenure.

The complications are compounded by the confluence of several major regional and global events that occurred near the beginning of Medvedev's term in office. These include the August 2008 war with Georgia, the September 2008 onset of the acute phase of the global financial crisis, and the November 2008 election of Barack Obama as US president. The result was a fundamentally altered international context from the one that had existed when Putin left the presidency in May 2008. These shifts produced openings in several directions for the Russian leadership to change the course of Russian foreign policy; the option they chose is indicative of underlying Russian foreign policy orientations and preoccupations.

Finally, the rapid evolution of BRICS itself during this period poses its own set of constraints. As discussed in the second chapter, the onset of the 2008 financial crisis was a catalyst for BRICS's development as a coordinated group. It is therefore an unequal comparison to consider Medvedev's policy toward BRICS against Putin's earlier stage setting. Although Putin had cued up the foreign minister meetings, Medvedev was the first Russian president to meet formally with his BRIC counterparts (in July 2008) and was at the helm when world events suddenly gave BRIC a perfect entrée onto the international stage. Therefore, it is hard to determine whether the increased emphasis Medvedev gave to BRIC in his first year was because of Russian political leanings, because of his own inclinations, or simply because the context changed and the opportunity presented itself.

By the same token, that early phase of BRIC's international prominence did not last. By 2011 the group was focused primarily on building up intra-BRICS cooperation. The intra-BRICS agenda supported Russian goals for economic modernization. It detracted focus, however, from the element of the group that had always most interested the Russian leadership and that Putin had developed through his rhetoric as president: BRICS as a balance against the West and a way to gain leverage in Russia's ongoing attempts to revise the post–Cold War international institutional architecture. Although Medvedev was less vocally anti-American than Putin, he was no less committed to bringing about a multipolar world. When BRICS turned inward, the group was no longer explicitly useful for that project.

As a result of the changing international context and the changes within BRICS itself, BRICS did not penetrate Russian foreign policy beyond official rhetoric either during Medvedev's term or for the first two years of Vladimir Putin's third term. Further, the rhetoric itself stayed fairly shallow. Although leaders could have highlighted the growing economic and development agenda, the focus stayed on the role BRICS could play in changing the international order.

Although leaders remained frozen on the international aspect of BRICS, Russian academics and experts at state research institutions considered BRICS in a more nuanced fashion. They produced a plethora of books, reports, and analyses about current and potential areas of BRICS cooperation. In some ways this intellectual output filled in gaps that the narrow official approach to BRICS left open, thereby showing a deeper thinking about BRICS among the intellectual elite than was evident in the ruling elite. These scholars produced a framework of ideas and goals for BRICS that could be further developed if desire (or need) arose. But while the work was often supported with state funds, the analysis was not incorporated into official discourse. This suggests that the goal of supporting BRICS research projects was part of the overall Russian attempt to build a façade of BRICS policy rather than an indication of deepening official interest in the details of the topic.

This chapter proceeds as follows: the first section considers official approaches to BRICS from 2008 through 2013, with particular reference to how changing relations with the West and other international projects affected how officials portrayed the role of the BRICS group and its importance to Russia. The second section analyzes the unofficial approach to BRICS during this era, looking in particular at the material produced in state universities and research institutes. Finally, the third section draws those two prior analyses together to explain why the Russian approach to BRICS was so loud but so empty, even when BRICS itself was developing rapidly.

A Note on Medvedev

The ambiguity of Medvedev's de facto power vis-à-vis Putin, who was prime minister when Medvedev was president, makes it more difficult to ascribe to his speeches the same agenda-setting power as to those given by Putin. The challenge is that Medvedev was neither puppet nor free agent. Instead, he was somewhere in between, but the precise balance is unknown. Further, it is unlikely that the balance remained constant throughout Medvedev's four-year term.

The question of how independent Medvedev was is of particular importance in considering foreign policy, the realm in which he was constitutionally supreme. There are conflicting opinions on this issue. Gordon Hahn, for example, argues that in the first two years of the tandemocracy, "except for sporadic forays into foreign policy, Putin . . . settled into the economic policymaking as premier and avoid[ed] involvement in the president's prerogatives, at least in public."[1] By contrast, Angela Stent, citing an unnamed US official, argues that Medvedev wished to "establish his own power base" but was unable to do so for fear of threatening Putin.[2] Although the context is a more general question of which leader in the tandem held more power, it suggests that in all areas, including foreign policy, Medvedev's actions were constrained. In addition, the 2008 Foreign Policy Concept, which Medvedev approved shortly upon taking office, vested some foreign policy power in the cabinet and the office of the prime minister.[3]

Given these unknowns, the approach to the analysis will be as follows. At the basic level, I assume that Medvedev was not merely a stooge but rather represented a faction of the elite who for some period was ascendant over Putin's traditional power ministry clan.[4] Therefore, his words had weight. Indeed, even assuming Putin was quite powerful behind the scenes, Medvedev, especially in his first two years, presented a different vision for Russia than that which Putin had put forth during the final years of his second presidential term. Whatever the power dynamics, it is clear that Medvedev was permitted to do so, and this is significant. As argued in the first chapter, the words of the leader matter. Whether Medvedev was "allowed" to be reform-oriented and less anti-Western in his foreign policy or whether he was independent enough to present those ideas over Putin's objections, his speeches reflected a visible shift in direction in Russian policy.

Just because those views were promulgated at the highest level, though, does not mean elite infighting had ceased and everyone had acquiesced to the new priorities. Russian elite opinion has never been monolithic. When Putin was president in his first two terms, he commanded sufficient respect and power that it is fair to consider his statements as representatives of the overwhelmingly dominant portion of the ruling elite (as distinct from the intellectual elite). Medvedev was seen as president conditional only on Putin's good will. Therefore, although Medvedev's words and speeches will be given pride of place, in this chapter more supporting documents, such as speeches by the foreign minister, will be drawn in as additional support.

BRICS in Russian Official Policy

As a result of both exogenous forces and internal group dynamics, BRICS underwent enormous change and evolution between 2008 and 2013. Russia's official position on BRICS and its utility for Russian foreign policy, however, remained essentially static. This is a result primarily of renewed efforts to strengthen US/EU-Russian relations, an increased emphasis on economic development as a goal of foreign policy, and changes in the trajectory and focus of the BRICS group that diverged from Russian goals for the forum.

2008: The Year That Everything Could Have Changed

By every measure 2008 was a watershed year in international politics and economics.[5] Domestically, both Russia and America held presidential elections, and each brought in a leader whose stance appeared quite different from his predecessor's and whose election was a landmark event. In Russia the election of Dmitry Medvedev marked the first peaceful transfer of power via election in Russian history.[6] In the United States, Barack Obama became the country's first African American president, and his election was a symbol both domestically and internationally of a repudiation of the divisive policies of the George W. Bush era.[7]

Relations between Russia and the United States also suffered a severe shock in 2008. The August war with Georgia was vivid evidence that bilateral relations had been allowed to drift dangerously. American and Russian analysts called for a more pragmatic approach to the bilateral relationship. As one Russian expert put it, "Washington needs to think strategically about Moscow, not ideologically or theologically."[8] An American expert argued, "The crisis in Georgia brings us face-to-face with the reality that the United States and Russia have squandered the opportunity to build a relationship that works for both parties."[9] Although the dividends did not begin to materialize until 2009, this sudden jolt spurred both sides to renew their emphasis on the bilateral relationship in ways that had implications for each country's wider foreign policy stance.

The shocks were not just domestic and bilateral. In September 2008, after a tense weekend of closed-door negotiations at the Federal Reserve Bank of New York, the US government declined to bail out Lehman Brothers, a multinational financial services firm headquartered in midtown Manhattan. On September 15, 2008, Lehman collapsed, sending shockwaves through the international financial system. In addition to roiling international markets, Lehman's demise intensified an ongoing discussion about the creation of new international financial governance architecture because of the signal it sent about America's capacity for leadership and ability to impose its vision for world order.[10]

The combination of the decline in bilateral Russian-American relations as a result of the war in Georgia with the more general global questioning of America's role in the world following the beginning of the financial crisis had a noticeable effect on Russian rhetoric. During his first address to the Federal Assembly, President Medvedev blamed both the Georgia war and the financial crisis on irresponsible American policy.[11] He also listed BRIC as a group with responsibility and importance for global governance, arguing, "The mistakes and crises of 2008 are a lesson to all responsible nations that it is time for action. We need to radically reform the political and economic systems. Russia, in any event, will insist on this. We will work together on this with the United States, the European Union, the BRIC countries and all parties with an interest in reform. We will do everything possible to make the world a fairer and safer place."[12] The message was clear: for Russia (rhetorically), the United States and the system it dominated had been overtaken by events, and Western powers would not have a monopoly on solving the problem they created.

Part of the reason the Russian leadership was so quick to condemn the profligacy of Western policy was that while Western markets were troubled beginning in 2007, the effects hit Russia only after Lehman crashed. Indeed, "until 2008, Russia was hailed as an economic miracle, enjoying rapid GDP growth, macroeconomic stability, and an unprecedented rise in real disposable income (more than 10 percent per annum on average over eight years)."[13] In January of 2008, before the depth of the crisis was clear but when the problems in the US economy were already evident, the Russian finance minister Alexei Kudrin stated that Russia would be an "island of stability" amid the recessions hitting Western economies.[14] In August 2008 Russia also had the world's third-largest national currency reserves, after China and Japan.[15]

It is worth noting that this illusory stability bred ambition and a misreading of the willingness of BRIC partners to launch a frontal attack on US dollar supremacy. According to then–US treasury secretary Henry Paulson, Russia in 2008 approached China about a coordinated sale of their shares in distressed US government–sponsored enterprises Fannie Mae and Freddie Mac.[16] China owned substantial holdings in both companies, and their willingness to hold the securities through the crisis provided vital support to the US economy.[17] Selling off their shares in Fannie Mae and Freddie Mac would have sent the markets into further turmoil and could have crashed the dollar. The Chinese demurred and told Paulson of Russia's proposal.[18] While it did not come to fruition, Russia's proposal is indication of their willingness to take extreme measures to lessen US dominance and their hope to use BRIC and its members to accomplish that aim.

Despite this early confidence, however, the effect of the global crisis was already evident in Russia when Medvedev gave his address to the Federal Assembly in November 2008. By October of that year, the Russian stock market had lost 80 percent of its May 2008 value.[19] Plunging commodities prices, capital flight, and bailouts of inefficient state companies tore through the country's foreign currency reserves.[20] Of all G20 economies, Russia's suffered the worst effects as a result of the 2008 crisis. These economic realities, however, did not stop Medvedev from capitalizing on the global discontent with US international leadership that the crisis had magnified and crystalized.

Medvedev's call to reconstruct global governance architecture to be more inclusive was not a new feature of Russian political rhetoric. Its roots trace back at least to Evgenii Primakov's calls to establish a multipolar world in the late 1990s and, in some guises, to the Soviet era as well. Medvedev's mention of BRIC as a force in bringing about a new world order was not entirely new; although this is the first annual address to mention the group, the sentiment is similar to that expressed by Putin in Munich in 2007. What is significant about this statement is twofold: first, Putin spoke generally about the rise of the BRIC countries as a new force in international politics. Medvedev, in the statement quoted above and again later in the same speech, explicitly referred to BRIC as an organized group conceptually on par with the G8 in terms of its role as a forum responsible for global governance. In doing so, he also implicitly highlighted the value Russia sees in its membership in that group.[21]

This new emphasis on BRIC followed statements made by Russian foreign minister Sergei Lavrov after the first stand-alone meeting of the BRIC foreign ministers in Ekaterinburg, Russia, in May 2008. The meeting was initiated by Russia. Following the meeting, Lavrov told the press:

Russia attaches great significance to its development in the BRIC format. This is a format which is not far-fetched, but derives from real life. It derives from the fact that the high rates of economic growth exhibited by our countries largely ensure the steady development of the world economy. Now that there is much talk about reforming the prevailing global financial-economic architecture, we have something to discuss, especially the protection of our common interests, including responsibility for the state of affairs in the present-day world.[22]

When Lavrov gave his press conference, the heads of state had never met formally as BRIC. The group had only just held its first stand-alone conference, as opposed to sideline meetings at other events. When Medvedev spoke, the leaders had held a sideline at the Hokkaido G8 but had not held their first summit. Russian political leaders therefore appear to have included BRIC as a significant group as a signal of Russia's aspirations and intentions for the future.[23]

The Foreign Policy Concept that Medvedev signed in July 2008 undergirded the aspirations expressed in both Medvedev's and Lavrov's statements.[24] The new concept, the first since 2000, operationalized many of the innovations from the 2007 review of foreign policy, including the idea of Russia once again being prepared to be an international leader and the centrality of the civilizational dimension of international relations. In another signal of Russia's shift away from a Western-centric approach toward a more fully multivector foreign policy, the concept also explicitly mentions the Troika (the Russia-India-China configuration) and BRIC as two forums Russia will actively use, in addition to the G8, in its quest to design a more stable world system.[25]

The 2008 concept, however, also suggests a greater emphasis on economic stability and international economic integration than did its predecessor from 2000. Although it proposes a need to reshuffle international governance and represents a Russia more assured of its place, it also is less combative about that place than the concept Putin adopted in his first presidential term.[26] Instead, the document proclaims the importance of "network diplomacy," announcing Russia's intention to "cooperate not as part of unwieldy military-political alliances, but with flexible, shifting groups of countries as necessary."[27] In other words, Russia wishes to be everywhere and part of every discussion, driving toward the goal of enhanced international power through increased economic growth. It is a continuation of the long-standing emphasis on Russia as an independent international actor. The emphasis on economics, however, is new.

The decrease in pugilistic rhetoric was also visible in how Lavrov spoke about BRIC in his press conference following the 2008 Ekaterinburg meeting of the foreign ministers. In the quotation above, Lavrov framed BRIC as the logical outgrowth of "real life."[28] BRIC is presented as a group prepared to take responsibility for improving global governance architecture, motivated to act in concert because of shared common interests. Although these sentiments are not substantively different from what Putin said in Munich, the gloss is one of global cooperation rather than global confrontation. Put another way, BRIC here is presented as one of many tools in Russia's pocket that the country could and would use to pursue its interests. It is by no means a replacement for other international partnerships. This presentation is also more in line with the tone of later BRICS summit declarations and accords with the official BRICS position that its formation has been a response to objective shifts in global economic power.

The moderation in rhetoric was not the only indication that BRIC would not supersede traditional partnerships in Russia's foreign policy priorities. In 2008, concurrent with the increased public emphasis on BRIC as a force in global governance, Medvedev also looked West. During the World Policy Conference in Evian, France, the Russian president outlined his proposal for a new European Security Treaty (EST).[29] He struck many of the same themes as he would in his 2008 address to the Federal Assembly the following month as well as in the 2008 Foreign Policy Concept. His statements, however, were all nested within a firm argument that Russia is an integral part of the Euro-Atlantic world.[30]

The EST proposal was poorly thought out and very vague on details. It also included suggestions that would clearly be anathema to NATO and the European Union, including a minimization of each of their roles in European security architecture.[31] Nevertheless, it was also the first major international policy proposal of Medvedev's presidency. Although he did not elaborate on the details until October 2008, Medvedev actually first presented the proposal at a meeting in Berlin before any of the 2008 crises hit.[32] This suggests that improving relations with the West was a higher priority for Medvedev than was elevating and strengthening BRIC. The EST remained a priority even after the Russo-Georgian War in August 2008 and the onset of the financial crisis, as evidenced by the release of the full draft treaty in November 2009. Therefore, while BRIC was an important rhetorical device in 2008, it did not displace the traditional focus on relations with the West.[33]

This is not to argue that Medvedev ever intended a return to the 1990s policy of (perceived) subordination of Russian national interests to Western leadership. Quite the contrary: the EST was itself indicative that Medvedev, like his predecessor, was committed to the goal of renegotiating post–Cold War institutional architecture. Unlike Putin, however, the proposal for revision centered on the Euro-Atlantic space. In Munich, Putin presented a Russia fed up with the West and ready to shift its focus to entirely new quarters. With the EST, whatever its faults and impracticalities, Medvedev highlighted that while the creation of a new world order was the international political priority of his presidency, he would aim to do so from a Western-oriented perspective. The proposal is also evidence of the ongoing tension in Russian elite discourse over trying to be accepted by the West and trying to compete with or balance against it.

It is worth noting that while the EST was a firm indication of Medvedev's political goals, his economic goals were somewhat different. Most important, the global financial crisis for the first time forced Russia to develop a comprehensive economic policy toward China. While economic relations had existed on paper for some time, such as a memorandum of understanding between China and Gazprom from 2006, the Russian side was not convinced of the worth of those deals.[34] After the global financial crisis, and especially after the precipitous drop in Russian GDP in 2009, that changed.[35] In 2010 China became Russia's largest trading partner.[36] That same year the Ministry of Economic Development and Trade announced the intention to increase Chinese FDI in Russia by $10 billion over the next ten years, from $2 billion to $12 billion.[37] The unwillingness of Western banks to lend to Rosneft and Transneft (state oil and oil transit companies) after the financial crisis hit Russia in 2009 also acted as a spur to increase Russian-Chinese energy relations.[38]

2009–11: Stasis

Rhetorical emphasis on BRIC subsided after 2008. This was a result of improved Russian-US and Russian-NATO relations, specifics of Medvedev's policy priorities, and changes within BRIC itself. Throughout the remainder of Medvedev's term and into the beginning of Putin's return to the presidency, the approach to BRICS in Russian foreign policy remained unchanged. It served the specific role of "rhetorical balancing"—with varying degrees of confrontational overtones—without becoming a real priority for the leadership.

US-Russian relations improved dramatically following the election of Barack Obama. There was optimism on both sides that with two leaders who came of age at the end of the Cold War, the historical baggage of the relationship could finally be jettisoned in favor of a new, modern partnership. Most important, though, was the presence in Washington of an administration that appeared willing to take a pragmatic rather than value-driven approach to US-Russian relations.[39] This new approach was motivated both by the shock of the collapse in relations following the Russo-Georgian War as well as a move among American experts to consider US policy toward Russia more holistically, as one piece of America's larger foreign policy goals and objectives.[40]

The "US-Russia Reset" got off to a rocky start when US secretary of state Hillary Clinton gave Minister Lavrov a button accidentally mislabeled "overload" instead of "reset." Despite these rough beginnings, however, the new approach bore significant early fruit. Following a sunny first meeting between the two leaders at the London G20 in April 2009, the two countries concluded a much-needed successor to the lapsed Strategic Arms Reduction Treaty agreement and established the Bilateral Presidential Commission, which included working groups on areas such as energy, democracy and human rights, and counterterrorism. Much to the benefit of the United States and its NATO allies, the Reset also produced an agreement on the Northern Distribution Network, which provided a more reliable transit route to resupply troops in Afghanistan.[41]

Perhaps the most important benefit of the Reset from the Russian perspective was the cancellation of planned missile defense sites in Poland and the Czech Republic in favor of the phased, adaptive approach. As discussed in the previous chapter, missile defense has long been an irritant in US-Russian relations. US administrations have always held that the purpose of a missile defense system in Europe is to protect European allies from Iran and that the system would have no effect on the Russian nuclear deterrent. Russia, however, maintains that the system undermines strategic stability and poses a threat to Russian national interests. The sites in Poland and the Czech Republic were especially distasteful to the Russian leadership because they were to be situated on the territory of former Warsaw Pact allies. President Obama emphasized that the switch to the phased, adaptive approach was driven by a new threat assessment rather than a desire to placate Russia. He also reportedly sent a secret letter to Medvedev early in his first term offering to withdraw the plan for sites in Poland and the Czech Republic if Russia agreed to cooperate on sanctioning Iran.[42] On hearing of the cancellation of those plans, MID stated that it was a positive sign that indicated America's interest in developing US-Russian relations.[43]

The move to the phased, adaptive approach, along with the de facto freeze of the question of Georgian and Ukrainian accession to NATO, paved the way for deeper cooperation on missile defense under both bilateral and NATO auspices. At the bilateral level, the Arms Control and International Security Working Group of the Bilateral Presidential Commission included discussions on how to cooperate on missile defense.[44] The Euro-Atlantic Security Initiative—a high-level, trilateral, track-2 project—coordinated a working group on missile defense that included the former chief of staff of the Strategic Rocket Forces on the Russian side, the former director of the Missile Defense Agency on the US side, and a former defense minister of Poland, among other experts.[45] Most impressive, during the 2010 NATO summit in Lisbon, President Medvedev addressed the alliance and supported the broad strokes of a joint missile defense project.[46] Although the project was presented in less conciliatory terms during his annual address to the Federal Assembly the following week, it was nevertheless a milestone in post–Cold War relations between Russia and the West.[47]

The upswing in relations with Russia's traditional partners, though, was not the only reason BRIC was a low priority. As discussed above, Medvedev was more oriented toward economic liberalization and international economic integration than Putin had been by the end of his first tenure as president. This new approach was hinted at in the 2008 Foreign Policy Concept. It is most apparent, however, in Medvedev's 2009 article "Rossiia, vpered!" ("Forward Russia!"), which focused mostly on domestic goals.[48] Although it also included some discussion of foreign policy, that discussion was more fully fleshed out in the unofficial 2010 survey of Russian foreign policy that was leaked to the Russian edition of *Newsweek*.[49] MID would not confirm that the leaked document represented a new doctrine, but analysts and newspapers accept it as a genuine reflection of the Medvedev team's foreign policy outlook at the time. Further, the ministry did confirm that the paper was prepared in response to President Medevedv's exhortation to use Russian foreign policy to drive investment.[50]

In part, the new orientation toward economic modernization and diversification put forth in both "Rossiia vpered!" and the leaked foreign policy paper was spurred by necessity. Unlike its BRIC partners, which managed to get through the 2008 crisis largely unscathed, Russia's GDP plummeted by 7.9 percent in 2009.[51] As a result, the confidence that marked the end of Putin's time in office was no longer sustainable; in order to modernize, Russia needed foreign capital.[52]

The text of the leaked 2010 paper, however, suggests that the focus on economic modernization and integration was not simply a result of immediate necessity. Entitled "Program for the Effective Exploitation on a Systemic Basis of Foreign Policy Factors for the Purposes of the Long-Term Development of the Russian Federation," the document details goals for Russia's economic relationship with countries in every region of the world.[53] Unlike previous concepts and surveys, which all speak explicitly about the need to construct a new world order, the main thrust of the 2010 foreign policy program is how to promote balanced economic relations across the globe as a way of speeding Russian development. The United States and Europe are seen as essential to this process as potential sources of high technology. The program also asserts that increasing economic integration with the Asia-Pacific Region is of paramount importance as part of the larger project of developing the Russian Far East. Nevertheless, the sections on China and India are remarkably short, and in the preamble, written as a cover letter to Medvedev, Lavrov states that the United States and Europe are the most "desirable partners."[54]

Lavrov's preamble is the only section of the program that reads like other Russian foreign policy documents. In it he identifies the United States as a source of global political and economic instability, and he stresses the importance of BRIC coordination in effecting changes in IMF quotas. Lavrov also argues that one of the primary goals of US policy is "to marginalize multilateral formats where the United States is not a member, including BRIC and the [Shanghai Cooperation Organization]."[55] The overriding message of the preamble is that Russia must modernize its economy in order to maintain its seat at the international decision-making table.

Neither "Rossiia vpered!" nor the program endorses a wholesale restructuring of the Russian economy. The article criticizes the Russian economy's dependence on natural resources and its endemic corruption as well as excessive reliance on the state. It does not, however, envision mass privatization, and the proposal it puts forward for transforming the Russian economy into a high-tech and digital leader remains ultimately state-driven. Similarly, although the program focuses on building economic relations in order to gain access to advanced technology, discussions are primarily about state-to-state relations rather than through the private sector. Neither document dwells on small- and medium-sized enterprises, often seen as the bedrock of successful market economies. The upshot is that even as Medvedev and his advisers were proposing large-scale modernization, their proposals demonstrate Russia's ongoing skepticism of global economic norms.

The idea of economic modernization via the BRIC mechanism is also absent from the leaked program, including in the discussion of bilateral relations with the individual countries themselves. This absence reinforces the notion that Russia was not really interested in the economic potential of the group. By the time the program was leaked to *Russkii Newsweek*, BRIC had already held two summits. Although the group was still in its infancy, the joint statement from the second summit included a commitment to cooperate in the energy sphere on research and development and high-tech transfer.[56] The group had also agreed to explore a wide range of sectoral cooperation and had held the first Business Forum in Rio de Janeiro the day before the leaders' summit in Brasilia.[57]

If Russia valued these developments, the growing intragroup economic agenda should have been incorporated into the official framing of BRIC in speeches and documents from that point onward. In some ways it was. In his 2010 address to the Federal Assembly, President Medvedev spoke of the importance of "economic diplomacy" and the need to build "modernization alliances" with the BRIC countries, among others.[58] The 2011 speech contains a similar, though weaker, exhortation.[59] In both cases, though, the mention of the economic potential of BRICS was entwined with a statement on the role of BRICS in increasing Russia's international voice. During this time, economics and internal development of BRICS as a mechanism became the principal priorities for the group, as demonstrated in the summit declarations beginning with the 2011 Sanya Declaration. Regardless of these developments, in most statements, Medvedev still focused primarily on BRICS as a narrow rhetorical political tool in Russia's ongoing international balancing act.

Even Medvedev's speeches at the BRICS summits often emphasized BRICS on the international stage over the intra-BRICS agenda. In the press statement following the first BRIC summit in Ekaterinburg in 2009, President Medvedev emphasized the primacy of the foreign ministries in coordinating BRIC. The implication was that other ministries, including those charged with economic development and cooperation, would play secondary roles.[60] Similarly, in his speech at the fourth summit in New Delhi in 2012, Medvedev proposed that

> a gradual transformation of BRICS into a fully-developed mechanism of interaction on major issues in global economy and politics could become our strategic goal. Such a step forward is only possible through joint efforts on the concept. I would like to suggest that our Foreign Ministers begin this work.
>
> The adoption of the forum's foreign relations strategy is also long overdue as it will help anchor the BRICS in the international relations system, to expand and strengthen the gravitational field which is already being formed around our five countries.[61]

He did also praise burgeoning intra-BRICS cooperation, but not to do so would have been impolitic. However, besides touting the growing BRICS Business Forum, Medvedev seemed most interested in increasing BRICS's role in the larger international system or, at a minimum, how intra-BRICS cooperation would support that goal.[62] He was much less enamored with the benefits of BRICS cooperation for Russian economic development or the other less political aspects of intra-BRICS coordination.

2012–13: Putin's Return and the Rise of the Eurasian Union

When Putin returned to the Russian presidency in 2012, it might have been logical to assume a renewed emphasis on BRICS. The group was now a more established actor with a growing independent agenda, including a preliminary agreement to form a BRICS development bank.[63] In addition, most of Medvedev's much-vaunted efforts in improving relations with the West and modernizing the Russian economy had failed to deliver on their initial promise. Joint cooperation on missile defense collapsed for good in November 2011.[64] In addition, the NATO intervention in Libya, which Russia had allowed to go forward when it abstained from the UNSC vote, had led to the brutal murder of Muammar Gaddafi. This event had a decisive effect on how Putin understood US intentions toward regimes of which it did not approve.

Putin's fears following the murder of Gaddafi were sharpened with the onset of protests in Russia following rigged parliamentary elections in December 2011. Those protests coincided with the arrival of Michael McFaul, a principal architect of the Reset, as the new US ambassador to Russia. The protests and McFaul's academic specialty in democratization prompted accusations from Moscow that the United States was trying to foment a "color revolution" in Russia, just as it had in Georgia and Ukraine (per the Russian interpretation).[65] After McFaul gave a speech on US-Russian relations at the Higher School of Economics in Moscow the following May, MID released an official statement accusing McFaul of crossing the boundaries of diplomatic decency.[66] McFaul's statements about avoiding linkages between American relations with countries in the former Soviet space and American relations with Russia provoked particular ire.[67] The Reset was dead, and the importance of BRICS could conceivably have expanded in its wake.

It did not. Instead, Putin turned his focus to the Eurasian Union, a project he proposed in one of a series of articles he wrote as part of his 2011–12 presidential campaign. Putin detailed a vision to bring together many of the former Soviet Republics into a customs union and free trade area, with some features that mirrored the operation of the European Union.[68] This was a renewal and expansion of a project that had been nominally part of Russian foreign economic policy since the mid-1990s, but Putin's article gave the plan new life.

As discussed in the first chapter, Russia's interest in the idea waxed and waned in the intervening years between the initial proposal in the 1990s and its emergence as a central tenet of Putin's foreign policy during his third presidential term. Indeed, for much of the post–Cold War era, Russian interest in pursuing the Eurasian Union had been lukewarm. Among other issues, the country was largely unwilling to undertake policies (e.g., tariff reductions) that would have made the nominal customs union formed in 1995 anything more than a piece of paper.[69]

The turning point came in 2009, when then–prime minister Putin announced that Russia would withdraw its bid to join the WTO in favor of a joint bid as a customs union with Belarus and Kazakhstan. Putin made his announcement during the annual St. Petersburg International Economic Forum, sometimes seen as Russia's version of the Davos World Economic Forum and a time when foreign eyes are more focused on Russia than they might be otherwise. The announcement came as a surprise to many both in and outside of Russia.[70] Although the Russian leadership ultimately reversed the statement and affirmed that Russia would seek individual WTO accession, efforts to build and strengthen the Customs Union continued. The Customs Union officially went into effect in 2010, and the laws on making the Customs Union a single economic space entered into force in January 2012.[71] Integration with the former Soviet space has nominally been the top priority in Russian foreign policy since the end of the Kozyrev era. Putin's new vision, however, gave that vague priority a specificity and explicit prominence it had not previously enjoyed.

In the years after Putin's announcement during the 2009 St. Petersburg forum, the Russian conception of the Eurasian Union took on a more political angle.[72] This caused friction with the other members, particularly Kazakhstan, which also has not benefited as much economically from the Customs Union as it anticipated.[73] In December 2013 Kazakh president Nursultan Nazarbayev came out against further politicization of the project, and serious conceptual differences over the future of the Eurasian Union exist among Belarus, Kazakhstan, and Russia (the core members). Nevertheless, even if the project stays strictly in the economic realm and does not progress to political cooperation, this iteration of the project has proved more durable than past efforts.

BRICS, by contrast, remained primarily in the realm of rhetoric. The discussion of BRICS and its role in global affairs in Putin's 2012 and 2013 addresses to the Federal Assembly recalled the rhetoric of 2006 and 2007 in its emphasis on BRICS over Western organizations. However, his statements reflected neither advancement in the approach toward the group nor the strides the group had made toward institutionalization over the preceding years.[74] Similarly, although the Foreign Policy Concept Putin approved in 2013 highlighted BRICS over the G8 in the discussion of how Russia would use its international connections to build a new world order, the concept otherwise ignored BRICS in the details of Russian foreign policy plans and priorities.[75]

Putin's press statement following the Durban summit in 2013 reinforced the perception that he was more interested in the idea of BRICS rather than the nuts and bolts of intra-BRICS cooperation. The theme of the Durban summit was

"BRICS and Africa: Partnership for Development, Integration, and Industrialization."[76] Russia is the only member of the BRICS group that does not have strong economic relations with South Africa and other countries on the continent. Putin could have used the occasion of the Durban summit to push for deeper ties. Instead, he focused on the work of the BRICS Business Forum, which, if successful, would theoretically bring substantive financial benefit to Russia, but beyond that the statement seemed almost perfunctory. He slipped in references to Russia's taking a leading role in promoting the group's development and reminded the audience that the member countries were "global growth leaders." However, there was little in the short address to suggest that it was a group in which Putin found specific benefit beyond the aura of membership itself.[77]

The official "Concept of the Participation of the Russian Federation in BRICS" was approved in March 2013 just ahead of the BRICS summit in Durban.[78] It is a useful window into the duality of the Russian approach to BRICS before the onset of the crisis in Ukraine.[79] On the one hand, the document lays out a long-term goal of further institutional formalization of the BRICS association and lists the ways the BRICS group can support Russian foreign policy and domestic economic goals.[80] On the other hand, the text emphasizes maintaining informal links and not institutionalizing the group to the point that it overrides bilateral relations.[81] The BRICS concept is more detailed in its vision for the group than the speeches of either Putin or Medvedev had been on the topic. However, it does not include ideas that had not already been raised in either BRICS meetings or similar BRICS conceptual documents.[82]

This lack of conceptual innovation, especially from the country that sees itself as the intellectual architect of BRICS, is revealing. It indicates that through the end of 2013, Russian policies and intentions toward BRICS remained both narrow and shallow. BRICS was another table to sit at and a useful theoretical alternative to Western clubs. It also was a convenient rhetorical weapon to show both domestic and international audiences that Russia had other friends besides Europe and the United States. However, it was not taken seriously as a real alternative option for Russia. As Alexander Sergunin argues, "BRICS for Russia seems to represent mainly a vehicle for *global normative transformation*, while for achieving specific geopolitical objectives Moscow prefers to use other organizations . . . which are *regional* in scope and more *practical* in their outlook."[83] In other words, the real value of BRICS to Russia was in the ability to speak about and tout its existence and maturation as an international group, as a way of pushing back against global norms with which it disagreed. The substance of cooperation was much less important.

BRICS in Russian Intellectual Circles, 2008–13

In contrast to the narrow official approach, the period between 2008 and 2013 saw an enormous output of academic analysis on BRICS and the role of Russia in

BRICS. Some of that was a response to the evolution of the forum. As BRICS added working groups and expanded its membership to include South Africa, research expanded correspondingly. However, in some cases research in Russia predated the inclusion of those topics in BRICS. Overall, the work of Russian academics on BRICS between 2008 and 2013 was broader and more nuanced than the official presentation of the project in government speeches and concepts.

The academic books range from region-specific analysis about BRICS and Africa or Latin America, often produced in preparation for or as a consequence of a BRICS summit, to detailed conference reports and publications covering a plethora of topics.[84] Some books explore BRICS from angles of particular concern to Russia, such as natural resource cooperation.[85] Articles in academic journals also delve into the details, examining topics ranging from comparative foreign direct investment among the BRICS countries to the potential for BRICS to play a bigger role in Russian foreign economic policy and how China uses BRICS to burnish its own image.[86]

This flowering of BRICS research becomes more interesting when contextualized by the fact that the line between state and academia in Russia is somewhat blurred. Most of the main research institutions as well as the most prominent universities are state owned. Russian educational institutions such as the constellation of institutes under the Russian Academy of Sciences (RAN) are considered "budgetary institutions," which are a special class of institutions created by the state to serve specific, non-commercial purposes.[87] Budgetary institutions are usually financed from the federal or local government budget.[88] Formally, although the majority of funding comes from government dollars, educational institutions have full autonomy over the direction of research, faculty selection, and financial activity.[89] They also are supposed to have rights over their capital assets, including property, and are allowed to rent these out as they see fit.[90]

The role of the Ministry of Education, and the state more generally, with respect to educational institutions is officially limited to enforcing standards, accreditation, and other similar roles.[91] In practice, however, the laws regarding state control over educational institutions are poorly and unevenly enforced, largely as a result of ambiguities in the legislative language.[92] In addition, RAN has been undergoing a long and controversial reform process that has altered how funding is dispensed. The reform has incurred accusations that the government (and Putin himself) is exerting more direct control.[93] In 2013, when a bill to reform RAN was introduced into the Duma, Prime Minister Medvedev stated, "Academic science should provide full-fledged expert support to the state in priority areas."[94] The 2013 bill was extremely controversial, in part because its authorship remains unclear; the Ministry of Education and Science denied that it drafted the bill, and the confusion never lifted.[95]

In addition to state financing of research, there is a great deal of cross-fertilization between universities, institutes, and government. For example, Vyacheslav Nikonov is simultaneously a member of the Duma, the dean of the

School of Public Administration at Moscow State University, and the chair of the Presidium of NKI BRIKS. In addition, both the Moscow State Institute of International Affairs (MGIMO) and NKI BRIKS are administratively part of the Russian Ministry of Foreign Affairs.

President Medvedev himself established NKI BRIKS in 2011 as the Russian arm of the BTTC.[96] It acts as a coordinating body for BRICS research in Russia at a variety of institutes and universities.[97] Since the spring of 2012 NKI BRIKS has also published a semiregular bulletin that summarizes main BRICS research worldwide. In addition, in 2013, the institute released *Strategiia Rossii v BRIKS: tseli i instrumenty* (*Russia's Strategy in BRICS: Goals and Instruments*), which details Russia's goals toward and possible strategies within the BRICS group.[98]

The different types and levels of association with the federal government mean there is a continuum of research independence. Work that is released by one of the institutes of RAN, especially if it is not listed as an NKI BRIKS publication on the website, is likely further from state influence than, for example, *Strategiia Rossii v BRIKS*. At the same time, though, because of the cross-fertilization, much of the research could be considered part of a track 2–level project rather than something wholly separate from government discourse. This is not to argue that every time a Russian scholar published a book or article on BRICS it was automatically because of a government directive; indeed, it may have been more about an effort to play to government goals in order to attract more funding. Rather, the point is that despite the fairly unidimensional official discussion of BRICS at the highest official levels, government money was making possible more nuanced input from universities and research institutes.

In some cases, government also engaged with academia directly. In 2011 MGIMO sponsored a large conference addressing the issues of BRICS in world politics and intra-BRICS cooperation as a means of modernization.[99] Vadim Lukov, the ambassador in MID tasked with coordinating Russia's engagement with BRICS, took part, as did ambassadors from other BRICS countries. Between 2008 and 2013 (and onward), the MID journal *Mezhdunarodnaia zhizn* (*International Affairs*) published articles about BRICS by officials, including Lavrov and Lukov, as well as local and foreign academics.[100]

Because these works are not part of official government discourse, they have greater freedom to explore and propose a wider array of possible roles for BRICS on the global stage. Some build directly off of common BRICS themes, such as the details of monetary cooperation within the group and the likelihood of various options for trade and monetary cooperation.[101] Other suggestions seem quite radical: for example, one contribution from the MGIMO conference suggests that it would be unwise to rule out military cooperation among the BRICS countries, especially if the United States and NATO continue their destabilizing policies.[102] This suggestion is not entirely without support: in 2013 NKI BRIKS sponsored a conference about instituting military cooperation among the BRICS countries.[103] Following the conference, Nikonov stated that the situation in Syria was an impetus for exploring military cooperation.[104] However, there is not wide-spread support for including a military dimension in BRICS cooperation, and becoming a military alliance would undercut the general BRICS position that they are not a bloc aligned against any other blocs in the international system.

The academic analysis is also not all unstintingly adulatory. Even among those analysts who support Russia's membership in BRICS and find it to be in line with Russia's strategic objectives, there is no illusion that BRICS is prepared to replace the G7 or that it is a grouping without internal divisions among its members.[105] There is also recognition that in order to be sustainable, BRICS must develop its own positive agenda rather than simply standing against perceived Western excesses.[106] Suggestions involve coordination on efforts to include BRICS curren-cies in the international reserves of other countries, economic and technological cooperation to support modernization, and cooperation on counterterrorism and narcotrafficking.[107] Most (though not all) of the authors agree that while BRICS holds potential if handled properly, the group is still in its institutional infancy.

Strategiia Rossii v BRIKS represents an effort to define a clear and robust posi-tive agenda for BRICS that supports Russian foreign policy goals and ambitions. The book covers a wide array of topics ranging from older issues of reforming the international financial system to newer frontiers such as the possibilities of coop-eration in the civil nuclear sphere. It includes contributions from both regional and functional experts from some of the most respected universities and research institutes in Russia.[108] The collection is a detailed effort to make BRICS into a full-fledged international grouping with distinct and specific mandates that sup-port Russian foreign policy and foreign economic policy objectives.

The problem with *Strategiia Rossiia v BRIKS* is that it is in large part a review of existing levels of cooperation. The articles it includes do not push the idea forward conceptually much more so than did the official BRICS concept. This suggests a larger point about the type of demand the research answered. Publish-ing a book about possible directions in which BRICS could develop was useful in terms of optics. It showed that BRICS was a topic Russia took seriously. But it was also part of constructing the larger Russian BRICS Potemkin village. As serious as individual scholars are about the prospects of BRICS, the official infrastructure surrounding them is more about showing that the infrastructure exists rather than facilitating BRICS research.

This points to a broader conclusion. From the nexus of the official rhetoric about BRICS as a new alternative for global order and the academic analysis of the details emerges Russia's real goal toward BRICS before the Ukraine crisis. For all the mentions of BRICS in high-level speeches and research produced at state or near-state institutions, the official interest in BRICS before 2014 was primarily as a rhetorical feint to help Russia boost its international standing and punch above its weight in global decision-making. Academic research supported that goal insofar as it gave the appearance of BRICS being high on the agenda. The fact that official discourse was for the most part disinterested in the ideas coming out of the state research institutions indicates that Russian political leaders were more interested in talking about the institutionalization of BRICS than actually implementing that goal.

BRICS as Bridge?

Russia's desire to use BRICS to increase its weight in the international system is among the more standard explanations of Russia's policy toward the group. Where previous analysis falls somewhat short is in defining precisely how Russia hoped to use BRICS to magnify its voice, especially since BRICS would seem at first to be a "second best" solution. Coordination with these large emerging countries did give Russia a bigger voice in some international organizations (such as the IMF and the G20). It did not, however, produce similar effects in Euro-Atlantic organizations, such as NATO or the G8, which are the prime locus of Russian dissatisfaction with the current system.[109] The rise of BRICS certainly did nothing to make Western states take Medvedev's EST proposal seriously.

But there is another angle that is worth considering. As much as the effort to institutionalize BRICS was designed to give Russia (rhetorical) parallel options to further accommodation with the West, there was also a hope that the country could use its unique position as a member of both the G8 and BRICS to increase its influence in both.[110] The aim was not just to gain influence in general international organizations but was also about looking for a way to position the country such that it could increase its leverage in those clubs with which it was most concerned. BRICS initially offered Russia an opportunity to portray itself as the link between (old) Western institutions and the emerging powers, with the goal of using its membership in both and its dual emerging- and established-power identity to increase its voice on both sides.

Unsurprisingly, these hopes went largely unrealized. In the period from 2008 to 2010, when BRICS coordination was most successful on the world stage, membership in the group did make Russia's foreign policy look more balanced, showing relations with rising powers even as Russia assented to the Reset. It did not, however, increase Russia's leverage vis-à-vis traditional powers except within the limited arena of the IMF. Once the BRICS agenda began to focus more on building intra-BRICS cooperation, it no longer served the same use of providing Russia with a non-Western pseudo-analog to the G8. The burgeoning BRICS agenda, which focused primarily on economic modernization and socioeconomic challenges of developing countries, was not irrelevant to Russia's needs. Yet it was not what Russia sought or wanted out of the forum.

Until it was suspended from the G8 in 2014, Russia was a member of both the old and the new global governance frameworks. Further, the same Russian diplomat was responsible for Russian activities within the G8, the G20, and BRICS.[111] Russia is also historically a power that desires the role of norm-setter, rather than norm-taker, on the international stage. Russia hoped that its membership in the G8 combined with the efforts to make BRICS seem like the next big thing in global governance would help push the traditional powers to make adjustments while not forcing Russia to relinquish its seat at the most prestigious international tables. The idea of BRICS as a bridge, therefore, has a dual meaning. In one sense, Russia hoped it could act as a bridge between the old and the new. In the other, Russia hoped that BRICS would provide a bridge to what it had always desired but membership in the G8 had not provided: a place at the top of the international power hierarchy.

Russia has a long tradition of positioning itself as a bridge, both civilizational and otherwise, between Europe and Asia or, more recently, between the United States and China.[112] What is interesting about the BRICS project is that Russia used it simultaneously to balance against the West and as a mechanism for increasing its value to the West. However, since Russia's investment in the project did not expand much beyond rhetorically extolling the group's virtues, the group was less effective than it might have been for either objective. By 2013 BRICS had pushed two rounds of reforms in the IMF (via the G20), expanded to include another member state, and begun seriously considering creating its own development bank and currency pool. Although the agenda remained speculative, the group had progressed sufficiently from its beginnings that, had the Russian leadership wished, it could have legitimately touted those accomplishments. The failure of the political leadership to convey these achievements indicates that the Russian leadership did not incorporate the evolution of BRICS into its approach to the group.

Conclusion

Russian policy toward BRICS between 2008 and 2013 was a lot of show and very little substance. The period saw rapid development of the BRICS mechanism itself and expanded opportunities for both rhetorical framing and concrete cooperation. Nevertheless, the approach of the Russian ruling elite remained frozen in its original conception of BRICS as a rhetorical tool of international politics. The leadership did not incorporate the changes within the forum into either its rhetoric or policy planning.

By contrast, the academic community showed more appreciation of the possibilities of the evolving BRICS mechanism. Reports covering every angle of Russia's participation in BRICS, including suggestions that would likely be rejected by the other BRICS members, emerged in concert with the expanding BRICS agenda and membership. These analyses provided a framework onto which Russian leaders could overlay substance if they wished.

As 2013 drew to a close, it became clear that this framework would be put to use sooner than anticipated. The Euromaidan Revolution in Ukraine turned regional politics upside down and pushed long-standing Russian foreign policy doctrines from the realm of rhetoric to one of concrete consideration. The next chapter explores how the repercussions of Maidan, and Russia's reaction to them, changed the approach to BRICS and catapulted the group up the list of Russia's foreign policy priorities, at least in the immediate aftermath of the crisis.

Notes

Epigraphs: Medvedev, "Address to the Federal Assembly of the Russian Federation," November 30, 2010; and Lavrov, "BRIKS—globalnyi forum novogo pokoleniia," 3.

1. Hahn, "Medvedev, Putin, and Perestroika 2.0," 252.

2. Stent, *Limits of Partnership*, 220.

3. Mankoff, *Russian Foreign Policy*, 17.

4. On the power ministries forming Putin's political base, see Taylor, *State Building in Putin's Russia*.

5. Parts of this and the following section draw heavily on Salzman, "U.S. Policy toward Russia."

6. Henry Kissinger, "Unconventional Wisdom about Russia," *New York Times*, July 1, 2008, https://www.nytimes.com/2008/07/01/opinion/01iht-edkissinger.4.14135943.html.

7. Jeff Zeleny and Nicholas Kulish, "Obama, in Berlin, Calls for Renewal of Ties with Allies," *New York Times*, July 25, 2008, https://www.nytimes.com/2008/07/25/us/politics/25obama.html.

8. Trenin, "Thinking Strategically about Russia," 5.

9. Gottemoeller, "Russian-American Security Relations after Georgia," 1.

10. Baranovsky, "Vvedenie," 295; and Weber, *End of Arrogance*, 110.

11. Medvedev, "Annual Address to the Federal Assembly," November 5, 2008.

12. Ibid.

13. Aven, foreword to *Russia after the Global Economic Crisis*, xi.

14. Andrew E. Kramer, "Russia Talks of a Stability beyond Ties to the U.S.," *New York Times*, January 25, 2008, https://www.nytimes.com/2008/01/25/business/worldbusiness/25ruble.html.

15. Åslund, Guriev, and Kuchins, *Russia after the Global Economic Crisis*, 1.

16. Robert Peston, "Russia 'Planned Wall Street Bear Raid,'" *BBC News*, March 17, 2014, http://www.bbc.com/news/business-26609548.

17. Paulson, *On the Brink*, 273–74.

18. Peston, "Russia 'Planned Wall Street Bear Raid.'"

19. Åslund, Guriev, and Kuchins, *Russia after the Global Economic Crisis*, 1.

20. Aven, foreword to *Russia after the Global Economic Crisis*, xi; and Andrew E. Kramer, "A $50 Billion Bailout in Russia Favors the Rich and Connected," *New York Times*, October 30, 2008, https://www.nytimes.com/2008/10/31/business/worldbusiness/31oligarch.html.

21. Medvedev, "Annual Address to the Federal Assembly of the Russian Federation," November 5, 2008.

22. Ministry of Foreign Affairs of the Russian Federation, "Transcript of Remarks and Response to Media Questions."

23. In June 2008 Brazilian foreign minister Celso Amorim published an article (in Portuguese) entitled "The BRICs and the Reorganization of the World." This suggests

that by mid-2008 Russia was not the only BRIC country to be integrating the group into its foreign policy position. See Stuenkel, *BRICS and the Future of Global Order*, 12–13.

24. Ministry of Foreign Affairs of the Russian Federation, "Foreign Policy Concept of the Russian Federation," July 2008.

25. Ibid.

26. Ibid.

27. Ibid.

28. Ministry of Foreign Affairs of the Russian Federation, "Transcript of Remarks."

29. Medvedev, "Speech at World Policy Conference."

30. Ibid.

31. Weitz, "Rise and Fall of Medvedev's European Security Treaty," 1.

32. Ibid.

33. Kremlin, "Draft of the European Security Treaty."

34. Alexander Gabuev, interview with the author, September 5, 2014, Moscow.

35. Ibid.

36. Mankoff, *Russian Foreign Policy*, 194.

37. Ibid., 195.

38. Lo, *Russia and the New World Disorder*, 146.

39. Salzman, "U.S. Policy toward Russia," 10.

40. Ibid., 11.

41. Stent, *Limits of Partnership*, 231.

42. White House, "FACT SHEET: U.S. Missile Defense Policy"; and Peter Baker, "Obama Offered Deal to Russia in Secret Letter," *New York Times*, March 2, 2009, https://www.nytimes.com/2009/03/03/washington/03prexy.html.

43. Baker, "Obama Offered Deal to Russia in Secret Letter."

44. Department of State, Office of Website Management, "Arms Control and International Security."

45. EASI Working Group on Missile Defense, "Missile Defense: Towards a New Paradigm." The author worked on EASI.

46. Simon Tisdall, "Lisbon: The Most Exciting Post-Cold War NATO Summit?" *Guardian*, November 15, 2010, http://www.theguardian.com/commentisfree/cifamerica/2010/nov/15/lisbon-nato-summit. The EASI Working Group on Missile Defense came together after Lisbon but built on that momentum.

47. "Warning of New Arms Race, Medvedev Calls for Cooperation with West on Missile Shield." *RadioFreeEurope/RadioLiberty*, January 12, 2010, http://www.rferl.org/content/russia_medvedev_parliament/2234566.html.

48. Medvedev, "Rossiia, vpered!"

49. Ministry of Foreign Affairs of the Russian Federation, "O programme effektivnogo ispolzovaniia na sistemnoi osnove vneshnepoliticheskikh faktorov v tseliakh dolgosrochnogo razvitiia Rossiiskoi Federatsii."

50. Nikolaus von Twickel, "Leaked Paper Calls for Friendlier Foreign Policy," *Moscow Times*, May 13, 2010, http://www.themoscowtimes.com/news/article/leaked-paper-calls-for-friendlier-foreign-policy/405884.html.

51. Michael Stott, "Russia's New Foreign Policy Puts Business First," Reuters, May 25, 2010, https://www.reuters.com/article/us-russia-policy-idUSTRE64O28020100525.

52. Ibid.

53. Ministry of Foreign Affairs of the Russian Federation, "O programme effektivnogo."

54. Ibid.; and McDermott, "Kremlin Contemplates a Seismic Shift in Russian Foreign Policy."

55. Ministry of Foreign Affairs of the Russian Federation, "O programme effektivnogo."

56. BRIC Leaders, "BRIC Summit—Joint Statement."

57. Ibid.

58. Medvedev, "Address to the Federal Assembly of the Russian Federation," November 30, 2010.

59. Ibid.

60. Medvedev, "Press Statement Following BRIC Group Summit."

61. Medvedev, "Russian President's Address at the BRICS Summit."

62. Ibid.

63. BRICS Leaders, "Delhi Declaration"; and David Smith, "Brics Eye Infrastructure Funding through New Development Bank," *Guardian*, March 28, 2013, https://www.theguardian.com/global-development/2013/mar/28/brics-countries-infrastructure-spending-development-bank.

64. Stent, *Limits of Partnership*, 228.

65. Remnick, "Watching the Eclipse"; and Mitchell, *Color Revolutions*, 193.

66. Ministry of Foreign Affairs of the Russian Federation, "Zaiavlenie MID Rossii v sviazi s vyskazyvaniiami Posla SShA v Moskve M. Makfola."

67. Miriam Elder, "Michael McFaul, US Ambassador to Moscow, Victim of Kremlin 'Twitter War'," *Guardian*, May 29, 2012, https://www.theguardian.com/world/2012/may/29/michael-mcfaul-twitter-attack-russia; Ministry of Foreign Affairs of the Russian Federation, "McFaul's Mention of 'Linkages'"; and Ministry of Foreign Affairs of the Russian Federation, "Michael McFaul's Analysis Is a Deliberate Distortion."

68. Putin, "Novyi integratsionnyi proekt Evrazii."

69. Naumkin, "Russian Policy toward Kazakhstan," 53.

70. Åslund, "Why Doesn't Russia Join the WTO?," 60.

71. Cooley, *Great Games, Local Rules*, 60.

72. Nursha, "Evolution of Political Thought," 33.

73. Ibid.

74. Putin, "Address to the Federal Assembly of the Russian Federation," December 12, 2012; and Putin, "Address to the Federal Assembly of the Russian Federation," December 12, 2013.

75. Ministry of Foreign Affairs of the Russian Federation, "Concept of the Foreign Policy of the Russian Federation."

76. BRICS Leaders, "eThekwini Declaration."

77. Putin, "Press Statement Following the BRICS Summit."

78. Ministry of Foreign Affairs of the Russian Federation, "Concept of Participation of the Russian Federation in BRICS."

79. Ibid.

80. Ibid.

81. Ministry of Foreign Affairs of the Russian Federation, "Foreign Policy Concept of the Russian Federation."

82. For example, Saran, Singh, and Sharan, "Long-Term Vision for BRICS."

83. Sergunin, "Understanding Russia's Policies towards BRICS: Theory and Practice," 11. Emphasis in original.

84. Deich and Korendiasov, *BRIKS-Afrika*; Davydov, *BRIKS—Latinskaia Amerika*; and Okuneva and Orlov, *Voskhodiashchie gosudarstva-giganty BRIKS*.

85. Kozlovskii, Komarov, and Makrushkin, *Braziliia, Rossiia, Indiia, Kitai, IuAR*.

86. Bobrova, "Priiamie inostrannye investitsii"; Isachenko, "Strany BRIKS"; and Antonov, "BRIKS kak imidzhevaia kopilka."

87. Batkibekov et al., *Perfection of the System of Management*, 6.

88. Ibid.

89. Ibid., 29.

90. Ibid., 27.

91. Ibid., 30.

92. Ibid., 31.

93. Allakhverdov and Pokrovsky, "Putin"; MacWilliams, "Academy Agrees to Post-Soviet Crash Diet"; and Gelfand, "What Is to Be Done about Russian Science?"

94. "Russian Academy of Sciences System Is Obsolete, Will Be Reformed—Medvedev," Interfax: Russia & CIS General Newswire, June 27, 2013, http://search.proquest.com/doc view/1372021043/abstract/C863079ADF004875PQ/2?.

95. Dezhina, "Special of Structural Reforms in Russian Science," 44. One of the more controversial aspects of the law was that it stripped RAN of the right to act as lessor on federal properties. Since some parts of RAN are situated in central Moscow on properties that would fetch extremely high rents on the open market, this is a blow to RAN revenue and may also be one of the government motivations for stripping RAN of the right to act as lessor.

96. "About the Committee," NKI BRIK, http://www.nkibrics.ru/pages/about (in Russian). Russia is the only BRICS country whose BTTC member was chartered by the government. Other countries designated BTTC institutions are often close to the government (e.g., the Observer Research Foundation in India) but were not formed by presidential mandate specifically to coordinate research for BRICS.

97. Georgii Toloraya, interview with author, May 14, 2014, Moscow.

98. Nikonov and Toloraya, *Strategiia Rossii v BRIKS*.

99. Okuneva and Orlov, *Voskhodiashchie gosudarstva-giganty BRIKS*.

100. Lukov, "BRIKS—Faktor Globalnogo Znacheniia"; Lavrov, "BRIKS—globalnyi forum novogo pokoleniia"; and Sin, "Strany BRIKS."

101. Khmelevskaia, "Valiutnoe partnerstvo BRIKS"; and Isachenko, "Strany BRIKS," 86–87.

102. Orlov, "BRIKS," 45.

103. "BRICS Explore Political, Military Cooperation."

104. Ibid.

105. Panova, "Mesto Rossiia v BRIKS"; and Grishaeva, "Rossiia i BRIKS," 304.

106. Panova, "Mesto Rossiia v BRIKS."

107. Larionova et al., "Vozmozhnosti sotrudnichestva v BRIKS," 204; and Panova, "Russia in the BRICS."

108. Nikonov and Toloraya, *Strategiia Rossii v BRIKS*.

109. Roberts, "Russia's BRICs Diplomacy," 42. The G20 has overtaken the G7/G8, but that is less a consequence of the rise of the BRICS group and more a result of the global response to the 2008 financial crisis.

110. Shubin, "Ot BRIK k BRIKS," 305; and Ministry of Foreign Affairs of the Russian Federation, "Concept of Participation of the Russian Federation in BRICS."

111. Research Centre for International Cooperation and Development, "Meeting with Vadim B. Lukov Ambassador-at-Large of the Russian Ministry of Foreign Affairs."

112. Tsygankov, *Whose World Order?*, 96–97; and Lo, *Russia and the New World Disorder*, 50.

5

From Bridge to Bulwark (and Back Again)

Russia and BRICS after the Onset of the Ukraine Crisis

> This year, as has been the case many times during crucial historical moments, our people have demonstrated national enthusiasm, vital endurance, and patriotism. The difficulties we are facing today also create new opportunities for us. We are ready to take up any challenge and win.
>
> —Vladimir Putin, December 2014

> The escalation of hostile language, sanctions and counter-sanctions, and force does not contribute to a sustainable and peaceful solution, according to international law, including the principles and purposes of the United Nations Charter.
>
> —BRICS foreign ministers, March 2014

AS FALL TURNED TO WINTER IN 2013, RUSSIAN FOREIGN POLICY AND ELITE political rhetoric seemed to have settled into a familiar pattern. President Putin frequently decried the danger of "value-based approaches" in international relations, and BRICS was fully integrated, along with the G20, the G8, and the SCO, into sound bites about the new world order.[1] Even as Putin criticized American foreign policy, Russian-Western cooperation continued on some issues, including the Northern Distribution Network, which was slated to play a critical role in the planned US drawdown from Afghanistan.[2] Russia was preparing to host its second G8 summit in January 2014. The deteriorating situation in Syria brought the United States and Russia to the table as partners, albeit partners with vastly different visions for how to bring the conflict to an end. In short, there was nothing to suggest that the tense accommodation between Russia and Western powers would not continue just as it had for the majority of the post–Cold War era.

Things were changing, however, and quickly. In November 2013 the long-simmering integration dilemma between Russia and Europe exploded into an open tug-of-war over Ukraine's economic affiliation and integration. As the situation in Ukraine, fueled by domestic politics and foreign meddling, spiraled out of control, Russia found itself no longer on the margins of the Euro-Atlantic order but unambiguously in conflict with it. As a result, a decade of rhetoric about the importance of BRICS both to Russia and to the future of the global order took on a much deeper resonance. In the wake of the geopolitical tensions set off by the crisis in Ukraine, Russian leaders began to bring their endorsement of BRICS from the realm of rhetoric to one of serious consideration as a viable alternative for Russian foreign policy. It also made Russia's latent anti-Western agenda for the BRICS group much more explicit, raising questions about how far the other BRICS countries might be willing to go in their support.

This chapter begins with a review of the crisis in Ukraine through 2014 and the varying responses to those events by Western powers and the BRICS countries. It then turns to how Russia's approach to BRICS altered at the practical and rhetorical levels as a result of the rupture with the West. This in turn leads to analysis of the role of anti-Western sentiment within the group as both a motivating and dividing factor.[3] The chapter concludes with an assessment of the extent to which the change in the Russian approach to BRICS since the onset of the crisis in Ukraine was short-lived rather than durable and what the reversion to the mean may suggest for the future of the group.

The Crisis in Ukraine (2013–14)

The crisis in Ukraine brought to the fore tensions that had been alternately ignored and inflamed since the end of the Cold War. Despite its long roots, though, the crisis moved remarkably swiftly once the situation finally boiled over. Understanding the details and timeline is critical to understanding both Russian and Western reactions to the different phases of the crisis as well as why Russia so suddenly found itself in need of alternative partners.

Euromaidan and the Ouster of Viktor Yanukovych

The Euromaidan Revolution began when protesters gathered in Kyiv's Independence Square on the evening of November 21, 2013. Initially at issue was Ukrainian president Viktor Yanukovych's decision not to sign the Deep and Comprehensive Free Trade Area (DCFTA) agreement with the European Union, but the protests were later fueled by Yanukovych's use of force against the protesters as well as revelations about the astonishing level of corruption within his regime. Although the roots of the protests were mutlifactorial, the public narrative quickly became that of a proxy fight between Russia and the West for control over Ukraine's political and economic future. Putin had lobbied hard for Ukraine to join the developing Eurasian Union (EEU); EU laws made membership in the customs union that forms the core of the EEU incompatible with the DCFTA.[4] Observers interpreted Yanukovych's decision not to sign the DCFTA as a choice of Moscow over the West. This interpretation was reinforced by the deal Yanukovych reached with Moscow in December 2013 for a $15 billion bailout and a sharp reduction in the price of gas.[5]

December 2013 and January 2014 witnessed a rapid deterioration of the situation. Protests spread to other cities in Western Ukraine, and citizens in the east, historically both Russophone and more Russophilic than Western Ukrainians, began protesting in fear of what was happening in Kyiv. Yanukovych at first refused to negotiate with the opposition and instead signed an anti-protest law in mid-January 2014. The law was repealed less than two weeks later, but by then the situation was moving forward on its own momentum. Yanukovych's violence against the protesters also increased: between February 18 and February 20, 2014, more than one hundred people in Kyiv were killed.[6]

After that spate of violence, though, it seemed that the crisis might be over. On February 21, 2014, Yanukovych and the main opposition leaders signed an EU-brokered deal that promised a "political resolution to the crisis."[7] The deal included agreement on a timeline for constitutional reform, parliamentary and presidential elections, and amnesty for the protesters.[8] Yet that very evening, owing to both pressure from the opposition and abandonment by his erstwhile allies, Yanukovych fled the capital, and the opposition took control of the government.[9] According to a Russian government–produced documentary in 2015, Russian military helicopters evacuated Yanukovych first to Crimea and shortly thereafter into southern Russia.[10] Yanukovych gave a press conference from the Russian town of Rostov-on-Don on February 28, 2014, in which he urged Russia to take action against the new Ukrainian government.[11] He then disappeared from the public eye.

The Annexation of Crimea and War in Eastern Ukraine

Russia immediately declared the ouster of Yanukovych the result of an illegal coup and delayed the bailout it had promised Ukraine while Yanukovych was still in power.[12] Russia also quickly took decisive action to protect its interests in Crimea, a historically Russian enclave that became part of the Ukrainian Soviet Socialist Republic in 1954. Crimea has both historic and strategic importance for Russia. It is the site of the 1945 Yalta Conference, in the old imperial Livadia Palace, and the Crimean port city of Sevastopol has been the home of the Russian Black Sea Fleet for more than two hundred years. The local population has a high percentage of retired Russian military personnel and a history of demanding independence from Ukraine.[13] Earlier secessionist efforts failed, leaving Crimea as an autonomous republic within Ukraine.

The official Russian narrative holds that the seizure of Crimea was a response to the unraveling situation in Kyiv. However, a document leaked to the Russian newspaper *Novaya gazeta* in February 2015 revealed that the Russian government had been preparing for a post-Yanukovych scenario weeks before his flight from

Ukraine.[14] *Novaya gazeta* reported that an oligarch submitted a document with a plan to take Crimea to the presidential administration sometime between February 4 and February 12 of 2014, while massive protests in Kyiv were still ongoing.[15] It described the dangers Russian leadership foresaw if the "Banderovskaia junta" of the Ukrainian opposition were allowed to prevail, and outlined a political and logistical strategy for Russia's intervention into the conflict. The strategy included separating Crimea and Eastern Ukraine from the rest of the country.[16] The seizure of Crimea and the stoking of hostilities in Eastern Ukraine did not deviate overmuch from this early plan.

On February 27, 2014, unmarked Russian military personnel seized the Crimean parliament building and began occupying local Ukrainian military bases.[17] This bloodless invasion was aided by local protests led by Sergei Aksyonov that had begun in response to the unrest in Kyiv. The Russian leadership quickly designated Aksyonov the legitimate leader in Crimea.[18] Under his leadership, the Crimean parliament voted to hold a referendum on independence from Ukraine.[19] On March 16, in outright violation of Ukraine's constitution, a reported 90 percent of Crimean residents voted to secede from Ukraine and join Russia.[20] In a landmark speech on March 18, 2014, President Putin formally announced Russia's annexation of the peninsula.[21]

Following the annexation of Crimea, pro-Russian separatists in southeastern Ukraine began to mount their own rebellions. Fighting continues throughout the region, despite several attempts at reaching a cease-fire. Russia largely refuses to acknowledge the presence of Russian troops in Ukraine, but there is significant evidence that Russia is providing ongoing material support to the separatists.[22] By September 2014 there was also increasing evidence that support for the separatists had progressed from the provision of arms to involvement of Russian soldiers in the conflict.[23] Russia has suffered casualties in the conflict in Ukraine, but this remains officially secret. Remains are transferred covertly while families are given false reasons for the death of their loved ones.[24] As of this writing, the conflict remains unresolved and unstable.

Vladimir Putin's Justification for the Annexation of Crimea and Its Implications

In some ways, Putin's March 18, 2014, speech announcing the annexation of Crimea was the logical extreme of the rhetorical approach he had cultivated over the preceding fourteen years. He highlighted Russia and Crimea's unique historical bond, tracing their joint history to Crimea as the place where Prince Vladimir accepted Christianity in 988 CE. Putin also emphasized that modern Russia, unlike the Russia of the 1990s, was ready and able to defend its national interests; chief among these is the protection of Russian citizens, language, and culture abroad.[25] This argument found particular resonance because one of the first actions of the new Ukrainian government was to ban Russian as the second official language in the country. Although the law was quickly overturned, it infuriated the population in Russian-speaking regions and was fodder for Putin's rhetoric at home.[26]

The speech also tied the annexation of Crimea with the tradition of veneration of World War II. Putin asserted that "Nationalists, neo-Nazis, Russophobes and anti-Semites executed this coup. They continue to set the tone in Ukraine to this day."[27] The connection between the victory over fascism in World War II and the fight against Ukraine in the present day is notable for two reasons. First, and most obviously, it points to the overwhelming domestic element of Putin's Ukraine policy. Just as Putin used the veneration of World War II in successive speeches and displays as part of rebuilding contemporary Russian national identity around a memory of unity, suffering, and ultimate victory, so too is the struggle against the "fascists and anti-Semites" in modern Ukraine aimed at bolstering Putin's domestic popularity and consolidating his political base. The argument was particularly convincing given the involvement of the far-right Ukrainian nationalist coalition Right Sector in toppling Yanukovych.[28] The annexation of Crimea was by and large extremely popular in Russia, and in the aftermath Putin's popularity soared.[29] The popularity of Crimean annexation also increased in the years immediately following. In March 2014, 64 percent of respondents to a Levada Center poll thought Crimea should be part of Russia; in March 2016 that number was 87 percent.[30]

The second significance of the nod to World War II is deeper than an effort to reinforce national unity. It is intricately tied to broader themes about Russia's role in the world. In the fight against German and Italian fascism, the Soviet Union played a decisive role in overcoming Hitler's terror and restoring world order. The main theme of Putin's speech on Crimea is that while Russia has continued to obey international law and respect world order, Ukraine and its Western supporters have become rogue states that threaten global stability. Putin presents a carefully constructed, if contradictory, argument that the annexation of Crimea was not in fact a violation of international law and, even if it was, it is no more a violation than the independence of Kosovo. He concluded the argument with a sweeping indictment of the current global order:

> The situation in Ukraine reflects what is going on and what has been happening in the world over the past several decades. After the dissolution of bipolarity on the planet, we no longer have stability. Key international institutions are not getting any stronger; on the contrary, in many cases, they are sadly degrading. Our western partners, led by the United States of America, prefer not to be guided by international law in their practical policies, but by the rule of the gun. They have come to believe in their exclusivity and exceptionalism, that they can decide the destinies of the world, that only they can ever be right. They act as they please: here and there, they use force against sovereign states, building coalitions based on the prin-

ciple "If you are not with us, you are against us." To make this aggression look legitimate, they force the necessary resolutions from international organisations, and if for some reason this does not work, they simply ignore the UN Security Council and the UN overall.[31]

In a mirror image of the rhetoric in the United States and much of Europe, Putin casts Russia as the responsible global citizen and the West as the outlaw.

There is another significance to that quotation: the explicit transformation of the crisis in Ukraine into a conflict between Russia and the West. Reiterating arguments that he had voiced on numerous previous occasions, Putin maintained that over the preceding twenty-five years, Russia had always been willing to cooperate with the West, but the interest was never reciprocated. Instead, Russia's national interests were systematically ignored and belittled. He accused NATO and the United States of repeatedly lying about their intentions, primarily with regard to the deployment of military personnel and infrastructure in the newer NATO members and the goals for the planned missile defense installations.[32] He concluded that section of his speech with the assertion that "with Ukraine, our western partners have crossed the line, playing the bear and acting irresponsibly and unprofessionally."[33]

As noted above, it was clear before this speech that Russia viewed US and EU intervention in Ukraine, both before and after the final collapse of the Yanukovych government, as a direct violation of Russia's national interests. Furthermore, American officials (unintentionally) were equally frank in their view of the "right" outcome of the conflict.[34] In a discussion between the US ambassador to Ukraine, Geoffrey R. Pyatt, and the assistant secretary of state for European and Eurasian affairs, Victoria Nuland, leaked by Russian intelligence, Nuland told Pyatt she believed that, of the two leading opposition figures, Arseniy Yatsenyuk rather than Vitali Klitschko should be part of a new Ukrainian government.[35] The idea of Yanukovych retaining power did not come up in the conversation. It matters, however, that in a speech aimed at both the domestic and international audience, the two pillars that Putin chose as his main framework for justifying his actions in Crimea were international law and the US disregard for it as well as a very explicit brand of anti-Americanism (and somewhat broader anti-Westernism).[36]

This framing has important implications both for how Russia positioned itself vis-à-vis BRICS and for how the BRICS countries responded both individually and collectively. Putin's gymnastics in trying to justify the seizure of Crimea, thin as the final argument may be, allowed him to fit the annexation within his broader narrative of the primacy of international law and national sovereignty.[37] These are persistent themes in his rhetoric. They also are the two basic tenets of the BRICS group. In cobbling together what Alexander Cooley terms a "patchwork of international principles, rules, and norms" to give his actions a veneer of legitimacy, Putin also provided other countries with just enough cover to stay silent.

Global Responses to the Annexation of Crimea
and the War in Eastern Ukraine

Globally, there were two basic responses to Russia's annexation of Crimea and ongoing covert actions in Ukraine: complete opprobrium and silence. The opprobrium came from the West and its allies, with the United States at the forefront. On March 17, 2014, just after the referendum in Crimea and the day before Putin confirmed the annexation, US president Barack Obama declared the new US policy of trying to isolate Russia for its behavior in Ukraine. He stated, "From the start, the United States has mobilized the international community in support of Ukraine to isolate Russia for its actions and to reassure our allies and partners. . . . And as I told President Putin yesterday, the referendum in Crimea was a clear violation of Ukrainian constitutions and international law, and it will not be recognized by the international community."[38] US sanctions had been approved two weeks previously, following the invasion of Crimea. In the March 17 statement, Obama announced an expansion of those sanctions. He claimed the moral high ground and the support of the international community for the US response to Russia's actions.

Three days later, after Putin had confirmed that Russia would absorb Crimea, Obama announced a further expansion of the sanctions. This time the sanctions covered not only top officials but also oligarchs known to support Putin and Bank Rossiia, the bank preferred by Russian senior leaders.[39] Just as in his previous press statement, Obama once again cloaked his statement in the mantle of international law. On March 20, he said,

> Over the last several days, we've continued to be deeply concerned by events in Ukraine. We've seen an illegal referendum in Crimea; an illegitimate move by the Russians to annex Crimea; and dangerous risks of escalation, including threats to Ukrainian personnel in Crimea and threats to southern and eastern Ukraine as well. These are all choices that the Russian government has made—choices that have been rejected by the international community, as well as the government of Ukraine.[40]

The wording here is important. In both statements, Obama says again and again that Russia's actions are "illegal" or "illegitimate." He asserts that Russia has lost the support of the international community and that it will be isolated for its actions.

The rhetoric from the EU, though somewhat more measured, made the same basic assumption. On March 13, 2014, the European Parliament demanded that Russia withdraw all its troops from Ukraine and condemned the Russian presence in Crimea as "a breach of international law."[41] It was initially harder to agree on sanctions in Europe, in part because European economies have much stronger ties with Russia than does the US economy. However, following Crimea's secession and absorption into Russia, the EU followed the US example. As the crisis continued unabated and devolved into armed conflict in Ukraine's east, both the United States and the EU passed successively harsher and more wide-ranging sanctions.[42] These have included banning travel for top Russian officials, sharply restricting access to capital for Russian companies and banks, and limiting Western exports of dual-use technology imports and some oil industry technology.[43]

Fierce as they may be, however, US and EU sanctions are not representative of a wider trend. Contrary to President Obama's press statements, the whole international community did not reject Russia's actions outright. On March 27, 2014, the United Nations General Assembly passed UN Resolution 68/262, titled "Territorial Integrity of Ukraine," which declared Crimea's secession from Ukraine invalid.[44] Of the 193 members of the General Assembly, 100 voted in favor of the resolution; 11, including Russia, voted against it; and 58 members abstained (24 countries were absent).[45] All four other BRICS countries numbered among the abstentions.[46] In aggregate, only slightly more than half of United Nations member states supported the resolution. This is hardly a basis for Obama's assertion that the international community as a whole had rejected Russia's actions in Ukraine.

The BRICS countries' abstentions on Resolution 68/262 and unwillingness to condemn Russian actions in Crimea should have come as no surprise to anyone paying attention to the group. Three days before the UN vote, at the Nuclear Security Summit in The Hague, BRICS had offered a quiet rebuke to those countries trying to isolate Russia. In response to rumored efforts by the Australian foreign minister to ban President Putin from the November 2014 G20 Summit in Brisbane, the BRICS foreign ministers issued a joint statement reminding observers that no G20 member has the authority to exclude another unilaterally.[47]

The Hague statement was the strongest coordinated message of BRICS unwillingness to be implicated in the West's attempt to isolate Russia. The votes on the UN resolution are somewhat different. The decision of the four other BRICS countries to abstain from the resolution is neither evidence of prior coordination nor all that surprising. BRICS countries reliably vote against resolutions that threaten their conception of the inviolability of national sovereignty and nonintervention.[48] While the resolution was aimed at condemning Russia's violation of those principles vis-à-vis Ukraine, in doing so it intervened in the private affairs of another sovereign state—Russia. The BRICS countries' votes in the UN do diverge, but those divergences are mainly (though not exclusively) on votes around nonproliferation.[49] Further, as discussed elsewhere, BRICS find Western application of international law biased, and that also likely played a role in the decision not to support the UN resolution on Crimea. Finally, much of the story of the success of BRICS is the malleability of its narrative; the vote need not have been precoordinated nor even taken for the same reasons. It is the cohesive appearance afterward that matters most.

Nevertheless, it is worth noting that BRICS membership may have played a role in Brazil's decision to abstain from Resolution 68/262. Historically, Brazil has been more likely than its BRICS peers to support human rights resolutions.[50] Since these are a subset of resolutions about questions of sovereignty, it follows that Brazil has at times allowed a concern for the former to trump the general commitment to the latter, which in turn implies a slight flexibility on sovereignty Brazil's BRICS partners do not share. However, the resolution on Crimea came during a moment of domestic vulnerability for Brazilian president Dilma Rousseff and during a year when Brazil held the BRICS chair. Rousseff may have calculated that it was more dangerous to risk alienating Russia and have them boycott the Fortaleza summit than to alienate the United States in abstaining from the resolution. A showing of good statesmanship at the Fortaleza summit was considered important for victory in the October 2014 Brazilian elections.[51]

Abstention is not the same thing as voting against a resolution; it is a much easier political choice to make.[52] Similarly, silence is not the same thing as support. Indeed, outright support for Russia was meager at best. It came mainly from client states, such as Belarus or Armenia, or states that are themselves very isolated from the rest of the world, including Syria and North Korea.[53] Nevertheless, silence does give room for maneuver. The breathing room this silence provided, combined with worsening political relations with the West and tightening economic conditions, changed how Russia talked about and interacted with the group in the period immediately following the onset of the crisis.

Intra-BRICS Practicalities after Ukraine

With the imposition of sanctions and the passage of Resolution 68/262, Russia found itself the target of an isolation campaign by the West and many of its allies. In response, Russia's political leadership looked to the BRICS countries individually and the BRICS group as a whole to fill the political and economic void left by the West. This section examines the details of what that meant in practice as well as the reasons it was a temporary phenomenon.

Some Caveats

Until February 2014 Russia's top leadership found the idea of BRICS politically and rhetorically useful only within a narrow set of parameters. The crisis in Ukraine changed that calculus in the short run, but it is tricky to separate out the precise extent to which the crisis caused a change in policy. This is because the crisis in Ukraine is still ongoing and because of three distinct factors that confound the analysis: the economic downturn in Russia and the other BRICS at the time, the path dependence of ongoing institutionalization before the crisis, and the confluence of Russia's 2015 chairmanship of BRICS with the crisis.

On the economic side, Western sanctions, a precipitous drop in the price of oil, and capital flight almost entirely stalled growth in the Russian economy in 2014.[54] Russia's real GDP contracted by 2.7 percent in 2015.[55] Combined with weaker economic performance in the other BRICS, economic conditions have not lent themselves toward Russian efforts to increase economic relations with its BRICS partners. As discussed in the second chapter, intra-BRICS economic relations are in general a poor proxy for the strength of the group. Nevertheless, to the extent that post-Ukraine Russian policies emphasize increasing economic ties with BRICS partners, it is worth noting that slow fulfillment of those goals may be due in part to global economic trends.

The second confounding factor in establishing how Russia's approach to BRICS changed as a result of the conflict with Ukraine is the group's prior movement toward institutionalization. The deliverables from the 2014 summit in Fortaleza provide a perfect example. The BRICS Contingency Reserve Arrangement gives Russia a theoretical alternative source of capital. This could prove quite useful, considering Western sanctions make it hard for Russian banks to get long-term financing in the West. However, the agreement on the Contingency Reserve Arrangement, as with the agreement on the BRICS bank, was in process long before the situation in Ukraine exploded. The simultaneous agreement on the Contingency Reserve Arrangement and the exclusion of Russia from Western markets was an interesting coincidence, but it offers no new information about Russian policy toward BRICS institutionalization.

The same can be said of the myriad new forums and groups that emerged over the course of 2014 and 2015. These include the BRICS Parliamentary Forum, the BRICS Civil Forum, and the BRICS Youth Forum. On the one hand, as President Putin asserted in his welcome to the parliamentary delegates in Moscow in June 2015, contact between lawmakers of the BRICS countries is a substantive step in the development of the BRICS group as an international association. He also said that the Parliamentary Forum "opened a qualitatively new level of engagement among the countries."[56] Similarly, the other forums all advance the goal of strengthening ties between the countries beyond the governmental level and push the group toward institutionalization. Putin and his government were strongly supportive of these efforts.

On the other hand, many of the seemingly new forums have long histories. The idea for the BRICS Youth Forum, for example, is in BRICS action plans as far back as the 2012 summit in New Delhi and mirrors a similar SCO initiative. Similarly, although the Ufa summit saw the first adoption of a formal strategy for economic partnership, the Fortaleza Declaration proclaimed that it was time to create such a strategy, suggesting work began under Brazil's 2014 BRICS presidency.[57] Further, some ideas that Russia pushed hard under its chairmanship, such as cooperation on energy, have been included in statements from the very first summit in Ekaterinburg. The agreements and groupings that emerged in the midst of the Ukraine crisis had a long lead time. The combination of Russia's chairmanship with the flurry of activity gave the appearance that after years of neglect Russia was working hard to make BRICS a true alternative to the West. Drawing that conclusion, however, neglects the reality that many of these projects were already in process before the crisis in Ukraine began.

The final confounding factor in understanding how the Ukraine crisis impacted Russia's approach to BRICS on a practical level is the very fact of Russia's chairmanship in 2015.[58] There are two issues here: one external and one internal. From the external perspective, the political rupture between Russia and the West makes it tempting to interpret everything Russia did vis-à-vis its 2015–16 BRICS chairmanship as essentially anti-Western.[59] Russia would have hosted the BRICS summit in 2015 regardless of its other international entanglements; to interpret what happened under its chairmanship as strictly a reaction to Ukraine would be incorrect. This is not to argue that Ukraine and the rupture with the West did not affect how that chairmanship was administered or what proposals Russia put forward (see below) but rather to offer the corrective that BRICS would likely have been a major feature in Russian politics in 2015 even without the extra pressures of the Ukraine crisis.

This leads to the internal aspect of Russia's chairmanship. Russian leaders tend to be event driven; for example, in the lead up to hosting the 2012 Asia Pacific Economic Cooperation summit in Vladivostok, the leadership spent a lot of time and money speaking about the importance of Russia's attachments in Asia. After the summit concluded, however, the focus shifted to the upcoming Olympics in Sochi, Russia, and the emphasis on relations in the East receded.[60] By the same token, the way Russia approaches BRICS in a chairmanship year is different from the approach in a nonchairmanship year. Just as it would be dangerous to read too much into Russia's emphasis on BRICS as a straight rejection of the West, it would be incorrect to see the sudden surge in interest in the group in 2015 as a total pivot in Russia's foreign policy without accounting for the extra interest driven by its hosting duties. Put differently, while the crisis in Ukraine changed the role of BRICS in Russian foreign policy, the crisis and its effect on relations with the West are not the only reason Russia invested so heavily in its BRICS membership in 2015.

The Importance of Optics

The above caveats notwithstanding, BRICS did become operationally useful for Russia after the onset of the Ukraine crisis. The BRICS countries' continued willingness to engage in both business and summitry with Russia is a powerful counter to the West's attempt to isolate the country politically and economically.[61] This is not just about symbolic international gestures, such as the vote on UN Resolution 68/262 or the statement in The Hague about excluding Russia from the G20. Gestures like these are good for short-term boosts, but they do not offer sustainable relief. More important are things like the May 2014 $400 billion gas deal between Russia and China, or the possibility of substituting meat imports from Brazil instead of the EU meat banned by Putin's "anti-sanctions."[62] The succession of BRICS-related events around Russia over the course of 2015 was no less important: they offered high-profile demonstrations that Western rhetorical censure and economic sanctions failed in their objective to isolate Russia.

A June 2015 tweet from Ian Bremmer, president of the consulting firm Eurasia Group, summed up the situation nicely. Bremmer tweeted a map with the caption, "The World is isolating Russia. As long as the World looks like this."[63] The map Bremmer tweeted is missing all of Africa, most of Asia, and everything south of Texas on the American continent. Indeed, it is basically a map of NATO, with a few additions. The world is not isolating Russia; the West is, and it has not attracted non-Western countries to its cause.

The sanctions have had an impact on the Russian economy, and trade with BRICS is insufficient to make up the budget shortfall created by the sanctions and the falling oil price. Further, the expected increase in trade with China and other BRICS has not materialized. This is partly because of some hesitation in China to engage in projects that directly contravene the sanctions.[64] It is further a by-product of the collapse in commodity prices, turmoil in Chinese markets, and the overall economic slowdown in emerging markets. It is also because the Russian business climate remains troubled, and BRICS businesses are no less concerned about property rights and returns on investment than are Westerners. Nevertheless, as Bremmer's map vividly demonstrates, Russia is not without partners. Considering that Russia's interest in BRICS has historically been primarily about the optics of the group, it is fitting that these optics of ongoing political and economic partnership became operationally important for the country.

The Short-Term Concretization of Russia's Goals toward BRICS

Although optics are always important to Russia's leadership, the change was more than just cosmetic. Whether as a result of the crisis or a result of its chairmanship, the Russian approach to BRICS, at least at the policy level, was far more concrete in 2015 than it was even two years previously. The best evidence of this concretization is a comparison between the "Concept of Participation of the Russian Federation in BRICS," approved in 2013, and the "Concept of the Russian Federation's Presidency in BRICS in 2015–2016," released on March 1, 2015.[65] As discussed in the previous chapter, the 2013 concept outlines a long list of areas in which Russia would like to see BRICS cooperation but displays little interest in either firm institutionalization or pushing the boundaries of how BRICS could evolve.

The 2015 concept, by contrast, is much more direct. The beginning of the document declares,

> A long-term objective of the Russian Federation in BRICS and, accordingly, a
> consistent goal of its presidency of the association is the gradual transformation of

BRICS from a dialogue forum and a tool for coordinating positions on a limited range of issues into a full-scale mechanism for strategic and day-to-day cooperation on key issues of world politics and the global economy. This objective will be achieved by consistently expanding the range of cooperation areas, actively promoting the common interests of BRICS countries on the international scene, and creating an extensive system of mechanisms for cooperation, primarily in the financial and economic sphere, which will gradually evolve into concrete institutions. All this is intended to raise BRICS to the level of an important element of the global governance system in the 21st century.[66]

As noted in the previous chapter, the 2013 concept does include the goal of making BRICS a "full-fledged mechanism of strategic and ongoing cooperation on key international political and economic issues."[67] That statement, however, is buried at the very end of the document. In 2015 the goal is in the second paragraph, setting the stage for the proposals that follow. As if to underscore the new commitment to making BRICS strong and permanent, the 2015 concept lists enhancing "the efficiency of BRICS by improving the reporting process for previous commitments assumed by member countries" as one of the core objectives of the Russian presidency.[68]

There are other departures, especially in terms of how BRICS acts as a subforum within larger organizations. For example, the 2013 concept speaks generally of coordination in forums such as the United Nations "on the basis of common interests."[69] The 2015 concept calls for "developing comprehensive cooperation in the UN."[70] The later document also pares down the goals, offering fewer potential areas of cooperation but each with more detailed and implementable proposals. This is likely in part due to the differing objectives of each concept: one is long-term and the other is specifically related to Russia's chairmanship. It is also evidence, though, of clearer thinking about the realm of the possible in BRIC and which areas best serve Russia's immediate objectives.

As a case in point, the 2015 concept specifically references Western sanctions on Russia as an impetus for strengthening intra-BRICS economic cooperation.[71] Indeed, many of Russia's suggestions for BRICS are aimed at creating a parallel system to that controlled by Western states, perhaps as a way of circumnavigating the West's attempted isolation of Russia. One of the proposals Russia put forth as chairman was to replace the US government with the UN International Telecommunications Union as the Internet Corporation for Assigned Names and Numbers (ICANN) overseer.[72] During his statement at the Fortaleza summit, Putin suggested that BRICS use GLONASS, Russia's navigation system, which is an alternative to the US Global Positioning System.[73] In May 2015 the Central Bank of Russia suggested that BRICS discuss creating its own version of the SWIFT system.[74]

Whether any of these proposals ultimately come to fruition (and BRICS has a several-year incubation period for new proposals), they are indicative of two important developments. First, they show that the combination of the Ukraine crisis and the chairmanship forced those involved in making Russia's BRICS policy to think seriously about how the forum could help Russia navigate its new global context. Second, the efforts to create a parallel system indicate that the rhetoric of building a new world order translated into Russia's operational approach to BRICS, at least during its tenure at the helm of the organization.

The concept for Russia's BRICS presidency not only shows an evolution of Russia's approach to BRICS in its relevant policy proposals. It also attempts to weave the group more closely into one of Putin's main regime legitimation efforts: the veneration of World War II. The eighth section of the BRICS presidency concept is "Awareness-Raising during Russia's Presidency," and the goals it lists are all aimed toward increasing awareness of BRICS on the international stage.[75] One of the proposed methods of doing so is

> to hold, together with the BRICS partners, a number of publicity campaigns devoted to the 70th anniversary of the victory in WWII. In political terms, the events are aimed at promoting the ideas of friendship and mutual understanding among the peoples of the BRICS countries; stiff resistance to attempts to revive the ideology and policies of Nazism, racism, anti-Semitism, and xenophobia in all their manifestations; and preventing the falsification of history, which seeks to undermine the foundations of the post-war world order.[76]

This brings the BRICS group directly into a major part of Russian policy and national identity. Given how Putin framed the reasons for Russia's involvement in the Ukraine crisis, it also set the BRICS group directly against the West.

BRICS versus the West in Post-Ukraine Russian Political Rhetoric

While the approach to BRICS became more multifaceted at the policy level, that change did not translate into more nuanced rhetoric at the highest political levels. Instead, the crisis in Ukraine did not change Putin's rhetorical approach to BRICS so much as it removed its veil. As argued previously, from the very beginning Putin primarily deployed Russia's membership in the group as a rhetorical alternative option to the West. A level of anti-Westernism was inherent in this approach, but it was framed in the context of creating a more fair and balanced world order. If anti-Westernism is conceived of as a continuum, the initial anti-Westernism was at the mild end. Although that framing remains in official group statements, much of Putin's rhetoric in the immediate aftermath of the onset of the Ukraine crisis framed BRICS as an explicitly anti-Western project, moving it to the more extreme end of the anti-Westernism spectrum.

In terms of evaluating anti-Western rhetoric after the Ukraine crisis, three Putin speeches are particularly telling. The first is the March 2014 speech discussed above, which announced the annexation of Crimea. The second is Putin's speech and question-and-answer session at the annual Valdai International Discussion Club in October 2014.[77] The third is the annual address to the Federal Assembly in December 2014.[78] These speeches are explicitly, angrily, anti-Western.

At Valdai, as in the March 2014 speech on Crimea, Putin accused the United States of being the source and cause of global instability. He stated, "The United States, having declared itself the winner of the Cold War, saw no need for [creating a new world order]. Instead of establishing a new balance of power, essential for maintaining order and stability, they took steps that threw the system into sharp and deep imbalance."[79] The result of these steps, in Putin's estimation, is a world in which "international law has been forced to retreat over and over by the onslaught of legal nihilism."[80] During the December address to the Federal Assembly, he sounded similar themes. In what was ostensibly a section about the need to cooperate on fighting international terrorism, the speech takes a tangent onto the lingering ill effects of the 2002 US abdication of the Anti-Ballistic Missile Treaty and subsequent plans to build missile defense installations in Europe.[81] Earlier in the speech he asserted that Europe and the United States would have devised another reason to levy sanctions even in the absence of a crisis in Ukraine because the real aim was "to contain Russia's growing capabilities, affect our country in some way, or even take advantage of it."[82] This phrasing is reminiscent of the warning in Putin's 2004 annual address about the ire Russian growth would incur but evolved to suit the new context. Putin here displays not only a deep dislike of the West and its policies but also a fundamental mistrust of its motives, making the possibility of cooperation, which he raises later in the speech, seem almost unimaginable.

In the Valdai speech, Putin contrasted the behavior of the West with that of BRICS, the SCO, and the other organizations Russia has helped found. Unlike the West, which is actively trying to isolate Russia and acts without regard for international stability, BRICS, the SCO, and the EEU provide stable partnerships that help Russia accomplish its "integration-oriented, positive, peaceful agenda."[83] Putin also framed these three organizations as open and nonconfrontational, with the goal of bringing governments together rather than forming exclusionary blocs.[84] The implicit negative parallel with NATO and the EU was unmistakable.

All three speeches also hark back to the theme of sovereignty that Putin developed over the course of his first two presidential terms. During the question-and-answer session at Valdai, in an unsubtle rebuke of US hegemonic claims (this time in connection with whether Kosovo's independence could serve as a precedent), he drew the following analogy:

> You may remember the wonderful saying: Whatever Jupiter is allowed, the Ox is not.
>
> We cannot agree with such an approach. The ox may not be allowed something, but the bear will not even bother to ask permission. Here we consider it the master of the taiga, and I know for sure that it does not intend to move to any other cli-

matic zones—it will not be comfortable there. However, it will not let anyone have its taiga either. I believe this is clear.[85]

This means Russia will do what it feels necessary to protect its own interests. Putin pushes his remonstration even further with the reference to "climatic zones," presumably a reference to Dmitry Medvedev's claim after the 2008 war with Georgia about a sphere of "privileged interests" in Russia's border regions.[86] The implication is that Russia will not be expansionist, but neither will it countenance incursions into its region of concern.

Unlike the earlier era's speeches touting Russia's ability and willingness to protect its interests, however, the speeches in 2014 are retrospective. Putin's claims during his March, October, and December 2014 addresses about Russia's willingness to take unilateral action to protect vital interests were made in the wake of the manifestation of that willingness. If the 2007 Munich speech was a warning shot, then these speeches were the end of the battle.[87] The annexation of Crimea was simply presented as a fait accompli; the bear did not ask for permission.

Yet the repeated protestations against Western policies and the persistent anti-Western rhetoric that accompanies them are also somehow hollow. Rather than a clean break from the West, the speeches betray an ongoing focus on justifying Russia's actions in the context of the West's own misdeeds. The speech at Valdai, for example, was supposed to be a programmatic speech.[88] Indeed, the theme of the conference was the need to build a new world order. Rather than offering suggestions on that theme, the address was instead a recrimination against both European and American policies since the end of the Cold War. Putin could have used the opportunity to outline his vision for how the different emerging elements of global governance, including BRICS, could be brought together into a coherent and workable system. He did not do that; instead, he spent most of the speech rehashing Western reactions to Ukraine and Russia's right to protect its interests.[89]

The emphasis on the transgressions of the West, as opposed to on a forward-looking vision, is emblematic of the continued Western orientation of the political elite. Orientation is not the same as alignment. According to Dmitri Trenin, Russia is now fully outside the Western sphere.[90] Another analyst referred to the break in relations following the annexation of Crimea as a "divorce process" of Russia from the West.[91] Instead, the orientation is a combination of a continued dominant identity as a first world country and also a deep and ongoing desire for recognition of great power status from the United States. As Fyodor Lukyanov put it, "The inability to abandon the West is the biggest obstacle to Russia's success in BRICS."[92] In other words, Russia's BRICS policies and efforts to build BRICS into a major organ of global governance are hampered by Russia's continued need for Western recognition. As much as Russia may wish to build a new world order, it is still fighting the battles of the old one.

Some of the analyses prepared in advance of the 2015 summit in Ufa bear out this reading. Consider, for example, *Perspektivy i strategicheskie prioritety voskhozhdeniia BRIKS* (*Prospects and Strategic Priorities for the Rise of the BRICS*), a study produced under the auspices of NKI BRIKS. The book purports to be an entire agenda for the future development of the group, including efforts at modeling possible growth patterns and exploring new areas for deepening the partnership.[93] Much of the introductory section, however, is devoted to a repetition of the traditional litany of the crimes of the West. At one point it goes so far as to assert that the ongoing crisis in Ukraine is an outright war that the United States and Europe are waging against Russia.[94] Introducing what is otherwise a comprehensive qualitative and quantitative analysis of BRICS with the conflict between Russia and the West (and an explicit recognition of the importance of BRICS to Russia given the rupture with the West) rather than the BRICS group's achievements to date belies Putin's contention in the Valdai address that BRICS is not about forming blocs against other parties.[95]

The West is omnipresent in more than official rhetoric and documents. Academics, too, often see conflict with the West as the seed from which BRICS has grown. The response of Boris Martynov, the deputy director of the Institute of Latin America of the Russian Academy of Sciences, to a set of questions about the development of BRICS in Russian foreign policy is a good illustration. The academic prefaced his response with the following statement: "For the beginning I must say that I do not like the USA (please, don't get offended: nothing personal, only business). When still a young man, I began to hate communists, for they always taught me how to live and what to do. Nowadays it seems that the US are trying to do the same with all the world. Sorry for them, for I knew many fine Americans. Partly my answers will be connected with that . . . opinion."[96] It was an honest and revealing preface. The answers that followed similarly framed the development of BRICS as a reaction against Western hegemony within the international system. For Martynov, BRICS was a global governance Hail Mary, whose goal is to salvage what it can from the current world order and devise a positive agenda to reverse what will almost certainly be a further descent in "anarchy."[97] But what is perhaps most salient about the answer is the assumption that in some ways, BRICS began with a profound disappointment in the United States.

If Martynov's answers suggest an almost wistful element to the anti-Westernism in Russia's BRICS policies, others are somewhat more confrontational. An article about an interview on the news station *Pravda* with Vladimir Davydov, the director of Institute of Latin America of the Russian Academy of Sciences, ran under the headline "BRICS Are the Main Geopolitical Enemy of the USA."[98] Davydov said that the BRICS countries need a common economic and information policy because the United States is not only trying to undermine Russia; it has designs on all the BRICS countries.[99] During an interview in Moscow in September 2014 Davydov was less combative, but he was adamant that the United States is no better or smarter than Russia and that BRICS is a way of counteracting Western encroachment.[100]

This issue of Western encroachment on Russian interests, or potential for encroachment, brings the anti-Western rhetoric down to the realm of the practical. In essence, anti-Westernism exists on two levels in Russia's approach to BRICS. The first is the fulminating anti-Westernism of Putin's speeches on US irresponsibility or Davydov's framing of BRICS as a geopolitical foe of the United States. These are high-profile, quotable, and likely intentionally inflammatory.[101] The second, represented by Russia's proposals during its BRICS chairmanship, is anti-Westernism as functionalism. Russia attempted to make BRICS a bulwark against the West through slow, steady, and low-profile (for the layman) suggestions. Operating together, these two levels make Russia's immediate post-Ukraine approach to BRICS much more comprehensively anti-Western than it was before the crisis.

(Russian) Anti-Westernism and the Rest of BRICS

Russia does not execute its BRICS policies in a vacuum. The responses of the other partners are critical for Russia's long-term success or failure to achieve its objectives in how it would see BRICS evolve. In the case of Russia's increased foreign policy emphasis on the importance of anti-Westernism in the BRICS group, the main question is the support of the other BRICS countries for that shift in approach. This brings to the fore an issue with which the group has struggled since its inception: the role and degree of anti-Westernism in BRICS both as a motivator for cooperation and even sometimes a raison d'être.

The role of anti-Westernism in BRICS is unresolved because of competing and contradictory interests within the group. On the one hand, as discussed in chapter 2, all the BRICS countries have more investment in their relations with Western countries than they do in relations with the other BRICS countries. Even though China is now the largest trading partner for Brazil, India, and South Africa and the top exporter to Russia, none of the BRICS countries feature in China's list of top five trading partners. All BRICS countries conduct significant trade with the United States and the European Union.[102] These strong economic ties are one reason that BRICS documents are so careful to emphasize that the group is not directed at any third parties and is not an anti-Western bloc.

There are also political reasons to temper any perceived anti-Western motivations. BRICS's overarching goal is to reshape global governance architecture such that the member countries have a larger voice in existing institutions. China in particular is well aware that it has been a prime beneficiary of the current system of global economic governance. While it wishes to see power redistribution and has become increasingly revisionist, the country's leaders do not wish to overturn the system entirely.[103] What this means in practical terms is that BRICS will need Western acquiescence and cooperation in order to achieve its aims. From that perspective, overt or alienating anti-Westernism would be counterproductive.

On the other hand, there is something inherently anti-Western in the group's initial coalescence. As discussed in the opening chapter, the beginning of BRICS as a political idea is deeply entwined with the global discontent with the United States that began to emerge in the wake of the invasion of Iraq.[104] While it was also a response to objective trends in the distribution of global economic power, those trends fueled discontent with US and European intransigence on the reform of global economic governance. The BRICS countries' silence on Crimea also happened in the context of renewed anger over the revelations of the US National Security Agency spying programs at home and abroad.[105]

Perhaps more importantly, though, there is also an intrinsic Pareto optimality problem with the BRICS demands.[106] The BRICS countries desire a reorganization of votes in international organizations (most prominently the IMF but elsewhere as well) so that voting weights better represent the current global distribution of economic capacity.[107] However, in demanding that reshuffling, the BRICS countries are by definition demanding that the shares of other countries, mainly in the EU, decrease. The BRICS hope to gain power through others' loss of power. There is no solution to the demand wherein some EU member states are not geopolitically and geoeconomically worse off afterward than they were beforehand.[108]

It is worth noting that in some ways the particular concerns about the governance structures of international financial institutions are more specifically anti-European than anti-American. While the BRICS countries may not like that the United States has effective veto power in the IMF, the bigger problem is that countries like the Netherlands and Belgium are overrepresented. As noted in the first chapter, several European countries that properly received large voting shares when the IMF was created in 1944 have been eclipsed in the intervening seventy years. For example, Mexico has a larger economy and a larger population than Belgium, but before the passage of the 2010 quota reform in 2016, the latter had more weight in the IMF.[109] Some of the motivation for BRICS, therefore, is also about trying to address legitimate concerns about the existing economic order, especially regarding international finance and international trade.

Indeed, the IMF itself takes this view. In an October 2015 report, two IMF economists argued that the world is "on the cusp of an epochal change in terms of economic power, the type of which has not been witnessed in the past 200–250 years."[110] As a result of that coming shift, "changes in global economic governance will have to be more substantive than the current incremental changes envisaged."[111] The authors base their claim on 2015 IMF projections that the BRICS group's share of global GDP would surpass that of the G7 by 2017.[112] They also argue that a revision of votes is ultimately in the interest of advanced economies because it will make global economic governance more stable.[113] Nevertheless, a radical restructure of the IMF executive board would require US acquiescence to meet the 85 percent threshold for change, and this is unlikely to be forthcoming.[114] Since European states stand to lose the most votes, they also are unlikely to support revision in the near term.

The BRICS group therefore walks a very fine line regarding its relationship with the West. It must be sufficiently oppositional in order to capitalize on the anti-Western sentiment and dissatisfaction with the current system among developing countries that spurred its rise to prominence. However, it cannot become so oppositional that it torpedoes either the main goal of the BRICS group as identified in summit declarations (reform but not revolution in the international system) or the national economic interests of BRICS member countries. Further, the group has to make sure that the perception of the group as an anti-Western alliance does not override the image of the group as one whose goal is to fix real and acknowledged problems in global economic governance.

The ongoing standoff between Russia and the West makes this balancing act more delicate, not least because of how it affected Russia's calculus for participation in the group. Other BRICS countries understand that the Western sanctions on Russia are not an attack on either the BRICS group or the other member countries individually.[115] However, none of the other BRICS are going to risk their own relationships with either the United States or the EU for Russia.

It is in some sense a question of degrees. As noted earlier, the BRICS countries (and others) have been happy to try to pick up the market share left by Western sanctions. This suggests there could be a certain amount of flexibility among the other BRICS partners in allowing Russia to make BRICS's anti-Westernism more overt. However, if Russian rhetoric (beyond that intended for domestic consumption) goes too far, then it is likely that China, India, and Brazil will push back.[116] These countries will not want BRICS to become an explicitly anti-Western alliance. The open question, therefore, is how the other BRICS balance cooperation in that group with the risks it poses, given the enduring split between Russia and the West.

One indicator is that, despite international pressure, none of the BRICS countries endorsed Western efforts to isolate Russia either financially or politically. While Chinese banks may not wish to contravene Western sanctions directly, Chinese companies do not feel bound to observe the ban on providing goods bound for Crimea.[117] In 2014 Russia brought Sergei Aksyonov, the Russian-appointed president of Crimea, as part of the delegation on Putin's state visit to India. The visit included a meeting between Aksyonov and Indian businessmen that resulted in a memorandum of understanding with a group that bills itself as the Indo-Crimean Partnership.[118] The BRICS countries are not choosing sides; China is also actively investing in Ukraine, including the acquisition in 2017 of a Ukrainian manufacturer of engines for military cargo aircraft.[119] Nevertheless, the willingness to transgress sanctions (e.g., by investing in Crimea) is important. Further, investment in Crimea is not uncontroversial, even in China.[120]

Ironically, the primary reason for BRICS's willingness to provide tacit support for Russia may be the West's reaction to Russia's activities. As the Brazilian academic and BRICS expert Oliver Stuenkel argues, "The BRICS's unwillingness to denounce and isolate Russia may have less to do with its opinion on Russia's intervention in Crimea per se and more to do with its skepticism of the West's belief that sanctions are an adequate way to punish whom it sees as international misfits."[121] Stuenkel does not argue that Russia has won the BRICS's silence (and therefore silent acquiescence) because the leaders of Brazil, India, China, and South Africa agree with Russia's actions in Ukraine. Instead, it is because of the tool employed by the West to express its disapproval. All the BRICS countries have at one time or another been the targets of Western sanctions. All are (officially) wary of sanctioning others.[122]

While the other BRICS countries may take issue with the specific stick employed to bring Russia back into line, that is not necessarily a sufficient explanation for the other BRICS countries' silence. Instead, the roots of the silence likely lie in a deeper and (from an American perspective) more worrying source. Stuenkel explains: "Especially for voices more critical of the U.S., the West's alarm over Crimea is merely proof that established powers still consider themselves to be the ultimate arbiters of international norms, unaware of their own hypocrisy. If asked which country was the greatest threat to international stability, most BRICS foreign policymakers and observers would not name Russia, Iran and North Korea, but the United States."[123] This is a damning statement. It may not be the raw anti-Western sentiment that courses through Vladimir Putin's speeches, but it is the same idea and even the same phrase. In this analysis, the United States is not the world's policeman. It has become instead a global bandit, and therefore its power must be constrained. As long as the BRICS countries agree on this basic point—and there is no reason to think positions are shifting—anti-Westernism will serve as a useful and effective rallying point reinforcing group cohesion.

Even as BRICS has shown a certain amount of solidarity on the Russia issue, there are tensions over Russia's anti-Westernism. At issue is what Marxism-Leninism called *perekhod kolichestva v kachestvo*—a change from one of quantity to one of quality. For Russia, politics have always been the dominant motivation for participation in BRICS; for the others, geo-economics is a stronger impetus.[124] In the years immediately following the onset of the crisis in Ukraine, however, the Russian approach to BRICS, and especially the attendant anti-Westernism that was always a strong component of that approach, underwent a shift so large that it became a qualitative shift. That shift has ultimately been a contributing factor in BRICS stagnation since the group's apex in 2014.

Consider the example of the BRICS Parliamentary Forum. Proposed by Russia during its 2015 presidency, the new forum quickly caused friction with the other BRICS partners.[125] India in particular came out against creating a permanent BRICS parliamentary assembly.[126] The head of the Indian delegation cited the risk of excessive institutionalization as his reason for voting against creating a permanent BRICS parliamentary body. Since even Russian foreign minister Sergei Lavrov is on record as opposing institutionalization, this reasoning may be a feint to hide deeper concerns.[127]

India and other BRICS may be more worried about how some Duma leaders framed the forum in terms of analogous bodies elsewhere. Leonid Slutsky, then chairman of the Duma Committee on CIS Affairs, said the following: "The European Union has its European Parliament. And the Eurasian Union is considering establishing a Eurasian Parliamentary Assembly. Cooperation under BRICS auspices has reached a sufficient level, where it is possible to speak about the necessity of dramatically raising inter-parliamentary coordination."[128] Comparing BRICS to the EU and the Eurasian Union presents a radically different vision for BRICS from what has been put forth thus far. It suggests not just a change in the level of institutionalization of the group but a qualitative change in how cohesive the group is expected to be with regard to its interactions with the outside world. Slutsky is likely not expressing the views of the higher political elite on this issue; he is not a member of United Russia (Putin's party) and at the time did not serve on a committee very involved with BRICS. Nevertheless, Russia fought hard for the parliamentary assembly. That it was unable to reach agreement on making it a permanent forum even when it held the BRICS chairmanship is indicative of the limits to which the other BRICS are willing to go in this partnership.[129] While the Parliamentary Forum persists, it remains weak, despite consistent Russian urging; the other members have acquiesced to meetings, but they have not agreed to give those meetings substance.[130]

The Next Big Idea: The Greater Eurasian Partnership

In the immediate aftermath of the onset of the crisis in Ukraine in 2014, Russia began thinking more clearly and concretely about ways BRICS could fill in gaps left by the demise of the relationship with Europe and the United States. That shift, however, did not last. By the Goa summit in October 2016, it was clear BRICS had slipped back into the rhetorical realm for the Russians. Instead, focus has shifted to the idea of the Greater Eurasian Partnership.[131]

The Greater Eurasian Partnership is still a rather amorphous idea, but the fundamental principle seems to be an economic and political space in Eurasia coordinated through networked relations among the major Eurasian multilateral groups.[132] These include the EEU, the Silk Road Economic Belt (the overland portion of China's Belt and Road Initiative), and the SCO, among others. The core of the Greater Eurasian Partnership is Sino-Russian relations and coordination between the EEU and Silk Road Economic Belt. During a summit in Moscow in May 2015, Putin and Chinese president Xi Jinping agreed to coordinate the two projects.

The shift toward reemphasizing regional over global reorganization is visible in Putin's 2015 address to the Federal Assembly. Despite hosting a successful joint summit with BRICS and the SCO that same year, the speech does not mention BRICS once. Instead, Putin focuses on Eurasia, saying: "I propose holding consultations, in conjunction with our colleagues from the Eurasian Economic Union, with the SCO and ASEAN members, as well as with the states that are about to join the SCO, with the view of potentially forming an economic partnership. . . . Of course, this partnership should be based on principles of equality and mutual interest."[133] The surprise is not that Putin is concerned first and foremost with consolidating Russia's primacy in Eurasia; the former Soviet space has always been Putin's prime foreign policy concern. What is surprising, however, is the omission of even the standard paragraph about Russia's commitment to BRICS as part of the new democratic world order. Considering Russia still formally held the BRICS presidency in December 2015 (it switched to India in February 2016), this omission is jarring and indicates the extent to which BRICS had fallen on the list of foreign policy priorities.

BRICS regained its previous rhetorical role in both the 2016 Foreign Policy Concept and in Putin's 2016 address to the Federal Assembly, but the emphasis and concrete goals that marked the Russian approach to BRICS in the immediate aftermath of the onset of the Ukraine Crisis are missing.[134] That absence is unremarkable in Putin's speech since his framing of the group never really went beyond its rhetorical use. It is striking, however, that the Foreign Policy Concept devotes no space to elaborating a vision of BRICS in line with the goals articulated in the 2015 concept of the Russian Federation's presidency of BRICS in 2015–16. Instead, the stress is on building up the EEU and other regional (non-Western) organizations.

There are several interconnected reasons for the demotion of BRICS after its brief stint in the Russian foreign policy limelight (in addition to the natural demotion following the end of Russia's chairmanship). The first is a combination of a sense of failure to achieve goals and overall disillusionment with the BRICS process. Portions of the Russian government, especially the Duma, pushed hard to make BRICS a political body with some heft after the crisis in Ukraine. Those efforts were unsuccessful because of both disagreement within the Russian government (for example, within MID) and opposition from BRICS partners (such as on the Parliamentary Forum, discussed above).[135] Facing the failure to transform BRICS into an organized platform capable of more than loose policy coordination on a narrow set of issues, Russia's leaders set their sights elsewhere.

The sense of failure at the official level is combined with a deep sense of failure and disillusionment at the expert level. As discussed earlier, in January 2015 Boris Martynov spoke about BRICS in terms of his disillusionment with the West. During a follow-up interview with Professor Martynov in March 2017, the scholar instead expressed profound disappointment that BRICS had not become a vehicle for formulating and pushing an alternate set of global norms.[136] What was the point of BRICS, he asked, if it was promoting the same norms about economics and international relations as everybody else? Martynov did not rule out that

BRICS could revive if its members recommit (and, in the case of Brazil and South Africa, weather their domestic crises), but he was overall pessimistic about the group's future. During a follow-up interview the previous week, Martynov's colleague Vladimir Davydov was similarly far less animated about the prospects of BRICS than he had been three years previously.[137]

There is, however, more than disillusionment in Russia's reversion to form on BRICS. It also represents a pragmatic realization of the limits of the group and the realities of Russia's current international position. In Dmitri Trenin's estimation, Putin has moved on from trying to lead a movement and is instead quite rationally focusing on Russia's immediate neighborhood. The difference from the pre-Ukraine regional approach is that the focus of the neighborhood has shifted from West to East.[138]

Conclusion

In 2006 Dmitri Trenin published an article in *Foreign Affairs* entitled "Russia Leaves the West," in which he argued that "Russia's leaders have given up on becoming part of the West and have started creating their own Moscow-centered system."[139] Since 2006 was the year BRIC held its first official meeting, Trenin would seem to have been prescient in his observation. However, a retrospective analysis suggests certain nuances. If in 2006 Russia was beginning to build its own solar system, to use Trenin's analogy, then this new system was at least adjacent to the Western one. Indeed, as discussed in the previous chapter, one of Moscow's initial goals toward BRICS was to strengthen its own hand through strategic cooperation with both old and new power centers.

This initial goal coincided with the goals of Russia's other BRICS partners. Although the group has always been something of a Rorschach test for its members, with each country having its own goals and rationale for participating, all used it as a way of maximizing their voice in the international arena without directly challenging the reigning hegemon. Russia has historically been the most willing to paint BRICS with an anti-Western brush, but it has also been cognizant of the limits of that approach. In Russian elite political discourse, BRICS has been the symbol of an alternative to the West but not more than that. This made managing conflicting views on anti-Westernism within the group easier.

In the immediate aftermath of the Ukraine crisis, that balance disappeared, at least from Russian official formulations. Instead of Russia as the cord that connects BRICS and the traditional powers together, the new image was of shackles being broken.[140] BRICS became Russia's battering ram against the old system. The crisis in Ukraine and the collapse in relations with the West also briefly forced Russia to take its BRICS diplomacy more seriously. Whereas before the crisis BRICS existed primarily as a rhetorical weapon, in 2014 and 2015 it was an organ whose prospects Russia took seriously beyond its use for imagery and optics.

That shift in perspective on BRICS did not last. Russia really has left the West, but it has done so only for its immediate East instead. Russia's outlook is now best exemplified by another piece from Trenin, this one published in April 2015. In *From Greater Europe to Greater Asia? The Sino-Russian Entente*, Trenin argues: "In lieu of a Greater Europe from Lisbon to Vladivostok, a Greater Asia from Shanghai to St. Petersburg is in the making."[141] As with the Greater Eurasian Partnership that began to take shape in Putin's rhetoric later that year, Sino-Russian relations form the heart of Greater Asia. Both by need and change in vision, that relationship is Russia's new primary focus.

Russia's step back from BRICS and move toward Greater Eurasia was not entirely unprompted. It is also in some ways a reciprocal response to shifts in Indian and Chinese foreign policy between 2014 and 2016 that led both countries to reevaluate their participation in BRICS. The next chapter tells that story and brings together the final element of the narrative about BRICS on the global stage.

Notes

Epigraphs: Putin, "Address to the Federal Assembly of the Russian Federation," December 4, 2014; and "BRICS at Hague Slam Attempts to Isolate Putin."

1. Putin, "Address to the Federal Assembly of the Russian Federation," December 12, 2013.

2. Stent, *Limits of Partnership*, 232.

3. Parts of this chapter, including the title, draw on Salzman, "From Bridge to Bulwark."

4. Valentina Pop and Andrew Rettman, "Merkel: Ukraine Can Go to the Eurasian Union." EUObserver, August 25, 2014. https://euobserver.com/foreign/125331.

5. Diuk, "Euromaidan."

6. "Ukraine Crisis: Timeline," *BBC News*, November 13, 2014, https://www.bbc.com/news/world-middle-east-26248275.

7. "Agreement on the Settlement of Crisis in Ukraine—Full Text," *Guardian*, February 21, 2014, http://www.theguardian.com/world/2014/feb/21/agreement-on-the-settlement-of-crisis-in-ukraine-full-text.

8. Ibid.

9. Andrew Higgins and Andrew E. Kramer, "Ukraine Leader Was Defeated Even before He Was Ousted," *New York Times*, January 3, 2015, https://www.nytimes.com/2015/01/04/world/europe/ukraine-leader-was-defeated-even-before-he-was-ousted.html.

10. "Putin Reveals Secrets of Russia's Crimea Takeover Plot," *BBC News*, March 9, 2015, http://www.bbc.com/news/world-europe-31796226.

11. Shaun Walker, "Viktor Yanukovych Urges Russia to Act over Ukrainian 'Bandit Coup,'" *Guardian*, February 28, 2014, https://www.theguardian.com/world/2014/feb/28/viktor-yanukovych-russia-ukraine-coup.

12. James Marson, Alan Cullison, and Alexander Kolyandr, "Ukraine President Viktor Yanukovych Driven from Power," *Wall Street Journal*, February 23, 2014, https://www.wsj.com/articles/protesters-take-control-of-kiev-1393067503.

13. Serge Schmemann, "Crimea Parliament Votes to Back Independence from Ukraine," *New York Times*, May 6, 1992, https://www.nytimes.com/1992/05/06/world/crimea-parliament-votes-to-back-independence-from-ukraine.html.

14. "Predstavliaetsia Pravilnym Initsiirovat Prisoedinenie Vostochnykh Oblastei Ukrainy K Rossii," *Novaia Gazeta*, February 25, 2015, http://www.novayagazeta.ru/politics/67389.html.

15. Ibid.

16. Ibid.

17. Shuster, "Putin's Man in Crimea"; and Simon Ostrovsky, "Sneaking into a Ukrainian Military Base: Russian Roulette in Ukraine (Dispatch 2)," YouTube, March 4, 2014, https://youtu.be/Y57vy4vWb-E.

18. Shuster, "Putin's Man in Crimea." In a Russian state–produced documentary about the annexation of Crimea, Putin claims that he had never heard of Aksyonov before these events, and that Crimean politicians chose him as their representative. For more, see Kondrashov, *Crimea*.

19. Shuster, "Putin's Man in Crimea."

20. Anderson, "Thugs on the Streets for Crimea's Referendum"; and Ilya Somin, "Russian Government Agency Reveals Fraudulent Nature of the Crimean Referendum Results," *Washington Post*, May 6, 2014, https://www.washingtonpost.com/news/volokh-conspiracy/wp/2014/05/06/russian-government-agency-reveals-fraudulent-nature-of-the-crimean-referendum-results/?utm_term=.ff7210792fcb.

21. Putin, "Address by President of the Russian Federation," March 18, 2014.

22. Czuperski et al., "Hiding in Plain Sight."

23. Benjamin Bidder, Moritz Gathmann, Christian Neef, and Matthias Schepp, "Undeclared War: Putin's Covert Invasion of Eastern Ukraine," *Spiegel Online*, September 2, 2014, http://www.spiegel.de/international/world/russia-expands-war-in-eastern-ukraine-amid-web-of-lies-a-989290.html.

24. Simon Ostrovsky, "The Kremlin's Secret War: Russia's Ghost Army in Ukraine (Full Length)," *Vice News*, March 6, 2015, YouTube, https://www.youtube.com/watch?v=C66mAkS1ZfM.

25. Putin, "Address by President of the Russian Federation."

26. "Ukraine Crisis: Timeline."

27. Putin, "Address by President of the Russian Federation."

28. Embody, "Beware Ukraine's Rising Right Sector."

29. "Support for Putin Soars in Ukraine Crisis," Reuters, Thursday, May 14, 2014, accessed August 5, 2018, http://www.reuters.com/article/2014/05/15/us-russia-putin-support-idUSBREA4E0L620140515.

30. Levada Center, "Crimea: Two Years Later," press release, June 10, 2016, https://www.levada.ru/en/2016/06/10/crimea-two-years-later/. It is worth noting, however, that this sentiment does not extend to paying for the peninsula's upkeep and reconstruction.

31. Putin, "Address by President of the Russian Federation."

32. Ibid.

33. Putin, "Obrashchenie Presidenta Rossiiskoi Federatsii," March 18, 2014.

34. "Ukraine Crisis: Transcript of Leaked Nuland-Pyatt Call," *BBC News*, February 7, 2014, http://www.bbc.com/news/world-europe-26079957.

35. Ibid.

36. Anti-Americanism is a specific subset of anti-Westernism.

37. Cooley, "Scripts of Sovereignty," 7.

38. Obama, "Statement by the President on Ukraine," March 17, 2014.

39. Obama, "Statement by the President on Ukraine," March 20, 2014.

40. Ibid.

41. European Parliament, "European Parliament Calls on Russia."

42. "Ukraine Crisis: Timeline."

43. Ibid.

44. United Nations General Assembly, "68/262." The United States was unable to push through a UNSC resolution affirming Ukraine's sovereignty and territorial integrity because Russia vetoed the attempt. China abstained from the vote. See Chappell, "Russia Vetoes U.N. Security Council Resolution."

45. United Nations, "General Assembly Adopts Resolution."

46. Stuenkel, BRICS and the Future of Global Order, 148.

47. Lisa Cox, "Russian President Vladimir Putin May Be Banned from G20 Summit in Brisbane," Sunday Morning Herald, March 20, 2014, https://www.smh.com.au/politics /federal/russian-president-vladimir-putin-may-be-banned-from-g20-summit-in-brisbane -20140320-353t9.html; and Department of International Relations and Cooperation of South Africa, "BRICS Ministers Meet."

48. Hooijmaaijers and Keukeleire, "Voting Cohesion," 402.

49. Ibid., 398.

50. Ferdinand, "Rising Powers at the UN," 385.

51. Stuenkel, BRICS and the Future of Global Order, 150.

52. Ferdinand, "Rising Powers at the UN," 384.

53. United Nations General Assembly, "68/262."

54. World Bank Group, "Global Economic Prospects, January 2015," 26.

55. IMF, "World Economic Outlook, April 2017: Gaining Momentum?," 202.

56. BRICS 2015, "Vladimir Putin napravil privetstvie." June 8, 2015, http://brics2015 .ru/news/20150608/155027.html.

57. "Strategy for BRICS Economic Partnership," 3.

58. Russia formally assumed the BRICS presidency on April 1, 2015. The chairmanship began in April 2015 and concluded in April 2016.

59. Timofei Bordachev, interview with the author, December 14, 2014, Moscow.

60. Alexander Gabuev, interview with the author, December 5, 2014, Moscow.

61. Dmitri Trenin, "Moscow Takes BRICS Summit as New Launch Pad for Global Influence," Global Times, January 26, 2015, http://www.globaltimes.cn/content/904034 .shtml.

62. Lucy Hornby, "China and Russia Set to Finalise Gas Deal," Financial Times, March 8, 2015, https://www.ft.com/content/c0c385ea-c55f-11e4-bd6b-00144feab7de; Kenneth Rapoza, "Putin's European Food Ban Bad for Russia, Good for Brazil," Forbes, August 10, 2014, https://www.forbes.com/sites/kenrapoza/2014/08/10/putins-european-food-ban -bad-for-russia-good-for-brazil/#485210d419ab; and Kenneth Rapoza, "Following Food Ban, Russia Moving on from Europe," Forbes, August 18, 2014, https://www.forbes.com /sites/kenrapoza/2014/08/18/following-food-ban-russian-moving-on-from-europe/#1bf 336e41888.

63. Ian Bremmer, Twitter (photo), June 7, 2015, https://twitter.com/ianbremmer/status 607671649891164161.

64. Gabuev, "Russia Has a China Problem, Too"; and Gabuev, "Sino-Russian Trade after a Year of Sanctions."

65. Ministry of Foreign Affairs of the Russian Federation, "Concept of Participation of the Russian Federation in BRICS"; and Ministry of Foreign Affairs of the Russian Federation, "Concept of the Russian Federation's Presidency in BRICS in 2015–2016."

66. Ministry of Foreign Affairs of the Russian Federation, "Concept of the Russian Federation's Presidency."

67. Ministry of Foreign Affairs of the Russian Federation, "Concept of Participation."

68. Ministry of Foreign Affairs of the Russian Federation, "Concept of the Russian Federation's Presidency." Georgii Toloraya, director of NKI BRIKS, underscored this objective when he spoke at an event hosted by the Center for Global Interests in Washington, DC, on June 12, 2015.

69. Ministry of Foreign Affairs of the Russian Federation, "Concept of Participation."

70. Ministry of Foreign Affairs of the Russian Federation, "Concept of the Russian Federation's Presidency."

71. Ibid.

72. Stuenkel, "Politics of Next Year's BRICS Summit." The US government relinquished oversight of ICAANN in October 2016. ICAANN is now an independent body.

73. Putin, "Speech at BRICS Summit Plenary Session," July 15, 2014.

74. Tass, "Tsentrobank Rossii predlagaet obsudit ideiu sozdaniia analoga SWIFT v ramkakh BRIKS," *Vedemosti*, May 29, 2015.

75. Ministry of Foreign Affairs of the Russian Federation, "Concept of the Russian Federation's Presidency."

76. Ibid.

77. Putin, "Address to Valdai International Discussion Club." The Valdai International Discussion Club is an annual gathering of international Russia experts sponsored by the Russian government.

78. Putin, "Address to the Federal Assembly of the Russian Federation," December 4, 2014.

79. Ibid. Putin here is speaking of political rather than economic imbalances.

80. Ibid.

81. Putin, "Address to the Federal Assembly of the Russian Federation," December 4, 2014.

82. Ibid.

83. Ibid.

84. Ibid.

85. Ibid.

86. Andrew E. Kramer, "Russia Claims Its Sphere of Influence in the World," *New York Times*, August 31, 2008, accessed August 5, 2018, https://www.nytimes.com/2008/09/01/world/europe/01russia.html.

87. On Munich as a warning shot, see Dmitri Trenin, interview with the author, December 2, 2014, Moscow.

88. Fyodor Lukyanov, interview with the author, December 13, 2014, Moscow.

89. Ibid.

90. Trenin, interview.

91. Viktoria Panova, interview with the author, September 19, 2014, Moscow.

92. Lukyanov, interview.

93. Sadovnichy, Yakovets, and Akaev, *Perspektivy i strategicheskie*.

94. Ibid., 38.

95. Putin, "Address to Valdai International Discussion Club." He only mentioned BRICS once in the address, and then only briefly in the same sentence as the Shanghai Cooperation Organization and the Eurasian Union.

96. Boris Martynov, email to the author, January 2015. Communication was in both Russian and English. This response was in English.

97. Ibid.

98. "Vladimir Davydov: BRIKS: Glavnyi geopoliticheskii vrag SShA." *Pravda*, January 14, 2015, http://www.pravda.ru/news/world/14-01-2015/1243757-davydov-0/.

99. Ibid.

100. Vladimir Mikhailovich Davydov, interview with the author, September 22, 2014, Moscow.

101. This could be for domestic political reasons since anti-Westernism is a large part of Putin's domestic political strategy.

102. Brancato, "Trends in Economic Development"; and Vlaskin, Glinkina, and Lenchuk, "Sotrudnichestvo so Stranami," 318.

103. Nicolas, "China and the Global Economic Order," 12; and Lo, "New Order for Old Triangles?," 13.

104. Laidi, "BRICS against the West?," 2.

105. Stuenkel, "G7 and the BRICS in the Post-Crimea World Order," 7.

106. In economics, a Pareto optimal solution is one in which no one can be made better off without making someone else worse off.

107. Ünay, "Reality or Mirage?," 84.

108. This is one of the reasons the 2010 IMF quota reforms remained stalled in the United States Congress until the end of 2015, even though the US share was not implicated in the reform.

109. Nicolas, "China and the Global Economic Order," 9.

110. Mohan and Kapur, "Emerging Powers and Global Governance," 4.

111. Ibid.

112. Ibid., 7.

113. Ibid., 50.

114. During the Obama administration, this was more an issue of intransigence from the legislative branch than from the executive branch.

115. Davydov, interview.

116. Nandan Unnikrishnan, interview with the author, September 22, 2014, Moscow; and Oliver Stuenkel, interview via Skype with the author, December 4, 2014.

117. Gabuev, "Friends with Benefits?"

118. Ellen Barry, "Putin and Modi Reaffirm Bond between Russia and India," *New York Times*, December 11, 2014, https://www.nytimes.com/2014/12/12/world/asia/putin-and-modi-reaffirm-bond-between-russia-and-india.html; and Matt Siegel and Douglas Busvine, "Ukrainian President Slams India over Crimean Leader Visit," Reuters, December 11, 2014, https://www.reuters.com/article/us-india-russia-crimea/ukrainian-president-slams-india-over-crimean-leader-visit-idUSKBN0JP1AM20141212.

119. Charles Clover, "Chinese Deal with Ukraine Defence Group Raises Hackles," *Financial Times*, October 5, 2017, https://www.ft.com/content/e8aed9f4-a1dc-11e7-9e4f-7f5e6a7c98a2.

120. Chinese Expert on Russia, interview with the author, February 2017.

121. Stuenkel, "G7 and the BRICS in the Post-Crimea World Order," 6.

122. Laidi, "BRICS against the West?," 3.

123. Stuenkel, "G7 and the BRICS in the Post-Crimea World Order," 6.

124. Unnikrishnan, interview.

125. Petr Topychkanov, "Politika v ushcherb ekonomike: Kak Moskva mozhet possoritsia s BRIKS," *RBK*, June 10, 2015, http://daily.rbc.ru/opinions/economics/10/06/2015/557816e09a794704c5d016db.

126. Polina Khimshiashvili, "Indiia zatormozila rossiiskii proekt po sozdaniiu assamblei BRIKS," *RBK*, June 8, 2015, http://top.rbc.ru/politics/08/06/2015/55758db99a7947dff14d5646.

127. Topychkanov, "Politika v ushcherb ekonomike."

128. Slutsky, quoted in Khimshiashvili, "Indiia zatormozila rossiiskii."

129. Ibid. Some of the issue may be bureaucratic differences in how the parliaments in the different BRICS countries operate.

130. "BRICS Urged to Boost Parliamentary Cooperation," BRICS Post, October 26, 2017, accessed August 5, 2018, http://thebricspost.com/brics-urged-to-boost-parliamentary-cooperation/.

131. Dmitri Trenin, interview with the author, March 21, 2017, Moscow.

132. Putin, "Mezhdunarodnyi forum 'Odin Poias, Odin Put.'"

133. Putin, "Presidential Address to the Federal Assembly," December 3, 2015.

134. Putin, "Presidential Address to the Federal Assembly," December 1, 2016; and Ministry of Foreign Affairs of the Russian Federation, "Foreign Policy Concept of the Russian Federation," November 30, 2016.

135. Petr Topychkanov, interview with the author, March 20, 2017, Moscow.

136. Boris Martynov, interview with the author, March 21, 2017, Moscow.

137. Vladimir Mikhailovich Davydov, interview with the author, March 16, 2017, Moscow.

138. Trenin, interview, March 21, 2017.

139. Trenin, "Russia Leaves the West," 87.

140. Krestianinov, "BRIKS razryvaet dollarovye tsepi."

141. Trenin, "From Greater Europe to Greater Asia?," 11.

6

BRICS from Other Perspectives
The Views from India and China

BRICS cooperation has now reached a crucial stage of development. In assessing its performance, it is important to bear two things in mind: the historical course of global development and evolving international landscape and the historical process of development of the BRICS countries, both individually and collectively, in the context of which BRICS cooperation is pursued.

—Xi Jinping, September 2017

In the last decade, two generations of leader [*sic*] of our countries contributed to the emergence and establishment of BRICS. We acquired credibility, wielded influence and spurred growth. Now, the next decade is crucial. In an environment where we seek stability, sustainable development and prosperity. BRICS leadership will be crucial in driving this transformation. If we as BRICS can set the agenda in these areas, the world will call this its Golden Decade.

—Narendra Modi, September 2017

OF THE FOUR OTHER BRICS NATIONS, INDIA AND CHINA ARE BY FAR THE most important to Russia on strategic, political, and economic metrics. As the two other countries in the group with significant independent sway on the global stage, they also are the countries whose membership is most vital for the group to be taken seriously as a group of rising powers. Like Russia, both India and China have a history of anti-Westernism among large sections of their foreign policy elite, although it is more rooted in anticolonial sentiment than specific anti-Westernism. Despite the different origins, however, antipathy toward continued Western hegemony in the international system makes them perhaps more amenable to some of Russia's more overtly confrontational language. On the other hand, both India and China are also considerably more networked into the global economic system than Russia; they both have more to lose from efforts to make BRICS an explicitly anti-Western forum.

As discussed in the previous chapter, tension over the limits of anti-Westernism in the BRICS project has been present from the beginning. In understanding how it has evolved and where it may be producing new fissures, it is worth looking more carefully at the role BRICS plays in Indian and Chinese foreign policy. An analysis of how India and China incorporate BRICS into their foreign policy strategies and how each country's relations with Russia impact their participation in the group provide a useful counterpoint for understanding the evolution of the forum since its inception and why cooperation has flagged since 2014.

From the beginning, both India and China have approached BRICS primarily as a tool of geo-economics and soft anti-Westernism. Both countries value the group's long-term potential to shift some global norms, especially regarding economic development, but they in general do not see BRICS as primarily a geopolitical tool. This approach puts them at odds with Russia's priorities, and especially with the hard anti-Westernism that Russia sought to bring into the group in the immediate aftermath of the onset of the crisis in Ukraine. Further, since 2014, both India and China have for different reasons begun to deprioritize the forum in favor of other projects and partnerships. India has begun to move closer to the United States, and the simultaneous attenuation of Indo-Russian relations and deterioration of Indo-Chinese relations has made some in the Indian elite question the use of BRICS. In China, a more assertive foreign policy under President Xi Jinping and with frustration at the slow pace of intra-BRICS cooperation have combined in a foreign policy focused on Chinese initiatives such as the AIIB that seem to obviate similar BRICS projects. The result is a situation in which Russia's main BRICS partners are increasingly less invested in the forum.

This chapter proceeds as follows: it begins with a primer on Indian foreign policy, including a brief background on relations between Russia (and the USSR) and India. This leads to a discussion of India's approach to BRICS, especially since Narendra Modi became prime minister in 2014. Analysis then turns to an overview of main questions and objectives in Chinese foreign policy, including an overview of Russo-Chinese relations. This is followed by an exploration of BRICS in Chinese foreign policy under the leadership of Xi Jinping. The chapter concludes with an evaluation of the implications of the analysis for the future of BRICS.

BRICS in Indian Foreign Policy

Indian foreign policy is in transition. While enormous development challenges remain, India's economy has generally grown steadily since the 2008 global financial crisis, and its leadership is taking a more assertive role in regional and global politics. One of the prime challenges India faces is balancing its historic role as the (self-appointed) vanguard of the developing world while also claiming a place at the "high table" of international politics. This section explores the roots of these diverging strains in Indian foreign policy as well as the role BRICS plays in managing that dichotomy.

Indian Foreign Policy: A Brief Primer

For most of the Cold War, Indian foreign policy was shaped and defined by non-alignment. Jawaharlal Nehru, India's first prime minister and a leader in the independence movement, articulated nonalignment as a moral choice necessary for defending the hard-won battle for sovereignty.[1] It also gave a political name to the desire of developing countries and newly freed colonies to avoid alliance with either superpower bloc. In addition to dictating an avoidance of either military alliances or excessive integration into the American-led global market, nonalignment also mandated substantive engagement in global normative debates.[2] This manifested in particular in the rhetorical defense of the "third world" against colonialism and imperialism and bled into anti-Westernism as well.[3]

India never formally joined either Cold War bloc. Operationally, however, its moral stance on anticolonialism and anti-imperialism brought it closer to the Soviet Union than to the United States. By the mid-1960s the USSR was India's main trading partner, and by the mid-1970s India was dependent on the Soviet Union for technology and to some extent regional security.[4] The relationship was codified in the 1971 Indo-Soviet Treaty of Cooperation and Friendship, which followed on several large trade deals.[5] Although Indian leaders professed non-alignment rhetorically, foreign policy after the death of Nehru in 1964 was much closer to realism in practice for the remainder of the Cold War.[6]

The end of the Cold War and the collapse of the Soviet Union dealt a series of interlinked shocks to India. On the economic side, decades of autarky and import substitution had left the country badly in debt and severely underdeveloped. The country experienced a massive economic crisis in 1990–1991; GDP growth slowed, government debt ballooned, and in March of 1991 India entered a financial crisis as foreign reserves dwindled while foreign debt was coming due.[7]

The loss of India's superpower protector compounded these shocks, removing from play a major trading partner, arms supplier, and political ally that, among other things, provided "a virtual guarantee against Chinese nuclear blackmail."[8] The result was that at the beginning of the post–Cold War era, India found itself needing to recalibrate both its economic and foreign policy strategies.

In 1991 Prime Minister Narasimha Rao initiated the Look East policy, which shifted away from the Cold War–era focus on border conflicts with Pakistan and China and relationships with the superpowers and toward involving India more intensely in regional forums as well as toward a broader array of partners.[9] The Ministry of External Affairs created an economics division, underscoring the economic focus of the policy. Diplomatic efforts focused on improving relations with China, Japan, South Korea, and countries in Southeast Asia, especially via the Association of Southeast Asian Nations. The policy also touched on security and defense concerns as India offered naval support to nervous Chinese neighbors as a way of building cooperative relationships.[10] In this way Look East also helped India build a hedge against China.[11] Look East was combined with a broad effort to restructure the domestic economy and bring it more in line with the recommendations of international financial institutions.[12]

Look East was successful in reorienting Indian foreign policy and foreign economic policy, and it continues to be the basis of contemporary Indian strategy.[13] It also brought India closer to a more independent foreign policy than it had under nonalignment. While political relations with the Russian Federation have always been friendly, neither political nor economic ties ever recovered to their Cold War apex. Instead, Indian foreign policy has continued to prioritize "strategic autonomy," which was at the core of Cold War–era nonalignment.[14] The difference is that, in current circumstances, India is better equipped to work as an independent actor on the world stage than it was in previous eras.

There is some debate about whether current Indian foreign policy is best conceived of as "nonalignment 2.0" or, as Modi has tried to popularize, "multialignment."[15] Multialignment consists of building strong relations with major powers including the United States, seeking leading roles in multilateral institutions, and building overlapping partnerships on multiple issues with multiple partners.[16] While the latter gives a patina of deeper engagement with international institutions, both ultimately support a vision of India with many partners but no binding ties to constrain its actions on the world stage.

Similarly, both nonalignment and multialignment contain normative angles. India seeks to be one of the global powers that makes the rules of the road, especially in areas such as development and nonproliferation that affect core interests.[17] India sees itself as the representative for the developing world in the fight to advance an amended global order more favorable to developing countries. Not unrelated, the implicit and explicit anti-Western component of the anticolonialism in nonalignment has been moderated as India builds relations with the West, especially the United States, but it has not disappeared entirely.[18] The BRICS group fits perfectly within this broader strategic framework.

BRICS in Indian Foreign Policy

BRICS serves a variety of purposes in Indian foreign policy. It helps India punch above its weight in the global arena. It is a mechanism for increasing the country's global status, shining a spotlight on issues including infrastructure development that are lower priorities for Western-led institutions, and pushing specific reforms in international organizations. It presents at minimum a forum to sit with China to try and influence their position and at the extreme a possible way to constrain

China by netting it into a multilateral framework. Finally, it is used to manage domestic criticism of India's changing foreign policy. While all of these elements remain important, their relative importance has waxed and waned over time. The group as a whole has diminished in priority in recent years. This section explores each of these elements and discusses why the group is falling out of favor in the Indian foreign policy establishment.

As noted in the previous section, the BRICS rhetoric about multipolarity and creating "a just and democratic world order" fits squarely within long-standing Indian foreign policy language and positions. From that perspective, the existence of and participation in BRICS is in itself a political objective; it is a good format for meeting with the prospective poles of the coming multipolar order.[19] It also provides a demonstration of what a fairer organizational format might look like: one vote for each country regardless of size, respect for national interests, and cooperation on issues of common concern. This element remains important regardless of the other dynamics of the group.

The optics of BRICS is related to the extent to which the forum can be useful as a vehicle for changing global norms. Indeed, this is one of the top priorities for how India views the forum.[20] Further, it is not the norms that Russia has been most vocal about, such as sovereignty, the use and abuse of the responsibility to protect, or general respect for international law. Sachin Chaturvedi, who leads the Research and Information System for Developing Countries, a think tank under the Indian Ministry of External Affairs, got down into the weeds during an interview in January 2017. He mentioned the role of BRICS in challenging development norms of the Organisation for Economic Co-operation and Development and pushing back against the accepted use of genetically modified crops in agriculture.[21] Gulshan Sachdeva, a professor at Jawaharlal Nehru University in New Delhi, also looked to the role of BRICS in challenging global norms, especially around economic development. While Professor Sachdeva was less sanguine than Professor Chaturvedi about whether BRICS was an effective forum, he did point to norm evolution as a main deliverable for BRICS in the long term.[22]

The image of BRICS as a vehicle for increasing the voice of developing countries in global affairs is also useful in Indian domestic politics. As noted in the previous section, Indian foreign policy during the Cold War, especially under Nehru, emphasized advocating for and establishing global norms against oppression, colonialism, and other great power sins. These were core goals of both the Nonaligned Movement and the G77, a group of developing countries in UNGA. The identity of being a developing country remains deeply ingrained in India's approach to the world stage, not just from the perspective of poverty and economic development but as a political identity as well. As India has grown in both economic and political importance, and foreign policy positions and interests have shifted accordingly, some domestic factions have argued that India is abandoning its long-held principles and partners.[23] BRICS, with its mantle as a group of developing countries, is a useful counterargument to those accusations. It therefore serves a specific perception-management need in domestic politics.[24] Similarly, BRICS provides a helpful bridging mechanism between the G77 / Non-aligned Movement identity and Great Power identity.[25]

The optics of BRICS and the potential of the group to affect global norms, while important to India, are both abstract and long term. In terms of concrete goals for intra-BRICS cooperation, Indian leaders generally stress economic development as the primary target. This is especially evident in the framing of then–prime minister Manmohan Singh's plenary statement at the 2012 BRICS summit in Delhi. In what was by far his longest plenary statement, Singh enumerated ten main goals for BRICS: only the final goal ventured beyond economics into geopolitics, stressing the importance of managing conflicts and terrorism.[26] Singh's statements at the other four summits he attended were much briefer and similarly focused on intra-BRICS cooperation toward best practices, sustainable development, and progress within the Doha Round of trade negotiations.[27]

Singh's successor as prime minster, Narendra Modi, has largely followed a similar formula with his statements at BRICS summits. The main exception is the 2016 summit India hosted in Goa. Although Modi focused primarily on various forms of intra-BRICS economic cooperation, he also specifically called for increased security cooperation to combat terrorism.[28] Modi made pointed comments about the dangers of being selective in how the group identifies terrorist organizations (a clear barb at China's support for Pakistan), and he called for adoption of the draft UN Comprehensive Convention on International Terrorism.[29] While the exhortation to sign the UN agreement on terrorism is standard in Indian foreign policy rhetoric, it played a larger role in Modi's 2016 BRICS statement than it had in preceding years.

In part, this was a natural outgrowth of the attack on the Indian Army in India-administered Kashmir a month before the Goa summit.[30] However, it also emphasized a key problem within BRICS that is one of the contributing factors to why the group has fallen on India's list of international priorities. While there have always been profound differences among the BRICS countries, the way those differences manifest and the trouble they cause is changing. This is particularly true regarding shifting relations within the Russia-India-China triangle.

It is no secret that India and China have a troubled relationship. The two countries have unresolved border conflicts. They fought a war (which India lost) over the territory in 1962, and in the past several years India has accused China of intentionally fanning the flames of conflict in the region.[31] China's support for Pakistan is another point of friction in the relationship, and China's unwillingness to condemn Pakistan as the perpetrator in the September 2016 attacks was one of the main sticking points at the Goa summit. Further, bilateral political relations since Modi came to power have deteriorated.

On the other hand, China is one of India's most important economic partners. Trade turnover between the two countries increased tenfold between 2004 and 2011, and Chinese foreign direct investment into India has increased dramatically under Modi's tenure.[32] Indeed, as Bobo Lo points out, Sino-Indian relations exhibit both a power asymmetry and a dimensional asymmetry, with poor political relations but strong economic partnership.[33] The economic relationship is not untroubled: the trade relationship has grown more contentious as India's trade deficit with China has increased. There are also concerns about Chinese limitations on Indian companies operating in the Chinese market (and some Indian limitations on Chinese investment in strategic sectors). China, however, is India's largest trading partner, a status unlikely to change in the near term. The two countries also cooperate in numerous international forums, including BRICS, BASIC (BRICS without Russia), and now the SCO. The result is that India essentially pursues a hedging policy toward China.[34] India seeks to engage China on matters of mutual interest (e.g., climate change and economic cooperation) while still strengthening its position in the Indian Ocean and building partnerships with other states in the region as well as with the United States.[35]

None of this, of course, is new. While the economic relationship has strengthened in the time since the BRIC group first coalesced, the political tensions have been waxing and waning for decades. So why was India's long-standing position on international terrorism, and China's predictably negative response, during the Goa summit a harbinger of problems on the horizon for BRICS cooperation? There are three interrelated elements: economic slowdown across the BRICS, changes in the Sino-Russian and Indo-Russian relationships, and changes in the Indo-US relationship.

The first issue is the most self-explanatory. Although this study examines BRICS as a political construct and most of the group's external coordination is to do with the politics of global governance, the group has always drawn much of its power from the narrative of its members being large, rapidly growing economies. Economic slowdown harms that narrative and makes the BRICS group's claim to be the representative of future power centers less convincing. The countries are still growing: Chinese growth picked up in 2017, Indian growth neared 7 percent, and Brazil finally emerged from its worst recession ever in the second quarter of 2017.[36] The rates are no longer as awe-inspiring, however, especially to a developed world that has also resumed growth.

The economic slowdown across the group is compounded by profound political crises in two of its members, Brazil and South Africa. Brazilian president Dilma Rousseff was impeached on corruption charges in 2015 in a very controversial vote, and her predecessor was sentenced to ten years in prison for corruption in 2017.[37] The government of Rousseff's successor, Michel Temer, is similarly scandal-ridden, although Temer survived a no-confidence vote in October 2017.[38] In South Africa, President Jacob Zuma, always a controversial figure, was ultimately forced to step down in February 2018 amid numerous corruption scandals.[39] While the scandals in both Brazil and South Africa are long-standing, their explosion in domestic politics since 2014 has removed any space in the two countries for thinking strategically about BRICS in the long term. From the

Indian perspective, all of this combines to make BRICS a weaker (and therefore less attractive) vehicle for pushing its interests in global governance. This is especially so since Brazil and South Africa tend to buttress India's position.

Next is the issue of changes in several of the important bilateral relationships. As discussed in the previous chapter, the 2014 annexation of Crimea significantly affected Russia's international position and its approach to BRICS. The crisis and its fallout also pushed Russia much closer to China in ways that make India nervous.[40] Despite remaining fears about technology transfer (and theft), Russia elected to begin selling some of its most advanced arms to China in late 2016.[41] Russia also appears to be closer to China diplomatically, both as a major partner on China's Belt and Road Initiative (the BRI), via the planned coordination with the EEU, and through its ambiguous language on China's claims in the South China Sea.[42] Russian bureaucrats in MID frequently consult with their Chinese counterparts on issues of importance, and the two countries also coordinate positions in multilateral forums.[43] While the Sino-Russian relationship is by no means uncomplicated nor at the level of alliance, it has grown stronger since 2014 and is a relationship both sides see as high priority.

The strengthening of the Sino-Russian relationship has happened against a backdrop of the (unrelated) weakening of Indo-Russian relations. As noted in the previous section, post–Cold War Indo-Russian relations have never reached the level of the Cold War–era partnership. The 1990s was a decade of benign neglect, with both countries consumed with managing intense domestic turmoil and adapting to the new international environment. Since the turn of the millennium, political relations have steadied, but they have not deepened. For example, India frequently invites President Putin to extend his stay following official visits to see other parts of India, but Putin always refuses.[44] People-to-people relations have also declined, with many more Indians choosing to study in the United States than in Russia (a change from the days of the Cold War). The bedrock of the relationship—Russian arms sales to India—remains, but it is declining. Between 2009 and 2013, Russia accounted for 75 percent of arms purchases by India. For the period from 2012 to 2016, Russia's share declined to 68.3 percent, with the difference made up primarily by an increase in imports from the United States and Israel.[45] Although a large subset of the Indian bureaucracy, including much of the Ministry of External Affairs, remains predisposed toward close relations with Russia, the reality is that the bilateral relationship has been deprioritized in both capitals.[46]

The combination of strengthened Sino-Russian relations and diminished Indo-Russian relations are compounded by changes in Chinese policy. Samir Saran, the leading Indian expert on BRICS, identifies two core principles of the group: sovereign preponderance and democratic equity.[47] Sovereign preponderance is the preeminence of the state as an actor in international politics and the consequent inviolability of national borders. Democratic equity is the call for a more democratic international order. Saran argues that two recent Chinese initiatives, the AIIB and the BRI, violate these principles.[48]

The BRI, with its ambitious plan to build interconnected infrastructure across multiple states' borders and longer-term plans for trade and security linkages, violates sovereignty. From the Indian perspective, the proposed China-Pakistan Economic Corridor is particularly worrisome as it begins in Pakistani-controlled Kashmir, an area that India sees as Indian territory. If the project goes forward, it will effectively change the facts on the ground, making it impossible for India to ever regain influence in the region.[49] Although China has made efforts to multi-lateralize the BRI, including hosting a large summit with prospective partners in May 2017, India has deep concerns over the extent to which the BRI will allow China to exert undue influence in the region and the extent to which the China-Pakistan Economic Corridor in particular infringes on Indian sovereignty and interests.[50] India declined to send even an embassy representative to the BRI summit.[51]

The AIIB, on the other hand, poses problems for the principle of democratic equity. One of the hard-fought battles about the NDB was how voting shares should be allocated. China wanted votes allocated by level of contribution and was willing (and able) to pay more into the bank than the other four partners. The others disagreed, arguing that BRICS works on the model of "one country, one vote," and that voting shares in the NDB should accordingly be equal among all five parties. China lost; each country holds equal voting rights.[52] The AIIB, by contrast, a project that post-dates the NDB, is a Chinese-led affair that fills a similar niche to the NDB. In doing so, it threatens to replace a model of equal partnership (nominally) with one explicitly designed to maximize Chinese influence. As noted in the first chapter, officially the two projects are mutually reinforcing rather than iterative, but given both the comparative levels of capitalization as well as comparative membership, the AIIB is clearly the "big brother" of the two new institutions.

The combination of changes in bilateral relations among Russia, China, and India, combined with China's recent predilection for projects that supersede BRICS initiatives, has changed India's calculus for participating in the group. While India does derive status and other abstract benefits from participation, it also values the group as a place to sit with Russia on its side as a way of trying to moderate Chinese policy. There are now real concerns that Russia would not side with India in a dispute against China within the group or any of the other multilateral forums (e.g., RIC, the SCO) in which the three countries cooperate.[53] This makes the likelihood of concrete gains from BRICS less likely for India. It suggests a policy course wherein India will remain in the group to reap the status and nontangible gains but will devote less energy to maximizing intra-group cooperation.

There is another reason why India is now less interested in intra-BRICS cooperation: the relationship with the United States. Since Modi came into office in the spring of 2014, he has placed enormous emphasis on improving relations with the United States. Manmohan Singh had presided over a historic improvement in Indo-US relations, culminating in the 2008 123 Agreement on civilian nuclear cooperation.[54] After 2008, however, India began focusing elsewhere and relations lost momentum.[55] Modi reversed the backslide, both because of a belief that India could not achieve its security or developmental objectives without deep cooperation with the United States and in response to an increased threat perception from China.[56] As a result of these efforts, at the end of the Obama administration, Indo-American relations were at a historic high. While relations with Russia were not a significant factor in Modi's decision to upgrade relations with the United States, it has caused tension with some in Russia, who see it as India abandoning their erstwhile ally for that ally's main strategic competitor. The Trump administration, while causing some concerns in India over H1B visas and a laser focus on the trade deficit, has primarily continued to support positive US-Indian relations.[57]

There has been no single factor in the decline of BRICS on the list of India's international priorities, and the country still benefits from membership (and particularly the optics of membership). However, those benefits have decreased, relatively, since 2014 because of a variety of structural and relational changes. Whatever the cause, the result is that India has lost interest in the group and is less inclined to follow Russia's lead in building it into a strong alternative actor on the global stage.

BRICS in Chinese Foreign Policy

Chinese foreign policy has also undergone considerable shifts in the last several years, and these shifts have affected the role BRICS plays in Chinese strategic thinking. In China, however, the shift dates to 2012, when Xi Jinping took over the Chinese presidency from Hu Jintao. This section explores the larger dynamics of recent shifts in Chinese foreign policy and contextualizes Sino-Russian relations within that broader framework. The next section looks at where BRICS fits into the picture and how it has changed since Xi became president.

Chinese Foreign Policy: A Brief Primer

China's global position has undergone dramatic transformation since the turn of the millennium. Much of that is related to the country's impressive annual economic growth. China's GDP grew above 7 percent per annum every year between 2000 and 2014.[58] It is the second-largest economy in the world as measured by market exchange rates and the largest as measured in purchasing power parity.[59] While Chinese GDP per capita remains well below the average of GDP per capita in advanced economies (four times less than US GDP per capita in 2016), the gap is expected to narrow in coming decades.[60]

China's rapid economic growth and consequent growth in importance in the global arena have precipitated intense debates about China's role in global governance and international politics both within and outside of China. Abroad, especially among Western scholars, the question has primarily revolved around how to make China a "responsible stakeholder" in the existing system. Within China, much of the debate is about how to reconcile China's rising prominence with Deng Xiaoping's 1989 maxim of "biding time, hiding brightness, not taking the lead but doing some things."[61] Chinese scholars and leaders have traditionally interpreted this dictum as an exhortation to keep a low profile in global politics; China's economic rise has forced the issue of how many "things" China can do and how much it can take the lead on without violating what has long been the guiding principle of Chinese foreign policy.[62]

Hu Jintao, who led China from 2002 until 2012, tried to square the circle of increasing Chinese power by declaring "China's Peaceful Development Road."[63] While allowing for China's growth and development as a great power, Hu's foreign policy affirmed that Chinese growth would be a boon for international society and would not be a threat in global politics. The impetus for this policy was twofold. First, most Chinese leaders and scholars agree that China's main priority is economic development; it is therefore imperative to maintain a peaceful international environment as the best way to facilitate continued growth. Second, Chinese leaders wished to prevent an accumulation of power that would cause other states to balance against it, especially before China has reached its own power potential.[64]

While this strategy provided the guiding framework for Chinese foreign policy throughout Hu's leadership, it evolved somewhat following the 2008 global financial crisis. In part because of anger that the United States, the progenitor of the crisis, still expected China to yield to US preferences, Chinese foreign policy became more assertive after 2008. Examples include threatening to sanction US companies selling arms to Taiwan and taking a harder line on European leaders' meetings with the Dalai Lama.[65] As China gained relative power in the years following the financial crisis, the country began to give a more expansive definition of its core national interests, despite the negative impact this had on relations with both neighbors and the United States.[66]

The big change in foreign policy, however, came with Xi Jinping's installation as president of China and leader of the Chinese Communist Party in 2012. Xi has not explicitly renounced Hu's strategy of peaceful development (nor is he expected to do so), but his leadership has been markedly different than that of his predecessor. Xi himself is more of a strongman than Hu, and this is reflected in his foreign and domestic policy: examples include Chinese media's creation of a cult of personality around Xi and the country's more forceful stance in the South China Sea, among other arenas.[67]

Xi has also made bilateral relations with Russia a priority. The Chinese president chose Moscow for his first overseas trip, and he sees the China-Russia axis as a source of global balance and stability.[68] China benefits from close relations with Russia at multiple levels. At the most abstract, the two countries have compatible near-term goals for reforming the global order (limiting US power), and this is an area in which Russia has made clear its willingness to cooperate, both bilaterally and through forums including BRICS. China also benefits from Russia's willingness to be the more visible opposition in forums like the UNSC. Russia's free hand with its veto gives China the space to abstain (though it does not always do so), thereby avoiding setting itself up in direct confrontation with the West, especially the United States.

China also has concrete reasons to nurture the relationship with Russia. In 2016 57 percent of Chinese arms imports came from Russia.[69] The Chinese capacity for native arms development is growing rapidly, but in the short term it will continue to depend on Russia for a large volume of imports. China has also learned the geopolitical lesson of Ukraine: Russian acquiescence, if not outright support, is critical for the success of large transnational projects in Eurasia.[70] As China pursues its plans for the Silk Road Economic Belt (the overland portion of the BRI), which cuts directly through Russia's historic backyard in post-Soviet Central Asia, China is careful about taking Russian interests and security concerns to heart. The agreement to coordinate Silk Road Economic Belt with the EEU is evidence of this approach.

In a widely read 2016 article in *Foreign Affairs*, Chair of the Foreign Affairs Committee of the National People's Congress of China Fu Ying writes: "The Chinese-Russian relationship is a stable strategic partnership and by no means a marriage of convenience: it is complex, sturdy, and deeply rooted."[71] Fu makes clear that the relationship is not and will not become a formal alliance, but she warns against US meddling in Sino-Russian relations.[72] She also suggests that Russo-Chinese interactions could become a model for how large states could cooperate to solve problems of mutual concern.[73]

The idea that Sino-Russian relations could serve as a model for interstate cooperation fits with other statements Chinese leaders and scholars have made about redefining how major powers cooperate. During the 2013 summit at Sunnylands in California, President Xi proposed building a "new model of major-country relationship between China and the U.S."[74] The basis of the new relationship was three conditions: "avoidance of conflict, cooperation in global governance, and mutual respect for each other's internal systems."[75] Hu Jintao had similarly called for a reconceptualization of US-Chinese relations during the 2012 round of the China-US Strategic and Economic Dialogues, but Hu's proposal kept away from language that called explicitly for noninterference in domestic affairs.[76] The United States has not accepted China's proposed reformulation of the bilateral relationship.

Xi's presentation of his version of finding a new modus vivendi for US-China relations followed a similar, though more optimistic, statement during his first visit to Moscow as president. In a speech at MGIMO in March 2013, Xi proclaimed that the relationship between China and Russia is "the best relationship between major countries."[77] The formal proposal for a "New Model of Major

Power Relations" is generally attributed specifically to the US-China relationship. The difference in tone between how Hu and Xi framed the idea and the praise Xi lavished on Sino-Russian relations before Sunnylands suggests, however, that the updated proposal for revised US-China relations draws from the example of the bilateral relationship between Russia and China.

This is not to argue that China sees the United States and Russia as equal powers. It does not.[78] Unlike Russia, which sees the United States, China, and Russia as the coequal determinants of a new order based on power balancing, China sees Russia as a great power but not a system-defining power.[79] Nevertheless, Sino-Russian relations embody what China would wish to see in Sino-American relations: mutual respect, nonintervention, interest-based cooperation, and avoidance of conflict.

The idea of establishing models for how international relationships should operate in the new world order is not restricted to bilateral relationships. A 2016 article calling for strengthening and institutionalizing the RIC format argued that "closer RIC coordination represents a non-ideological pattern of major-power cooperation on regional security."[80] As discussed in the second chapter, RIC is not the most compelling example of strong and functional multilateral cooperation. Attempting to cast it as such is further evidence of the extent to which Chinese scholars and leaders are looking for a demonstration effect in how they manage their bilateral and multilateral partnerships. Under Xi's leadership, China is looking to show rather than tell how it would prefer to see global governance evolve.

One final note: when Chinese leaders speak about reforming global governance, they mean almost exclusively global economic governance.[81] With a permanent seat and a veto in the UNSC, China is well represented in organs of global political and security governance. Like Russia, China has serious concerns with the security order in its region, but it does not view BRICS as a vehicle for pushing for changes to the Asia-Pacific security order, except on the rhetorical level with calls for moving past Cold War thinking. This is a phrase that Russia uses frequently, but whereas for Russia the question is NATO, for China, the evidence of Cold War thinking is the persistence of US-led security arrangements in the Pacific.[82] At the practical level, China addresses these concerns through its own policies in the South China Sea as well as some military cooperation and joint exercises with Russia.

BRICS in Chinese Foreign Policy

China did not instigate BRICS cooperation, but the group does serve several purposes in Chinese foreign policy. While the Chinese government values the optics of BRICS as an equal partnership of rising powers cooperating on issues of mutual interest, geo-economics is China's main motivation for participating in the group. Chinese goals for BRICS are specific and tactical. These goals are twofold: pushing for substantive reform and reallocation of power in organs of global economic governance and, through the NDB and other mechanisms, countering the narrative of neoliberal policy as the only effective developmental program. Since 2014, however, the government has deemphasized the role of BRICS as its preferred method of exerting change in global governance. Instead, Xi's China is focused on its own initiatives, notably the AIIB, BRI, and the Silk Road Fund (a state-owned fund that helps channel investment for BRI). This shift is a result of three interrelated issues: changes in the utility BRICS has for China, changes in China's position in the world relative both to the rest of the BRICS countries and to the United States, and frustration with the incapacity of BRICS to implement its plans quickly.

BRICS originally served several core Chinese interests. China faces what one Chinese expert calls "the dilemma of rising powers."[83] China must simultaneously lobby for more status and representation in the international system while managing fears about its rise from both neighbors and other global powers. In its early days BRICS helped China alleviate some of the dilemma by both increasing China's leverage in larger multilateral forums (especially the G20) while also allowing China to hide behind louder members within the group to manage fears of Chinese power. The inclusion of India, Brazil, and South Africa in the group also strengthened BRICS's image as a force for lobbying on behalf of developing countries. This allowed China to prove its own bona fides as a developing country even as its GDP outstripped most of the other countries in that category.[84]

Since 2014, though, BRICS has in ways exacerbated rather than ameliorated China's rising power dilemma. In part this is because of the growing gap between China and the other BRICS countries on nearly every economic metric except for GDP per capita.[85] Another element that complicated the situation is the extent to which BRICS became part of the narrative Russia was creating about an entirely non-Western network, a goal that diverges from China's goals for the group. It also makes Chinese participation in the group seem like acquiescence to a confrontational stance against the West, which in turn aggravated Chinese efforts to allay US fears about a rising China.[86]

There is also the question of whether hiding in a larger group still serves Chinese interests. This is somewhat related to the previous discussion about differences between the leadership styles of Hu Jintao and Xi Jinping. Xi is more assertive and more a man of action; the plodding pace of BRICS development runs counter to his leadership style.[87] It also, however, is related to the previous discussion about China's political and economic trajectory relative to the other BRICS. At least for now, China does not want US-style global hegemony; nevertheless, it does aspire to play a leading role in the international system. Part of carving out its place is establishing institutions through which it can promote its own global vision, as the United States did with the Bretton Woods institutions after World War II. BRICS was useful for "hiding brightness," but it does not provide a platform through which to advance an overtly Chinese vision or agenda. AIIB and BRI, by contrast, are explicitly Chinese projects that can be shaped to fit China's international agenda.

It is worth noting that the content of the Chinese vision, and how it differs from the Western vision, remains ambiguous. The country has not articulated an alternative set of values, beyond pabulum statements such as "democracy with Chinese characteristics."[88] There is clearly a divide between China and the West on questions of human rights, sovereignty, and humanitarian intervention. China is also unlikely to develop a Western-style liberal democracy in the near to medium term, if ever. Beyond fiercely defending its own sovereignty and incursions thereof, however, China does not generally proselytize its own system beyond its borders.[89] On the economic front, where the AIIB would seem to be a prime organ for advancing differing norms of development financing, the bank is so far operating according to Western methods. AIIB's first projects are cofinanced with, among others, the Asian Development Bank and the European Bank for Reconstruction and Development, both part of the World Bank Group.[90] While the Silk Road Fund is not cooperating with World Bank Group banks, it is partnering with some Western firms for selected projects.[91]

The mixed messages of the AIIB as simultaneously a purveyor of new norms of development financing and a partner for World Bank Group banks points to the wider issue that China's perspective on liberal economic norms is muddled. On the one hand, at the 2017 Davos World Economic Forum, Chinese president Xi Jinping gave a forceful defense of economic globalization and the dangers of protectionism.[92] China has benefited enormously from the current international economic order, and Chinese leaders emphasize that they wish to make the current order more inclusive rather than design a new one from the ground up. On the other hand, the question of China's right to be designated a market economy by the WTO remains hotly contested, state-owned enterprises continue to dominate in many sectors, and China prefers developmental economics (development through, for example, large-scale infrastructure projects) to development through further market liberalization. China's closing domestic economy, further, belies Xi's rhetoric on globalization. Both the AIIB and the NDB fit with the theme of development economics, but the willingness of the AIIB to work with Western norms and partners suggests a stark contrast with how Russia has conceived of the NDB as an alternative to the Western system. China, furthermore, has always been careful to emphasize that the NDB is supplemental rather than detrimental to the current system.

This leads to the third cause of China's disenchantment with BRICS: frustration over its slow pace of decision-making and operationalization. This is in some ways a tautological problem. China, India, and Russia all now have alternative projects and relationships they prioritize over BRICS. For Russia, that is the Greater Eurasian Partnership; for India, it is improved relations with the

United States and increased concerns over China; and for China, it is BRI and AIIB. However, these projects, especially on the Chinese side, came about in part because BRICS proved to be less effective at building new institutions than China originally hoped. Some of this is to do with the issues discussed in the section on India, particularly the way slowing growth rates have made it harder to gloss over conflicting interests. It is also linked with the differences between Hu and Xi. Whereas Hu was content to let the group develop at its own pace as long as it served Chinese interests and did not hinder other items on China's agenda, Xi does not have this patience. Xi has not given up on BRICS, but unless the group proves itself to be action-oriented and ready to increase practical cooperation, especially in the areas of trade and investment, China under Xi's leadership will lose interest.[93]

Conclusion

China took over the BRICS presidency from India in January 2017.[94] Like Russia and India before it, China hosted a raft of BRICS-related events throughout the year, including an academic conference in June 2017 to which scholars from non-BRICS countries were invited.[95] The BRICS Summit, however, was not the most important conference on the 2017 calendar from the Chinese leadership's perspective. That designation belonged to the May 2017 Belt and Road Forum for International Cooperation. While China invested in hosting a successful BRICS summit, leadership attention was elsewhere.

India, after the failure of the Goa summit and the changes in the relationships with Russia and China, is similarly distracted. BRICS offers India few regional security or economic benefits at this point; it does not constrain China and it offers India no increased voice in regional development. Economic relations, always handled bilaterally among the BRICS countries anyway, are now shifting more toward BRI, a project about which India has intense concerns. For the Indian leadership, too, then, focus is on other projects and initiatives.

Neither China nor India will leave BRICS entirely. Both benefit from the optics of the group, and both value the support of the other members in their efforts to gain more representation in global economic governance. Further, this element of cooperation—especially coordination within the G20—is unlikely to be affected because it is an area in which all five countries benefit regardless of other changes in the external environment. Therefore, BRICS will revert to what it was before the drive for institutionalization began in 2011. It will remain a pressure group in the G20, and it will provide its members a platform from which to advance discrete shared interests.[96] It will not, however, fulfill the promise of the 2014 summit in Fortaleza and become a more substantial and institutionalized organization.

Notes

Epigraphs: Xi, "Working Together"; and "PM Modi's Speech at Brics Summit 2017: Key Highlights," *Livemint*, September 4, 2017, https://www.livemint.com/Politics/IhpujnSwYE 1Bxy5R7zZkgK/PM-Modis-speech-at-Brics-Summit-2017-Key-highlights.html.

    1. Malone, *Does the Elephant Dance?*, 48–49.

    2. Hall, "Multialignment and Indian Foreign Policy," 272.

    3. Chitalkar and Malone, "Democracy, Politics and India's Foreign Policy," 78.

    4. Mazumdar, "India's Search for a Post–Cold War Foreign Policy," 167.

    5. This agreement was signed only months before India invaded what was then East Pakistan (and is now Bangladesh), ostensibly on humanitarian grounds.

    6. Malone, *Does the Elephant Dance?*, 50–51.

    7. Ibid., 81.

    8. Ganguly, "India's Foreign Policy Grows Up," 43.

    9. Kelly, "Looking Back on Look East," 85–86.

    10. Ibid., 86–87.

    11. Ganguly, "India's Foreign Policy Grows Up," 44.

    12. Ibid., 43.

    13. Kelly, "Looking Back on Look East," 81.

    14. Khilnan et al., "Nonalignment 2.0," 6.

    15. Ibid., 6; and Hall, "Multialignment and Indian Foreign Policy," 272.

    16. Hall, "Multialignment and Indian Foreign Policy," 272.

    17. Ibid., 278.

    18. Ganguly, "India's Foreign Policy Grows Up," 42.

    19. Indian Diplomat, interview with the author, January 23, 2017, Delhi, India.

    20. Sachin Chaturvedi, interview with the author, January 23, 2017, Delhi, India; and Gulshan Sachdeva, interview with the author, January 23, 2017, Delhi, India.

    21. Chaturvedi, interview.

    22. Sachdeva, interview.

    23. Saran, "India's Contemporary Plurilateralism," 633.

    24. H.H.S. Viswanathan, interview with the author, January 17, Delhi, India.

    25. Saran, "India's Contemporary Plurilateralism," 624.

    26. Singh, "Prime Minister's Statement at the Plenary Session of the Fourth BRICS Summit."

    27. Singh, "Opening Remarks by the Prime Minister of India Dr. Manmohan Singh at the Plenary Session of the First BRIC Summit"; Singh, "Opening Statement by the Prime Minister of India Dr. Manmohan Singh at the Plenary Session of the BRIC Summit"; Singh, "Statement by the Prime Minister of India Dr. Manmohan Singh at the Plenary Session of BRICS Leaders"; and Singh, "Prime Minister's Statement at the Plenary Session of the 5th BRICS Summit."

    28. "Full Text of PM Narendra Modi's Speech at BRICS Leaders' Plenary Session," NDTV.com, October 16, 2016, http://www.ndtv.com/india-news/full-text-of-pm-narendra -modis-speech-at-brics-leaders-plenary-session-1474881.

    29. Ibid.

    30. "Militants Attack Indian Army Base in Kashmir 'Killing 17'," *BBC News*, September 18, 2016, https://www.bbc.com/news/world-asia-india-37399969.

31. Singh, "How to Tame Your Dragon," 149.

32. Wojczewski, "China's Rise," 32; and Ruchika Chitravanshi, "China Leaps 10 Spots with $956 Million FDI in India," *Economic Times*, June 25, 2016, http://economic times.indiatimes.com/industry/banking/finance/china_leaps_10_spots_with_956_million _fdi_in_india/articleshow/52909753.cms?prtpage=1.

33. Lo, "New Order for Old Triangles?," 15.

34. Wojczewski, "China's Rise," 23.

35. Ibid., 37.

36. Kevin Yao and Elias Glenn, "China's 2017 GDP Growth Accelerates for First Time in Seven Years," Reuters, January 18, 2018, https://www.reuters.com/article/us-china -economy-gdp/china-fourth-quarter-gdp-grows-6–8-percent-year-on-year-beats-expect ations-idUSKBN1F70OJ; BS Reporters, "India Inc Bets on 7% GDP Growth in 2017–18," *Business Standard*, December 2, 2017, https://www.business-standard.com/article/economy -policy/india-inc-bets-on-7-gdp-growth-in-2017–18–117120201044_1.html; and Joe Leahy, "Brazil Emerges from Its Worst Ever Recession," *Financial Times*, September 1, 2017, https://www.ft.com/content/b0886e9c-8f1b-11e7-a352-e46f43c5825d.

37. Ernesto Londoño, "An Impeached President, Reeling but Defiant," *New York Times*, April 13, 2017, https://www.nytimes.com/2017/04/13/opinion/an-impeached-president -reeling-but-defiant.html; and Ernesto Londoño, "Ex-President of Brazil Sentenced to Nearly 10 Years in Prison for Corruption," *New York Times*, July 12, 2017, https://www.nytimes.com /2017/07/12/world/americas/brazil-lula-da-silva-corruption.html.

38. Simon Romero, "Brazil's Leaders See Way Out of Scandal," *New York Times*, March 15, 2017, https://www.nytimes.com/2017/03/15/world/americas/brazil-congress-amnesty .html; Simon Romero, "Michel Temer Government in Brazil Reels as Dozens Face New Graft Investigations," *New York Times*, April 11, 2017, https://www.nytimes.com/2017/04/11/world /americas/brazil-michel-temer-investigation-petrobras-odebrecht.html; and Ernesto Lon-doño, "President Temer of Brazil, Dodges Corruption Prosecution, Again," *New York Times*, October 25, 2017, https://www.nytimes.com/2017/10/25/world/americas/brazil-michel-temer -corruption.html.

39. Foster, "Jacob's Ladder"; Lynsey Chutel and Lily Kuo, "What the 'State Capture' Report Tells Us about Zuma, the Guptas, and Corruption in South Africa," *Quartz Africa*, November 3, 2016, https://qz.com/825789/state-capture-jacob-zuma-the-guptas -and-corruption-in-south-africa/; Jason Burke, "Tens of Thousands March against Jacob Zuma in South Africa," *Guardian*, April 7, 2017, https://www.theguardian.com/world/2017 /apr/07/tens-of-thousands-march-against-jacob-zuma-in-south-africa; and E.C.S. "Why Jacob Zuma Resigned."

40. Dhruva Jaishankar, interview with the author, January 19, 2017, Delhi, India.

41. Denis Abramov, "In Arms Trade, China Is Taking Advantage of Russia's Desper-ation," *Moscow Times*, November 1, 2016, https://themoscowtimes.com/articles/in-arms -trade-china-is-taking-advantage-of-russian-desperation-55965.

42. Charap, Drennan, and Noël, "Russia and China," 33; and Thayer, "Does Russia Have a South China Sea Problem?"

43. Unnikrishnan and Purushothaman, "Trends in Russia-China Relations," 2.

44. Petr Topychkanov, interview with the author, March 20, 2017, Moscow, Russia.

45. "South Asia and the Gulf Lead"; and Blanchfield, Wezeman, and Wezeman, "State of Major Arms Transfers."

46. Topychkanov, interview; and Salzman, interview with an Indian diplomat. Perhaps the best example of the extent to which neither side is investing enough time in the relationship was the Russian decision to go forward with planned joint military exercise with Pakistan (the first ever) only two weeks after the terrorist attack in Kashmir in September 2016 and right before the annual Russia-India Summit.

47. Saran and Rej, "BRICS, Globalisms, and the Return of the State."

48. Samir Saran, interview with the author, Delhi, India, January 23, 2017. The way these two projects affect the Chinese approach to BRICS is discussed in following sections.

49. Topychkanov, interview.

50. Samir Saran, "Wahhabism, Meet Han-Ism: CPEC Betokens China's Search for Lebensraum in Pakistan and Pakistan Occupied Kashmir," *Times of India* (blog), May 12, 2017, https://blogs.timesofindia.indiatimes.com/toi-edit-page/wahhabism-meet-han-ism-cpec-betokens-chinas-search-for-lebensraum-in-pakistan-and-pakistan-occupied-kashmir/.

51. Suhasini Haidar, "Why Did India Boycott China's Road Summit?," *Hindu*, May 20, 2017, https://www.thehindu.com/news/national/why-did-india-boycott-chinas-road-summit/article18516163.ece/.

52. "Members and Share Allocations," New Development Bank, accessed April 21, 2017. http://www.ndb.int/about-us/organisation/members/.

53. Unnikrishnan and Purushothaman, "Trends in Russia-China Relations," vi.

54. Chitalkar and Malone, "Democracy, Politics and India's Foreign Policy," 83.

55. Pant and Joshi, "Indo-US Relations under Modi," 135–36.

56. Ibid., 133.

57. Madan, "When Modi Meets Trump"; and Moore, "Strengthen the U.S.–India Relationship."

58. "GDP Growth (Annual %)," World Bank, accessed August 6, 2018, http://data.worldbank.org/indicator/NY.GDP.MKTP.KD.ZG?end=2015&locations=CN&start=2000.

59. Alex Grey, "The World's 10 Biggest Economies in 2017," *World Economic Forum*, March 9, 2017, https://www.weforum.org/agenda/2017/03/worlds-biggest-economies-in-2017/; and PricewaterhouseCoopers, "The World in 2050," 2.

60. PricewaterhouseCoopers, "The World in 2050," 7.

61. Shambaugh and Xiao, "China: The Conflicted Rising Power," 40.

62. Ibid., 41.

63. Sutter, *Chinese Foreign Relations*, 5.

64. Ibid., 6.

65. Zhao, "Chinese Foreign Policy," 104–5.

66. Ibid., 104.

67. Sutter, *Chinese Foreign Relations*, 26–27; and Chan and Li, "New Chinese Leadership," 38–39.

68. Zheng and Lye, "China's Foreign Policy," 26.

69. Blanchfield, Wezeman, and Wezeman, "State of Major Arms Transfers." Ukraine is the second-largest supplier of arms to China, at 16.2 percent.

70. Charap, Drennan, and Noël, "Russia and China," 34.

71. Fu Ying, "How China Sees Russia," 96.

72. Ibid., 105.

73. Ibid., 100.

74. Xi Jinping, *Governance of China*, 306.

75. Xiang, "China and the International 'Liberal' (Western) Order," 109–10.

76. Hu Jintao, "Promote Win-Win Cooperation."

77. Xi Jinping, *Governance of China*, 301.

78. Lo, *Wary Embrace*, 82.

79. Ibid., 80–82.

80. Chen and Feng, "Russia-India-China Trio," 433.

81. Salzman, meeting with senior scholars from Nanjing Normal University, March 1, 2017, Nanjing, China.

82. Song Guoyou, interview with the author, Shanghai, China, March 2, 2017.

83. Think tank and university researcher, interview with the author, Beijing, China, February 2017.

84. Glosny, "China and the BRICs," 102.

85. Ming, "BRICS Development," 447.

86. Think tank and university researcher, interview.

87. Zhu Jiejin, interview with the author, March 2, 2017, Shanghai, China.

88. Xia Liping, interview with the author, March 2, 2017, Shanghai, China.

89. Charap, Drennan, and Noël, "Russia and China," 36.

90. Liu In, "Itogi pervogo goda ABII," 26.

91. "General Electric, China's Silk Road Fund to Launch Energy Investment Platform," Reuters, November 9, 2017, https://www.reuters.com/article/us-trump-asia-china-deals-ge/general-electric-chinas-silk-road-fund-to-launch-energy-investment-platform-idUSKBN 1DA057.

92. Xi, "Jointly Shoulder Responsibility."

93. Zhu Jiejin, interview. While there is no guarantee that either AIIB or BRI will themselves be successful, at least on both of those China has more decisive power to push the projects forward (and has accordingly allocated much higher resources to those projects than to BRICS).

94. "Xi Jinping Sends Letters."

95. "International Think Tanks Conference on BRICS," College of International Relations, HuaQiao University, accessed August 6, 2018, http://cir.hqu.edu.cn/info/1073/2053.htm.

96. On BRICS as a pressure group, see Raghavan, "BRICS: Still under Construction," 10.

Conclusion

Russia and BRICS in an Age of Strategic Uncertainty

BRICS IS NO LONGER A BIG STORY IN GLOBAL GOVERNANCE. THE STORY now is one of deep strategic uncertainty. The United Kingdom voted to leave the European Union; the United States elected and inaugurated as president a man with no political experience and seemingly little care for how US words and deeds affect how the country is perceived abroad. US-Russian relations remain unstable, plagued by the continuing crises in Ukraine and Syria and escalating anger over Russian interference in the 2016 US presidential election. Meanwhile, in the midst of rising economic nationalism across the developed world, China has rhetorically positioned itself as the new standard bearer for globalization and mutually beneficial economic development and integration. In his lengthy opening address at the May 2017 Belt and Road Forum, Xi Jinping laid out a detailed and multifaceted plan for linking China to near and distant neighbors through infrastructure, financing, and extensive people-to-people exchanges. Belt and Road, Xi affirmed, is open to all countries, not just those on the greater Eurasian landmass.[1] Senior officials from countries as far-flung as Argentina attended the summit, excited to be a part of the new, win-win plan for global development.[2]

Belt and Road, of course, faces considerable obstacles to success. These include protecting hard infrastructure assets in politically unstable regions and harmonizing soft infrastructure such as customs and trade regimes across multiple countries with questionable records on rule of law.[3] Corruption is a major risk and driving concern, and the logic of boosting domestic growth through exporting excess capacity remains questionable. Further, as Alexander Gabuev notes, there are no clear metrics against which to judge BRI as either success or failure.[4] Xi's May 2017 speech notwithstanding, the long-term goals of BRI are very broad, and Chinese scholars and policymakers alike are careful to speak of BRI as an "initiative" rather than a "project," suggesting it is best understood as an operating framework rather than a specific plan.[5]

The question here, however, is not whether BRI will succeed nor whether China is sincere in its professed defense of economic globalization. Instead, at issue is the remarkably swift shift in which countries are leading transformative efforts in global governance. This brings the story back to BRICS, and to Russia. While China has long been on a trajectory to challenge the United States as the global leader, Russia's BRICS initiative (and self-inflicted wounds by the West) opened the field much sooner than expected.

In her article "Building the New World Order BRIC by BRIC," Cynthia Roberts argues that the BRIC initiative was not an instance of strategic vision on the part of the Kremlin but one of successful opportunism.[6] Indeed, for all the hype from some quarters about Vladimir Putin as a grandmaster chess player, many experts agree that one of Russia's biggest foreign policy weaknesses is precisely its lack of a grand strategy.[7] What's more, when the idea to bring BRIC together as a political entity began percolating in Moscow, both Russia and the general international context were profoundly different from what they are today. There was no financial crisis either globally or within Russia, and US-Russian relations were cool but stable. Putin had already begun adjusting his rhetoric to reflect the emphasis on Russia's sovereignty and unique civilizational heritage, but these were the only harbingers of the changes to come.

Russia's tactical gambit paid off, however, with two strokes of extraordinary timing. First, when the global financial crisis erupted in 2008, BRIC—and Russia with it—was already there in the wings, ready to take its place in the spotlight. BRIC as a political force solidified amid the chaos of the financial crisis, but Russia had laid enough groundwork beforehand for the group to rise to the occasion. There was no guarantee that BRIC would not fizzle after its moment in the limelight during the acute phase of the financial crisis. The timeline of meetings and the August 2008 agreement to hold a leaders' summit, however, suggest the countries were already planning for a slow and steady build-up before fate and collateralized debt obligations intervened to make the group much more prominent much sooner than expected.

Russia benefited from another moment of exceptional timing in 2014. The same day the G7 countries announced they were suspending Russian membership in the G8, the BRICS foreign ministers issued a statement condemning rumored efforts to bar Putin from the November 2015 G20 summit in Brisbane.[8] One month after the aborted G8 summit in Sochi, the BRICS leaders met in Fortaleza and agreed to form and fund the group's first institutions. Just when Russia needed BRICS to be more than a talking point, the group demonstrated its serious intentions to continue building a system somewhat outside the Western order.

The story of the impact of BRICS on global order, however, is not only about Russia. In many ways, it is the response of the other BRICS countries to the crisis in Ukraine that makes clear the larger import of the group. The other BRICS countries have refused to join the West in condemnation of Russian actions, but not because they find those actions acceptable. Popular opinion of Russia is less negative in BRICS countries and the developing world than it is in Europe and North America, but on balance it still is not good, although developing countries have a lower threat perception of Russia than do Europe and the United States.[9]

Instead, the collective reticence in BRICS to condemn Russia is indicative of concerns about deeper structural problems in the administration of global governance. The BRICS countries are unwilling to be complicit in what they see as the West's arbitrary application of global rules and norms.

Indeed, a central element of concern for Russia and all the BRICS countries is continued Western ideational control of global governance. BRICS does not accept that it is the West's prerogative to determine which countries are considered "responsible stakeholders" or what it means to be a productive member of the international community. In this respect, the crisis in Ukraine is the proverbial canary in the coalmine. Russia's actions in Ukraine since the beginning of 2014 have violated core norms of the liberal international order. Russia has faced isolation, however, only from the United States and its allies. The silence of the BRICS countries is evidence that while the other four countries may not agree with Russian actions in Ukraine, they are not willing to stand behind the current system of norms and rules.

The unwillingness of the BRICS nations to defend the principles underpinning the current system is a direct challenge to Western ideational control of legitimating norms of global governance. BRICS has not offered alternative norms beyond noninterference in domestic affairs, nor are they likely to do so. Even without advancing an affirmative normative agenda, however, the BRICS countries have weakened the Western presumption of being the global norm-setter and, by extension, the foundations of the current order. In so doing, BRICS has allowed Russia to achieve its minimal objective for the group: constraining American global hegemony. Anything further is a bonus.

Having achieved that minimal objective, though, the future of BRICS is uncertain. Brazil and South Africa are beset by domestic crises; India is focused on relations with the United States and worries about more aggressive Chinese foreign policy; China is prioritizing the BRI; and Russia, reading the tea leaves, has shifted its gaze to the Greater Eurasian Partnership. Given that all five members continue to pay lip service to the importance of the group while focusing energies elsewhere, there are essentially three scenarios for future BRICS cooperation: implosion, constructive contribution, and stasis.

Implosion is the least likely outcome. Under this scenario, intra-BRICS tensions overwhelm the group and cooperation in the BRICS format ceases. The obvious route to this outcome would be a dramatic rise in tensions between any two of three Eurasian members, most likely China and India. Tensions would have to escalate to the point that areas of common interest are no longer sufficient to justify even minimal cooperation. If the group implodes, the detrimental effect BRICS has had on the stability of the current system stands but is ephemeral. Long-term questions of stability will be more about the interaction of how China behaves with whether the West is able to recover from its recent domestic turmoil.

This outcome is least likely for two reasons. First, there have long been fierce intragroup tensions in BRICS. Indeed, one of the most impressive parts of the BRICS story is the group's ability to slalom around areas of profound disagreement to cooperate on limited shared objectives. There is no reason to think a further increase in tensions would make that kind of narrow cooperation impossible. Indeed, the September 2017 summit in China, which followed directly on weeks of increased tension between China and India over the Doklam Pass in the Himalayas, is evidence of the group's plasticity in the face of intramember conflict.[10] Second, all the BRICS countries benefit from the optics of the group; in some cases, the optics of cooperation is in fact the primary benefit of the group. Since this type of shallow cooperation is easy to maintain even in the face of intense intragroup tensions, none of the countries are likely to abandon it.

Constructive cooperation is more likely than implosion, but only by a slender margin and only under certain conditions. Under this scenario, BRICS defines and operationalizes a positive agenda to patch holes in the current system while mitigating rhetoric about BRICS as an alternative rather than supplement to the existing order. BRICS would have to propose concrete, reasonable solutions for how to reform organs of global governance and Western norms that do not undercut core principles of the current system. The BRICS countries would also have to take on a level of global responsibility commensurate with their claim of global leadership; positions such as "differentiated responsibility," which India and China claim on climate change, would be insufficient. If BRICS pursues a policy of constructive contribution, the group would undo some of the damage it has wrought and be a net asset to global stability. The system under this scenario will morph from its current configuration, but it will not fracture.

Constructive contribution is more likely than implosion because BRICS has demonstrated an ability to delineate and implement a positive agenda. BRICS working groups on issues like taxation, trade, and environment already exist. If properly formulated and sufficiently resourced, these groups could expand the conversation on these issues in the appropriate global fora. While BRICS interests on questions of trade and taxation may diverge from current approaches, they are not necessarily detrimental to the integrity of the system. Similarly, in creating the NDB and the CRA, BRICS has created institutions that can fill holes in global infrastructure financing and provision of emergency liquidity. These groups and institutions are new enough that their futures, and their effect on the system, remain open questions. If they are integrated properly, treated appropriately by dominant institutions, and operate in ways that do not undermine existing norms, there is no reason they cannot strengthen the current order by bringing in wider voices and giving broader legitimacy to the rules.

Constructive contribution is a plausible outcome, however, only under certain conditions. These include a willingness within BRICS to reframe its approach and a West that is receptive to BRICS proposals. Thus far, neither of these has been forthcoming. On the BRICS side, rhetoric about being "an alternative" to the West is ultimately no more palatable or believable than being explicitly anti-Western. If BRICS is to choose the route of constructive contribution, it will have to speak clearly and with unity about massaging the current order rather than building a parallel option. Most important on this issue will be reigning in Russian rhetoric, whether for domestic or foreign consumption, about BRICS as a basis for a new world order rather than an opportunity to supplement the old one.

Receptivity in the West is no more promising. No matter how positive or softly framed the BRICS agenda, the group cannot take the path of constructive contribution if it has no willing partner. Rigidity, however, is a poor policy choice on the part of the West. Although they have different reasons for their reticence, both the EU and the United States (the most institutionally powerful parts of the West in global governance) have been disinclined to entertain suggestions of substantive changes to their leading roles in the current order. While that unwillingness is understandable from a realpolitik perspective, it ignores the rancor that such a response sows. If Western leaders do not make room for BRICS in existing institutions, BRICS have demonstrated the capacity to create their own outside the current system, governed by different rules.[11]

The final possibility, stasis, is by far the most likely. Under this scenario, BRICS continues to muddle through as it has since its 2014 apex. Leaders' summits, working group meetings, and photo ops happen regularly, and the optics benefits to cooperation remain. Rhetoric about the group continues to exist in a gray space somewhere between being constructive and reflexively anti-Western. The NDB and CRA would persist, but their operation and impact would be subsumed into the broader story about AIIB and China's efforts to establish its own institutional matrix. Under this scenario, BRICS is a persistent, destructive force in the global system; it leads to the gradual weakening of the integrity of the current order through its perpetual minor criticism without offering either operable solutions or plausible strength to achieve its aims.

This outcome is mostly likely because it is the one that happens through inertia as opposed to decisive action. None of the BRICS countries are motivated to kill the group, but all of them have chosen to prioritize other initiatives or problems. Stasis is most likely because it is not a choice at all.

These outcomes are not mutually exclusive; indeed, the most likely scenario is a mix of all three. However, two major intervening variables will affect what happens. The first is internal dynamics in the West. As Edward Luce argues in his book *The Retreat of Western Liberalism*, "the most mortal threat to the Western idea of progress comes from within."[12] Brexit, the election of Donald Trump, and the success (despite her ultimate defeat) of Marine Le Pen in France are all self-inflicted blows to the legitimacy of the Western claim to moral authority and ideational leadership of the liberal international order. America under Donald Trump will have to decide whether it still wishes to be the leader of the international system, and the answer is far from certain.[13] If America retreats into isolationism, Europe will have to decide if it can shoulder the burden alone.

The specter of Western retreat raises the question of what the role for BRICS is in a world in which the West has abdicated global responsibility. BRICS may now be pushing against an open door regarding criticisms of Western management of the system. If this source of unity for the group disappears, BRICS as a construct makes much less sense.

The other, and arguably more pressing, variable is Russia. Russia has always been ahead of its BRICS partners in terms of how much change it would like to see in global governance. All the other BRICS countries, but especially China and India, see themselves primarily as beneficiaries of the current system. They are integrated into global value chains, and they have seen their individual fortunes rise in both institutional representation and soft power projection. While they object to parts of the current system and the West's administration of it, they do not seek an entirely new order. Some of the changes they would prefer, especially tighter rules respecting national sovereignty, would constitute sea changes, but the BRICS countries apart from Russia are essentially evolutionary in their approach to the system. They sense that political and economic power is shifting in their direction, and they are content to wait for the inevitable.

Russia is different. It feels victimized by globalization, and Putin feels personally targeted by the West's interventionist approach to human rights and democracy. Since the onset of the crisis in Ukraine, sovereign globalization has transformed into import substitution and protectionism with limited regional integration with like-minded states. The narrative of "Fortress Russia" discernible during Putin's second presidential term has begun to manifest in political and economic policy. Whereas the other BRICS countries are active members of the international system, and especially global economic governance, Russia has never put down roots and now is turning evermore inward. The result is that, with the exception of the United Nations, Russia feels no real stake in the preservation of the existing governance system as a mechanism of protecting global power. Russia seeks a multipolar world; while its first choice would be a peaceful restructuring toward a great power concert, it feels sufficiently disconnected and insulated from the current order that it is willing to destroy it as a second-best solution.

The irony is that even though the other BRICS countries do not want to upend the current order entirely, their facilitation of Russian behavior since 2014 has done exactly that. Russian leaders spent a decade talking about BRICS as the future of international relations, as the true model of multicivilizational dialogue, and as the protector of national sovereignty. That rhetoric sharpened after the onset of the crisis in Ukraine, and it translated into a concerted effort to build a non-Western system. The BRICS countries, although more moderated in their joint statements, have never directly contradicted the Russian vision. Through

BRICS, whether wittingly or unwittingly on the part of its partners, Russia found an engine for cloaking its goals in a mantle of increasing democracy and representation and thereby transformed the image of the international liberal order.

Notes

1. Xi Jinping, "Work Together to Build the Silk Road."
2. "Argentine Experts Hail President Xi's Speech at Belt & Road Forum," *Xinhua*, May 15, 2017, http://www.xinhuanet.com/english/2017–05/15/c_136285421.htm.
3. Cooley, "Emerging Political Economy," 10.
4. Alexander Gabuev, "Shyolkovyi put v nikuda," *Vedemosti*, May 14, 2017, no. 4320, sec. Analitika: Povorot na vostok: Poyas bez puti, https://www.vedomosti.ru/opinion/articles /2017/05/15/689763-shelkovii-put.
5. Ibid.
6. Roberts, "Building the New World Order," 4.
7. Laura Bassett, "Mike Rogers: Putin Is Playing Chess, Obama Playing Marbles," *Huffington Post*, March 3, 2014, https://www.huffingtonpost.com/2014/03/02/mike-rogers -russia_n_4884922.html; Alexander Bolton, "Cruz: Putin Plays Chess, Obama Plays Checkers on Foreign Policy," *The Hill*, January 28, 2014, http://thehill.com/policy/international /196646-cruz-putin-plays-chess-obama-plays-checkers-on-foreign-policy; Fyodor Lukyanov, interview with the author, December 13, 2014, Moscow; and Dmitri Trenin, interview with the author, December 2, 2014, Moscow, Russia.
8. Department of International Relations and Cooperation of South Africa. "BRICS Ministers Meet."
9. Vice, "Publics Worldwide Unfavorable toward Putin, Russia."
10. Kallol Bhattacherjee, "With Doklam Standoff Resolved, PM to Visit China," *Hindu*, August 31, 2017, https://www.thehindu.com/news/national/with-doklam-standoff -resolved-pm-to-visit-china/article19583063.ece.
11. Shashi Tharoor, "Taking the BRICS Seriously," *Project Syndicate*, June 19, 2015, https://www.project-syndicate.org/commentary/cooperation-major-emerging-economies -by-shashi-tharoor-2015–06?barrier=accesspaylog. The West has a third option: making changes that give China and India substantively more powerful positions in organs of global economic governance while continuing to refuse to deal with BRICS as a group. This is in some ways the path already chosen, but the changes have thus far been insufficient to mollify India and China to the point that they stop pushing for those changes through BRICS.
12. Luce, *Retreat of Western Liberalism*, 11.
13. Hal Brands, "Is American Internationalism Dead? Reading the National Mood in the Age of Trump," *War on the Rocks*, May 16, 2017, https://warontherocks.com/2017/05 /is-american-internationalism-dead-reading-the-national-mood-in-the-age-of-trump/.

Bibliography

Acharya, Amitav. *The End of American World Order*. Hoboken, NJ: Wiley, 2014.

Adomeit, Hans. "Russia as a 'Great Power' in World Affairs: Images and Reality." *International Affairs* 71, no. 1 (1995): 35.

Allakhverdov, Andrey, and Vladimir Pokrovsky. "Putin: Reform Begins at Home." *Science* 306, no. 5698 (November 5, 2004): 957. http://science.sciencemag.org/content/306/5698/957.1.

Anderson, Jon Lee. "Thugs on the Streets for Crimea's Referendum." *New Yorker*, March 16, 2014. https://www.newyorker.com/news/news-desk/thugs-on-the-streets-for-crimeas-referendum.

Andreev, Yurii Valerianovich. "BRIKS: Cherez sotrudnichestvo—k bezopasnosti?" *Puti k miru i bezopasnosti* 45, no. 2 (2013): 127–28. http://new.imemo.ru/files/File/magazines/puty_miru/2013/13026_andreev.pdf.

Antonov, Ivan. "BRIKS kak imidzhevaia kopilka." *Mezhdunarodnaia zhizn*, no. 4 (May 2011).

Armijo, Leslie Elliott. "The BRICs Countries (Brazil, Russia, India, and China) as Analytical Category: Mirage or Insight?" *Asian Perspective* 31, no. 4 (2007): 7–42. https://www.jstor.org/stable/42704607.

Armijo, Leslie Elliott, and Cynthia Roberts. "The Emerging Powers and Global Governance: Why the BRICS Matter." In *Handbook of Emerging Economies*, edited by Robert E. Looney, 503–20. London: Routledge, 2014.

Aron, Leon Rabinovich. *Roads to the Temple: Truth, Memory, Ideas, and Ideals in the Making of the Russian Revolution, 1987–1991*. New Haven, CT: Yale University Press, 2012.

Åslund, Anders. *How Russia Became a Market Economy*. Washington, DC: Brookings Institution Press, 1995.

———. "Why Doesn't Russia Join the WTO?" *Washington Quarterly* 33, no. 2 (2010). https://doi.org/10.1080/01636601003661670.

Åslund, Anders, Sergei Guriev, and Andrew C. Kuchins, eds. *Russia after the Global Economic Crisis*. Washington, DC: Peterson Institute for International Economics Center for Strategic and International Studies New Economic School, 2010.

Aven, Peter. Foreword to *Russia after the Global Economic Crisis*. Edited by Anders Åslund, Sergei Guriev, and Andrew C. Kuchins. Washington, DC: Peterson Institute for International Economics / Center for Strategic and International Studies / New Economic School, 2010. https://catalyst.library.jhu.edu/catalog/bib_3578754.

Baev, Pavel. "Leading in the Concert of Great Powers: Lessons from Russia's G8 Chairmanship." In *The Multilateral Dimension in Russian Foreign Policy*. Edited by Elana Wilson Rowe and Stina Torjesen. London: Routledge, 2009.

Bajpaee, Chietigj. "Modi, India and the Emerging Global Economic Order." *Journal of Asian Public Policy* 9, no. 2 (May 3, 2016): 198–210. https://doi.org/10.1080/17516234 .2016.1165335.

Balcerowicz, Leszek. "Understanding Postcommunist Transitions." *Journal of Democracy* 5, no. 4 (1994): 75–89. https://doi.org/10.1353/jod.1994.0053.

Baranovsky, Vladimir Georgievich. "Vvedenie." In *Globalnaia perestroika*, edited by Alexander Alexandrovich Dynkin, 293–98. Moscow: Ves Mir, 2014.

Batkibekov, S., L. Grebeshkova, I. Dezhina, A. Zolotareva, E. Kitova, E. Kostina, T. Kuznetsova, I. Rozhdestvenskaya, S. Sinelnikov-Murylev, and S. Shiskin. *Perfection of the System of Management and Funding of Budget Institutions*. Vol. 1, *Increasing the Efficiency of Budget Expenditure on Funding Public Institutions and Management of Public Unitary Enterprises Perfection of the System of Management and Funding of Budget Institutions*. Moscow: Gaidar Institute, 2003. http://iep.ru/en/publications/publication/265.html ?highlight=WyJkZXpoaW5hW5hIl0=.

Baumann das Neves, Renato Coelho, and Tamara Gregol de Farias, eds. *VI BRICS Academic Forum*. Brasilia: Institute for Applied Economic Research, 2014. http://www.ipea .gov.br/portal/index.php?option=com_content&view=article&id=24280.

Béland, Daniel, and Robert Henry Cox. Introduction to *Ideas and Politics in Social Science Research*, edited by Daniel Béland and Robert Henry Cox, 3–20. New York: Oxford University Press, 2010.

Bell, Coral. *The Reagan Paradox: American Foreign Policy in the 1980s*. New Brunswick, NJ: Rutgers University Press, 1989.

Berlin, Isaiah. *The Soviet Mind: Russian Culture under Communism*. Washington, DC: Brookings Institution Press, 2004.

Biermann, Frank, Philipp Pattberg, Harro van Asselt, and Fariborz Zelli. "The Fragmentation of Global Governance Architectures: A Framework for Analysis." *Global Environmental Politics* 9, no. 4 (October 24, 2009): 14–40. https://muse.jhu.edu/article /362583.

Bin, Yu. "China-Russia Relations: Navigating through the Ukraine Storm." *Comparative Connections* 16, no. 2 (September 2014): 131–41, 174. https://csis-prod.s3.amazonaws .com/s3fs-public/legacy_files/files/publication/1402qchina_russia.pdf.

Biswas, Rajiv. "How China Is Reshaping Global Development." *DW*, November 19, 2014. https://www.dw.com/en/how-china-is-reshaping-global-development-finance/a -18072984.

Blanchfield, Kate, Pieter D. Wezeman, and Siemon T. Wezeman. "The State of Major Arms Transfers in 8 Graphics." Stockholm International Peace Institute, February 22, 2017. https://www.sipri.org/commentary/blog/2017/state-major-arms-transfers-8-graphics.

Bobrova, V. "Priiamie inostrannye investitsii v strankah BRIKS." *Mirovaia ekonomika i mezhdunarodnye otnosheniia*, no. 2 (2013).

Bobrovnikov, Alexander, and Vladimir Davydov. "Voskhodiashchie strany-giganty na mirovoi stsene XXI veka." *Latinskaia Amerika*, no. 5 (May 31, 2005): 4–20.

Borisoglebskaia, L. N., and V. M. Chetverikov, eds. *Razvitie stran BRIKS v globalnom prostranstve*. Moscow: INFRA-M, 2013.

Brancato, Ekaterina. "Trends in Economic Development, Cooperation, and Trade: BRICS' Position." Paper presented at the Russian International Studies Association (RISA), MGIMO—Moscow State Institute of International Relations, April 25, 2014.

BRIC Leaders. "BRIC Summit—Joint Statement." Second BRIC Summit, April 16, 2010, Brasilia, Brazil. http://www.brics5.co.za/about-brics/summit-declaration/second-summit/.

———. "The Leaders of the BRIC Countries (Brazil, Russia, India and China) Met during the G8 Summit in Japan." Tokyo, Hokkaido, Japan, July 9, 2008. http://www.brics .utoronto.ca/docs/080709-leaders.html.

"BRICS at Hague Slam Attempts to Isolate Putin." *BRICS Post* (blog), March 24, 2014. http://thebricspost.com/brics-at-hague-slam-attempts-to-isolate-putin/.

"BRICS Explore Political, Military Cooperation." *BRICS Post* (blog), September 20, 2013. http://thebricspost.com/brics-explore-political-military-cooperation/.

BRICS Foreign Ministers. "BRICS Ministers Meet on the Sidelines of the Nuclear Security Summit in the Hague." March 24, 2014. http://www.brics.utoronto.ca/docs/140324 -hague.html.

"BRICS Joint Statistical Publication." Rio de Janeiro: Instituto Brasileiro de Geografia e Estatística, 2014. http://brics.ibge.gov.br/downloads/BRICS_Joint_Statistical_Publica tion_2014.pdf.

BRICS Leaders. "Agreement on the New Development Bank," July 15, 2014, Fortaleza, Brazil. http://www.brics.utoronto.ca/docs/140715-bank.html.

———. "Delhi Declaration." Fourth BRICS Summit, March 29, 2012, Delhi, India. http://www.brics5.co.za/about-brics/summit-declaration/fourth-summit/.

———. "eThekwini Declaration." presented at the Fifth BRICS Summit: BRICS and Africa: Partnership for Development, Integration, and Industrialisation, Durban, South Africa, March 27, 2013. http://www.brics5.co.za/about-brics/summit-declaration /fifth-summit/.

———. "Sanya Declaration." Paper presented at the Third BRICS Summit, April 14, 2011, Sanya, China. http://www.brics5.co.za/about-brics/summit-declaration/third -summit/.

———. "Treaty for the Establishment of a BRICS Contingent Reserve Arrangement," July 15, 2014, Fortaleza, Brazil. http://www.brics.utoronto.ca/docs/140715-treaty.html.

BRICS Think Tank Council. "Realising the BRICS Long-Term Goals: Road-Maps and Pathways." 2017. https://www.orfonline.org/wp-content/uploads/2017/08/Brics.pdf.

"BRICS Urged to Boost Parliamentary Cooperation." *BRICS Post* (blog), October 26, 2017. http://thebricspost.com/brics-urged-to-boost-parliamentary-cooperation/.

Brown, Archie. *The Rise and Fall of Communism.* New York: Ecco, 2009.

Brütsch, Christian, and Mihaela Papa. "Deconstructing the BRICS: Bargaining Coalition, Imagined Community, or Geopolitical Fad?" *Chinese Journal of International Politics* 6, no. 3 (September 1, 2013): 299–327. https://doi.org/10.1093/cjip/pot009.

Bush, George H. W. "A Europe Whole and Free." Remarks to the Citizens in Mainz. Rheingoldhalle. Mainz, Federal Republic of Germany, May 31, 1989. https://usa.us embassy.de/etexts/ga6–890531.htm.

Callen, Tim. "PPP versus the Market: Which Weight Matters?" *Finance and Development,* March 2007. http://www.imf.org/external/pubs/ft/fandd/2007/03/basics.htm.

Chaadaev, P. Ia. *The Major Works of Peter Chaadaev.* Edited and translated by Raymond T. McNally. Notre Dame, IN: University of Notre Dame Press, 1969.

Chan, Irene, and Mingjiang Li. "New Chinese Leadership, New Policy in the South China Sea Dispute?" *Journal of Chinese Political Science; Dordrecht* 20, no. 1 (March 2015): 35–50. http://dx.doi.org/10.1007/s11366-014-9326-y.

Chappell, Bill. "Russia Vetoes U.N. Security Council Resolution on Crimea." *NPR.org*, March 15, 2014. http://www.npr.org/sections/thetwo-way/2014/03/15/290404691/russia-vetoes-u-n-security-council-resolution-on-crimea.

Charap, Samuel. "The Ukraine Crisis: Causes and Consequences." Presentation at the Russia-Eurasia Forum, Johns Hopkins School of Advanced International Studies, Washington, DC, October 28, 2015.

Charap, Samuel, John Drennan, and Pierre Noël. "Russia and China: A New Model of Great-Power Relations." *Survival* 59, no. 1 (January 2, 2017): 25–42. https://doi.org/10.1080/00396338.2017.1282670.

Charap, Samuel, and Jeremy Shapiro. "A New European Security Order: The Ukraine Crisis and the Missing Post-Cold War Bargain." Fondation pour la Recherche Stratégique, December 8, 2014.

Chen Dongxiao, and Feng Shuai. "The Russia-India-China Trio in the Changing International System." *China Quarterly of International Strategic Studies* 2, no. 4 (2016): 431–47. https://doi.org/10.1142/S2377740016500275.

Chitalkar, Poorvi, and David M. Malone. "Democracy, Politics and India's Foreign Policy." *Canadian Foreign Policy Journal* 17, no. 1 (March 1, 2011): 75–91. https://doi.org/10.1080/11926422.2011.563956.

Chung, Chien-Peng. "The Shanghai Co-Operation Organization: China's Changing Influence in Central Asia." *China Quarterly*, no. 180 (December 2004): 989–1009.

Clunan, Anne L. *The Social Construction of Russia's Resurgence: Aspirations, Identity, and Security Interests*. Baltimore: Johns Hopkins University Press, 2009.

Colton, Timothy. "Putin and the Attenuation of Russian Democracy." In *Putin's Russia: Past Imperfect, Future Uncertain*. Edited by Dale R. Herspring. 3rd ed. Lanham, MD: Rowman & Littlefield, 2007.

Cooley, Alexander. "The Emerging Political Economy of OBOR: The Challenges of Promoting Connectivity in Central Asia and Beyond." Washington, DC: Center for Strategic and International Studies, 2016. https://www.csis.org/analysis/emerging-political-economy-obor.

———. *Great Games, Local Rules: The New Great Power Contest in Central Asia*. Oxford: Oxford University Press, 2012.

———. "Scripts of Sovereignty: The Freezing of the Russia-Ukraine Crisis and Dilemmas of Governance in Eurasia." Center for Global Interests, 2015. http://globalinterests.org/wp-content/uploads/2015/01/Scripts-of-Sovereignty_Center-on-Global-Interests.pdf.

Cooper, Andrew F., and Kelly Jackson. "The Incremental Transformation of the G8 through the Heiligendamm Process." *Studia Diplomatica* 61, no. 2 (2008): 79–88.

Cooper, Julian. "Of BRICs and Brains: Comparing Russia with China, India, and Other Populous Emerging Economies." *Eurasian Geography and Economics* 47, no. 3 (2006): 255–84. https://doi.org/10.2747/1538-7216.47.3.255.

Czuperski, Maksymillian, John Herbst, Elliot Higgins, Alina Polyakova, and Damon Wilson. "Hiding in Plain Sight: Putin's War in Ukraine." Washington, DC: Atlantic Council, May 2015. http://www.atlanticcouncil.org/publications/reports/hiding-in-plain-sight-putin-s-war-in-ukraine-and-boris-nemtsov-s-putin-war.

Darden, Keith A. *Economic Liberalism and Its Rivals: The Formation of International Institutions among the Post-Soviet States*. Cambridge: Cambridge University Press, 2009.

Davydov, Vladimir Mikhailovich, ed. "BRIKS kak faktor stanovleniia politsentrichnogo rezhima mezhdunaronykh otnoshenii." *Mezhdunarodnaia zhizn* 5 (May 2011).

———. *BRIKS—Latinskaia Amerika: positsionirovanie i vzaimodeistvie*. Moscow, Russia: ILA RAN, 2014.

———. "Ekzamen krizisa dlia BRIK." *Latinskaia Amerika* 7 (2010).

Davydov, Vladimir, and Aleksandr Bobrovnikov. *Rol voskhodhiashchikh gigantov v mirovoi ekonomike i politike [shansy Braziii i Meksiki v globalnom izmerenii]*. Moscow: ILA RAN, 2008.

Degaut, Marcos. "Do the BRICS Still Matter?" Washington, DC: Center for Strategic and International Studies, October 2015. http://csis.org/files/publication/151020_Degaut _DoBRICSMatter_Web.pdf.

Deich, Tatiana Lazerevna, and Evgenii Nikolaevich Korendiasov, eds. *BRIKS-Afrika: partnerstvo i vzaimodeistvie*. Moscow: IAfr, 2013.

Department of International Relations and Cooperation of South Africa. "BRICS Ministers Meet on the Sidelines of the Nuclear Security Summit in the Hague." BRICS Ministry of External Relations, March 24, 2014. http://brics.itamaraty.gov.br/press -releases/21-documents/190-brics-ministers-meet-on-the-sidelines-of-the-nuclear -security-summit-in-the-hague.

Department of State, Office of Website Management, Bureau of Public Affairs. "Arms Control and International Security," May 27, 2010. http://www.state.gov/p/eur/ci/rs /usrussiabilat/c37312.htm.

Dezhina, Irina. "The Special of Structural Reforms in Russian Science." SSRN Scholarly Paper. Rochester, NY: Social Science Research Network, November 25, 2013. http:// papers.ssrn.com/abstract=2359349.

Diuk, Nadia. "Euromaidan: Ukraine's Self-Organizing Revolution." *World Affairs*, March–April 2014. http://www.worldaffairsjournal.org/article/euromaidan-ukraine's-self-organiz ing-revolution.

Dubin, Boris. "The Myth of the 'Special Path' in Contemporary Russian Public Opinion." *Russian Politics & Law* 50, no. 5 (October 9, 2012): 35–51. https://www.tandfonline .com/doi/abs/10.2753/RUP1061–1940500502.

EASI Working Group on Historical Reconciliation and Protracted Conflicts. "Historical Reconciliation and Protracted Conflicts." Carnegie Endowment for International Peace, February 3, 2012. https://carnegieendowment.org/2012/02/03/historical-reconciliation -and-protracted-conflicts-pub-46991.

EASI Working Group on Missile Defense. "Missile Defense: Towards a New Paradigm." Washington, DC: Carnegie Endowment for International Peace, February 2012. http:// carnegieendowment.org/files/WGP_MissileDefense_FINAL.pdf.

E.C.S. "Why Jacob Zuma Resigned." *Economist*, February 19, 2018. https://www.econo mist.com/the-economist-explains/2018/02/19/why-jacob-zuma-resigned.

Embody, Julia. "Beware Ukraine's Rising Right Sector." *National Interest*, August 12, 2015. http://nationalinterest.org/feature/beware-ukraines-rising-right-sector-13558.

Emerson, Michael. "Do the BRICS Make a Bloc?" *CEPS Commentary*, April 30, 2012. https://www.ceps.eu/system/files/ME%20Do%20the%20Brics%20make%20a%20bloc .pdf.

English, Robert. *Russia and the Idea of the West: Gorbachev, Intellectuals, and the End of the Cold War*. New York: Columbia University Press, 2000.

European Parliament. "European Parliament Calls on Russia to withdraw Military Forces from Ukraine." European Parliament, March 13, 2014. http://www.europarl.europa.eu/news/en/news-room/content/20140312IPR38707.

Ferdinand, Peter. "Rising Powers at the UN: An Analysis of the Voting Behaviour of BRICS in the General Assembly." *Third World Quarterly* 35, no. 3 (May 2014). http://dx.doi.org/10.1080/01436597.2014.893483.

Foster, Douglas. "Jacob's Ladder." *Atlantic*, June 2009. https://www.theatlantic.com/magazine/archive/2009/06/jacobs-ladder/307442/.

Friedman, Max Paul. *Rethinking Anti-Americanism: The History of an Exceptional Concept in American Foreign Relations*. Cambridge: Cambridge University Press, 2012.

Fu Ying. "How China Sees Russia: Beijing and Moscow Are Close, but Not Allies." *Foreign Affairs*, January–February 2016. https://www.foreignaffairs.com/articles/china/2015-12-14/how-china-sees-russia.

Fukuyama, Francis. "The Ambiguity of 'National Interest.'" In *Rethinking Russia's National Interests*. Edited by Stephen Sestanovich. Washington, DC: Center for Strategic and International Studies, 1994.

———. *The End of History and the Last Man*. New York: Free Press; Toronto: Maxwell Macmillan Canada, 1992.

Gabuev, Alexander. "Friends with Benefits? Russian-Chinese Relations after the Ukraine Crisis." Carnegie Moscow Center, June 29, 2016. https://carnegie.ru/2016/06/29/friends-with-benefits-russian-chinese-relations-after-ukraine-crisis-pub-63953.

———. "Russia Has a China Problem, Too." *Diplomat*, September 4, 2015. https://thediplomat.com/2015/09/russia-has-a-china-problem-too/.

———. "Sino-Russian Trade after a Year of Sanctions." Carnegie.ru Commentary, September 11, 2015. http://carnegieendowment.org/2015/09/11/sino-russian-trade-after-year-of-sanctions/ihte.

Ganguly, Sumit. "India's Foreign Policy Grows Up." *World Policy Journal; Durham* 20, no. 4 (Winter 2003–2004): 41–47. https://www.jstor.org/stable/40209888.

Gati, Charles. *Failed Illusions: Moscow, Washington, Budapest, and the 1956 Hungarian Revolt*. Washington, DC: Woodrow Wilson Center Press Stanford University Press, 2006. https://catalyst.library.jhu.edu/catalog/bib_2625052.

Gelfand, Mikhail. "What Is to Be Done about Russian Science?" *Nature* 500, no. 7463 (August 22, 2013): 379. https://www.nature.com/news/what-is-to-be-done-about-russian-science-1.13574.

Gilman, Martin G. *No Precedent, No Plan: Inside Russia's 1998 Default*. Cambridge, MA: MIT Press, 2010.

Glosny, Michael A. "China and the BRICs: A Real (but Limited) Partnership in a Unipolar World." *Polity* 42, no. 1 (January 2010): 100–129. http://dx.doi.org/10.1057/pol.2009.14.

Goddard, Stacie E., and Ronald R. Krebs. "Rhetoric, Legitimation, and Grand Strategy." *Security Studies* 24, no. 1 (January 2, 2015): 5–36. https://doi.org/10.1080/09636412.2014.1001198.

Gottemoeller, Rose. "Russian-American Security Relations after Georgia." Policy Brief. Foreign Policy for the Next President. Washington, DC: Carnegie Endowment for

International Peace, October 2008. http://carnegieendowment.org/files/russia_us
_security_relations_after_georgia.pdf.

Gould-Davies, Nigel. "Russia's Sovereign Globalization: Rise, Fall and Future." Research
Paper. London: Chatham House, The Royal Institute of International Affairs, January
2016. https://www.chathamhouse.org/publication/russias-sovereign-globalization-rise
-fall-and-future.

Grey, Alex. "The World's 10 Biggest Economies in 2017." World Economic Forum,
March 9, 2017. https://www.weforum.org/agenda/2017/03/worlds-biggest-economies-in
-2017/.

Grishaeva, L. E. "Rossiia i BRIKS: novyi etap sotrudnichestva." In *Voskhodiashchie
gosudarstva-giganty BRIKC: rol v mirovoi politike, strategii modernizatsii*. Edited by Liudmila Sergeevna Okuneva and A. A. Orlov. Moscow: MGIMO Universitet, 2012.

Gustafson, Thane. *Capitalism Russian-Style*. Cambridge: Cambridge University Press, 1999.
https://catalyst.library.jhu.edu/catalog/bib_2111533.

Gvosdev, Nikolas K., and Christopher Marsh. *Russian Foreign Policy: Interests, Vectors, and
Sectors*. Los Angeles, CA: Sage, 2014.

Hahn, Gordon M. "Medvedev, Putin, and Perestroika 2.0." *Demokratizatsiya* 18, no. 3
(Summer 2010): 228–59. https://www.researchgate.net/publication/290576472_Medve
dev_Putin_and_Perestroika_20.

Hall, Ian. "Multialignment and Indian Foreign Policy under Narendra Modi." *The Round
Table* 105, no. 3 (May 3, 2016): 271–86. https://doi.org/10.1080/00358533.2016.11
80760.

Hart, Andrew F., and Bruce D. Jones. "How Do Rising Powers Rise?" *Survival* 52, no. 6
(January 12, 2010): 63–88. https://doi.org/10.1080/00396338.2010.540783.

Hooijmaaijers, Bas, and Stephan Keukeleire. "Voting Cohesion of the BRICS Countries
in the UN General Assembly, 2006–2014: A BRICS Too Far?" *Global Governance* 22,
no. 3 (July 2016): 389–407. http://journals.rienner.com/doi/abs/10.5555/1075-2846
-22.3.389?code=lrpi-site.

Hopewell, Kristen. *Breaking the WTO: How Emerging Powers Disrupted the Neoliberal Project*.
Stanford, CA: Stanford University Press, 2016.

Hough, Jerry F. *The Logic of Economic Reform in Russia*. Washington, DC: Brookings Institution Press, 2001.

Hough, Jerry F., and Merle Fainsod. *How the Soviet Union Is Governed*. Cambridge, MA:
Harvard University Press, 1979.

Hu Jintao. "Promote Win-Win Cooperation and Build a New Type of Relations between
Major Countries." Address by H. E. Hu Jintao, President of the People's Republic of
China, at the Opening Session of the Fourth Round of the China-US Strategic and
Economic Dialogues, May 3, 2012. http://www.fmprc.gov.cn/mfa_eng/wjdt_665385
/zyjh_665391/t931392.shtml.

Hufbauer, Gary Clyde, Jeffrey J. Schott, Kimberly Ann Elliott, and Barbara Oegg. *Economic Sanctions Reconsidered*. Washington, DC: Peterson Institute for International
Economics, 2007. http://www.piie.com/publications/chapters_preview/4075/01iie
4075.pdf.

Hurrell, Andrew. "Hegemony, Liberalism and Global Order: What Space for Would-Be
Great Powers?" *International Affairs (Royal Institute of International Affairs 1944–)* 82,
no. 1 (2006): 1–19. http://www.jstor.org/stable/3569127.

IMF. "Press Release: IMF Managing Director Christine Lagarde Welcomes U.S. Congressional Approval of the 2010 Quota and Governance Reforms." December 18, 2015. http://www.imf.org/en/News/Articles/2015/09/14/01/49/pr15573.

———. "Press Release: Statement by IMF Managing Director Christine Lagarde on IMF Quota and Governance Reforms." December 21, 2014. http://www.imf.org/en/News/Articles/2015/09/14/01/49/pr14568.

———. "World Economic Outlook, April 2017: Gaining Momentum." April 2017. https://www.imf.org/en/Publications/WEO/Issues/2017/04/04/world-economic-outlook-april-2017.

Isachenko, T. M. "Strany BRIKS vo vneshneekonomicheskoi strategii Rossii: poisk alternativ." *Mezhdunarodnaia zhizn*, no. 11 (November 2011): 79–88.

Judah, Ben. *Fragile Empire: How Russia Fell in and out of Love with Vladimir Putin.* New Haven, CT: Yale University Press, 2013.

Kelly, Andrew. "Looking Back on Look East: India's Post-Cold War Shift Toward Asia." *Seton Hall Journal of Diplomacy and International Relations; South Orange* 15, no. 2 (Spring/Summer 2014): 81–93. http://heinonline.org/HOL/Page?handle=hein.journals/whith15&div=20&g_sent=1&casa_token=&collection=journals.

Kenen, Peter B. "Reform of the International Monetary Fund." Washington, DC: Council on Foreign Relations, May 2007. http://www.cfr.org/international-organizations-and-alliances/reform-international-monetary-fund/p13276.

Khilnan, Sunil, Rajiv Kumar, Pratap Bhanu Mehta, Prakash Menon, Nandan Nilekani, Srinath Raghavan, Syam Saran, and Siddharth Varadarajan. "Nonalignment 2.0: A Foreign and Strategic Policy for India in the Twenty First Century." New Delhi: National Defence College and Centre for Policy Research, 2012.

Khmelevskaia, Natalia Gennadievich. "Valiutnoe partnerstvo BRIKS: usloviia sozdaniia i instrumentarii sblizheniia interesov." In *Voskhodiashchie gosudarstva-giganty BRIKS: rol v mirovoi politike, strategii modernizatsii, sbornik nauchnykh trudov.* Edited by Liudmila Sergeevna Okuneva and A. A. Orlov. Moscow: MGIMO Universitet, n.d.

Kirshner, Jonathan. *American Power after the Financial Crisis.* Cornell Studies in Money. Ithaca, NY: Cornell University Press, 2014.

Kirton, John. "Explaining the BRICS Summit Solid, Strengthening Success." *International Organizations Research Journal* 10, no. 2 (2015): 1–29. http://www.brics.utoronto.ca/biblio/iorj-2015-02-kirton.pdf.

Klimovets, O. *Ekonomicheskie interesy Rossii v mezhdunarodnom partnerstve BRIK: monografiia.* Stavropol: Servisshkola, 2007.

Kondrashov, Andrey. *Crimea: The Way Home.* YouTube Documentary. March 17, 2017. https://archive.org/details/youtube-c8nMhCMphYU.

Kornegay, Francis A., Jr. "South Africa, the Indian Ocean and the Ibsa-BRICS Equation: Reflections on Geopolitical and Strategic Dimensions." ORF Occasional Paper #30, December 2011. Observer Research Foundation. https://www.orfonline.org/wp-content/uploads/2012/01/OccasionalPaper_30.pdf.

Kozlovskii, E. A., M. A. Komarov, and R. N. Makyshkin. *Braziliia, Rossiia, Indiia, Kitai, IuAR: strategiia nedropolzvaniia.* Moscow: NKI BRIKS, 2013.

Kramer, Mark. "The Myth of a No-NATO-Enlargement Pledge to Russia." *Washington Quarterly* 32, no. 2 (Spring 2009): 39–61. https://doi.org/10.1080/01636600902773248.

Krauthammer, Charles. "The Unipolar Moment." *Foreign Affairs* 70, no. 1 (January 1, 1990): 23–33. https://doi.org/10.2307/20044692.

Kremlin. "The Draft of the European Security Treaty." President of Russia, November 29, 2009. http://en.kremlin.ru/events/president/news/6152.

———. "The Leaders of the BRIC Countries (Brazil, Russia, India and China) Met during the G8 Summit in Japan." Japan, July 9, 2008. Tokyo, Hokkaido. http://www.brics.utoronto.ca/docs/080709-leaders.html.

Krestianinov, Viktor. "BRIKS razryvaet dollarovye tsepi." *Argumenty Nedeli*, no. 26 (July 17, 2014). http://argumenti.ru/politics/n446/352813.

Kuchins, Andrew C., and Igor Zevelev. "Russia's Contested National Identity and Foreign Policy." In *Worldviews of Aspiring Powers: Domestic Foreign Policy Debates in China, India, Iran, Japan, and Russia*. Edited by Henry R. Nau and Deepa M. Ollapally. New York: Oxford University Press, 2012.

Laidi, Zaki. "The BRICS against the West?" *CERI Strategy Papers* 11, no. 2 (2011): 1–12. http://www.sciencespo.fr/ceri/sites/sciencespo.fr.ceri/files/n11_112011.pdf.

Larionova, Marina. "BRICS: A Rising Global Governance Actor." Paper presented at the Russian International Studies Association, MGIMO–Moscow State Institute of International Relations, April 25, 2014.

———. "BRIKS v sisteme globalnogo upravleniia." *Mezhdunarodnaia zhizn*, no. 4 (April 2012): 2–14. http://dlib.eastview.com/browse/doc/27160066.

Larionova, Marina, Mark Rakhmangulov, Andrei Shelepov, Andrei Sakharov, and Nikolai Medyshevsky. "Vozmozhnosti sotrudnichestva v BRIKS dlia formirovaniia reshenii BRIKS iz 'dvadtsatki' po kliuchevym napravleniiam reformy mezhdunarodnoi finansovo-ekonomicheskoi arkhitektury v interesakh Rossii." *Vestnik mezhdunarodnoi organizatsii* 4 (2012): 199–238. http://iorj.hse.ru/en/2012—4/70750733.html.

Lavrov, Sergei. "BRIKS—globalnyi forum novogo pokoleniia." *Mezhdunarodnaia zhizn*, no. 3 (March 2012): 1–6.

———. "Face to Face with America: Between Nonconfrontation and Convergence." *Russian Politics & Law* 47, no. 3 (June 5, 2009): 45–60. https://www.tandfonline.com/doi/abs/10.2753/RUP1061–1940470304.

Legvold, Robert. "The Role of Multilateralism in Russian Foreign Policy." In *The Multilateral Dimension in Russian Foreign Policy*. Edited by Elana Wilson Rowe and Stina Torjesen. London: Routledge, 2009.

———. "Russian Foreign Policy during Periods of Great State Transformation." In *Russian Foreign Policy in the Twenty-First Century and the Shadow of the Past*. Edited by Robert Legvold. New York: Columbia University Press, 2007.

Light, Margot. "Foreign Policy Thinking." In *Internal Factors in Russian Foreign Policy*. Edited by Neil Malcom, Alex Pravda, Roy Allison, and Margot Light. Oxford: Oxford University Press, 1996.

Lipman, Maria, Lev Gudkov, and Lasha Bakradze. *The Stalin Puzzle: Deciphering Post-Soviet Public Opinion*. Edited by Thomas De Waal. Washington, DC: Carnegie Endowment for International Peace, 2013.

Liu In. "Itogi pervogo goda ABII." *Kitai*, February 2017.

Lo, Bobo. *Axis of Convenience: Moscow, Beijing, and the New Geopolitics*. Washington, DC: Brookings Institution Press, 2008.

———. "New Order for Old Triangles? The Russia-China-India Matrix." Russie.Nei. Visions. Notes de l'Ifri. Ifri, April 2017.

———. *Russia and the New World Disorder*. Washington, DC: Brookings Institution Press with Chatham House, 2015.

————. *Vladimir Putin and the Evolution of Russian Foreign Policy*. Oxford: Blackwell, 2002.

————. *A Wary Embrace: What the China-Russia Relationship Means for the World*. Lowy Institute Papers/Penguin Specials. Australia: Penguin Random House Australia, 2017. https://www.lowyinstitute.org/publications/wary-embrace.

Luce, Edward. *The Retreat of Western Liberalism*. New York: Atlantic Monthly Press, 2017.

Lukin, A. V. "Rossiia i Kitai v RIK i BRIKS." In *Voskhodiashchie gosudarstva-giganty BRIKC: rol v mirovoi politike, strategii modernizatsii*. Edited by A. A. Orlov and L. S. Okuneva. Moscow: MGIMO Universitet, 2012.

Lukov, Vadim. "BRIKS—faktor globalnogo znacheniia." *Mezhdunarodnaia zhizn* 6 (2011).

Lukyanov, Fyodor. "Putin's Russia: The Quest for a New Place." *Social Research* 76, no. 1 (Spring 2009): 117–50. https://www.jstor.org/stable/pdf/40972141.pdf.

————. "What Holds the BRICS Together?" *Russia in Global Affairs*, April 2, 2013. http://eng.globalaffairs.ru/redcol/What-holds-the-BRICS-together-15910.

Lula Da Silva, Luiz Inácio. "The BRICS Come of Global Age." *New Perspectives Quarterly*, July 20, 2010. https://doi.org/10.1111/j.1540–5842.2010.01175.x.

MacWilliams, Bryon. "Academy Agrees to Post-Soviet Crash Diet." *Science* 310, no. 5745 (October 7, 2005): 42. https://doi.org/10.1126/science.310.5745.42.

Madan, Tanvi. "When Modi Meets Trump: Where Do U.S.-India Relations Stand?" Brookings Institution, June 23, 2017. https://www.brookings.edu/blog/order-from-chaos/2017/06/23/when-modi-meets-trump-where-do-u-s-india-relations-stand/.

Magaril, Sergei. "The Mythology of the 'Third Rome' in Russian Educated Society." *Russian Politics & Law* 50, no. 5 (October 9, 2012): 7–34. https://www.tandfonline.com/doi/abs/10.2753/RUP1061–1940500501.

Makarychev, Andrey. *Russia and the EU in a Multipolar World: Discourses, Identities, Norms*. Soviet and Post-Soviet Politics and Society 127. Stuttgart: ibidem-Verlag, 2014.

Makarychev, Andrey, and Viatcheslav Morozov. "Multilateralism, Multipolarity, and Beyond: A Menu of Russia's Policy Strategies." *Global Governance* 17, no. 3 (July 2011): 353–73. http://journals.rienner.com/doi/abs/10.5555/1075–2846–17.3.353.

Malone, David. *Does the Elephant Dance? Contemporary Indian Foreign Policy*. Oxford: Oxford University Press, 2011.

Mankoff, Jeffrey. *Russian Foreign Policy: The Return of Great Power Politics*. 2nd ed. Lanham, MD: Rowman & Littlefield, 2012.

Martynov, B. F. "BRIK i degradiruiushchii miroporiadok." *Latinskaia Amerika*, no. 5 (May 2008): 4–20. http://dlib.eastview.com/browse/doc/17590915.

Mazumdar, Arijit. "India's Search for a Post–Cold War Foreign Policy: Domestic Constraints and Obstacles." *India Quarterly* 67, no. 2 (June 1, 2011): 165–82. https://doi.org/10.1177/097492841006700205.

Mboweni, Tito. "Brics Bank to Balance Global Order." *Global South Africans*, August 21, 2015. http://globalsouthafricans.com/latest/624-brics-bank-to-balance-global-order.html.

McDermott, Roger. "Kremlin Contemplates a Seismic Shift in Russian Foreign Policy." *Eurasia Daily Monitor* 7, no. 97 (May 19, 2010). https://jamestown.org/program/kremlin-contemplates-a-seismic-shift-in-russian-foreign-policy/.

Medvedev, Dmitry. "Address to the Federal Assembly of the Russian Federation." November 30, 2010, Moscow. http://eng.kremlin.ru/transcripts/1384.

————. "Address to the Federal Assembly." December 22, 2011, Moscow. http://eng.kremlin.ru/transcripts/3268.

———. "Annual Address to the Federal Assembly." November 5, 2008, Moscow. http://eng.kremlin.ru/transcripts/296.

———. "Press Statement following BRIC Group Summit." First BRICS Summit, June 16, 2009, Ekaterinburg. http://en.kremlin.ru/events/president/transcripts/4475.

———. "Rossiia, vpered!" *Gazeta.ru*, September 10, 2009. http://kremlin.ru/events/president/news/5413.

———. "Russian President's Address at the BRICS Summit." Fourth BRICS Summit, March 29, 2012, New Delhi. http://en.kremlin.ru/events/president/transcripts/14870.

———. "Speech at World Policy Conference." World Policy Conference, October 8, 2008, Evian, France. http://archive.kremlin.ru/eng/speeches/2008/10/08/2159_type829 12type82914_207457.shtml.

Mehta, Simi. "Understanding India's Economic Diplomacy." *Journal of Governance & Public Policy; Hyderabad* 6, no. 2 (December 2016): 61–68. https://search.proquest.com/docview/1894948420/abstract/2FCBA91218A7427APQ/7.

Ming Liu. "BRICS Development: A Long Way to a Powerful Economic Club and New International Organization." *Pacific Review* 29, no. 3 (May 26, 2016): 443–53. https://doi.org/10.1080/09512748.2016.1154688.

Ministry of Foreign Affairs of the Russian Federation. "Concept of Participation of the Russian Federation in BRICS," March 21, 2013. http://eng.news.kremlin.ru/media/events/eng/files/41d452b13d9c2624d228.pdf.

———. "Concept of the Foreign Policy of the Russian Federation," February 8, 2013. http://www.mid.ru/brp_4.nsf/0/76389FEC168189ED44257B2E0039B16D.

———. "Concept of the Russian Federation's Presidency in BRICS in 2015–2016." March 1, 2015. http://en.brics2015.ru/russia_and_brics/20150301/19483.html.

———. "Foreign Policy Concept of the Russian Federation," June 28, 2000. http://fas.org/nuke/guide/russia/doctrine/econcept.htm.

———. "Foreign Policy Concept of the Russian Federation," July 2008. http://archive.kremlin.ru/eng/text/docs/2008/07/204750.shtml.

———. "Foreign Policy Concept of the Russian Federation," November 30, 2016. http://www.mid.ru/foreign_policy/official_documents/-/asset_publisher/CptICkB6BZ29/content/id/2542248.

———. "McFaul's Mention of 'Linkages' Supposedly Put Forward by Russia in the Discussion of Pressing International Issues Is Also Unprofessional." Twitter. @mfa_russia, May 28, 2012. https://twitter.com/MFA_Russia/status/207171965499355136.

———. "Michael McFaul's Analysis Is a Deliberate Distortion of a Number of Aspects of the Russian-U.S. Dialogue." Twitter. @mfa_russia, May 28, 2012. https://twitter.com/MFA_Russia/status/207171509628837889.

———. "National Security Concept of the Russian Federation," January 24, 2000. http://www.mid.ru/bdomp/ns-osndoc.nsf/1e5f0de28fe77fdcc32575d900298676/36aba64ac09f737fc32575d9002bbf31!OpenDocument.

———. "O programme effektivnogo ispolzovaniia na sistemoi osnove vneshnepoliticheskikh faktorov v tseliakh dolgosrochnogo razvitiia Rossiiskoi Federatsii." *Russkii Newsweek*, May 11, 2010. http://perevodika.ru/articles/13590.html.

———. "Obzor vneshnei politiki Rossiiskoi Federatsii." Moscow, Russia, March 27, 2007. http://www.mid.ru/web/guest/foreign_policy/news/-/asset_publisher/cKNonkJE02Bw/content/id/378188.

———. "A Survey of Russian Foreign Policy." Moscow, Russia, March 2007. http://www
.mid.ru/brp_4.nsf/e78a48070f128a7b43256999005bcbb3/89a30b3a6b65b4f2c32572
d700292f74?OpenDocument.

———. "Transcript of Remarks and Response to Media Questions by Russian Minister of
Foreign Affairs Sergey Lavrov at Press Conference following Meeting of Foreign Ministers of Brazil, Russia, India and China (BRIC), Yekaterinburg," May 16, 2008. http://
www.mid.ru/en/vistupleniya_ministra/-/asset_publisher/MCZ7HQuMdqBY/content
/id/337980.

———. "Zaiavlenie MID Rossii v sviazi s vyskazyvaniiami Posla SShA v Moskve M.
Makfola," May 28, 2012. http://www.mid.ru/brp_4.nsf/0/7511BC12330A28A244257
A0C00591D4B.

Mishra, Abhishek. "IBSA and South-South Cooperation: An Appraisal." ORF *Expert
Speak* (blog), June 20, 2018. https://www.orfonline.org/expert-speak/ibsa-and-south
-south-cooperation-an-appraisal/.

Mitchell, Lincoln Abraham. *The Color Revolutions*. Philadelphia: University of Pennsylvania Press, 2012.

Mohan, Rakesh, and Muneesh Kapur. "Emerging Powers and Global Governance:
Whither the IMF?" Working Paper. Washington, DC: International Monetary Fund,
October 2, 2015. http://www.imf.org/external/pubs/ft/wp/2015/wp15219.pdf.

Momani, Bessma. "Another Seat at the Board: Russia's IMF Executive Director." *International Journal* 62, no. 4 (Fall 2007): 916–39. http://www.jstor.org/stable/
40204343.

Moore, Evan. "Strengthen the U.S.–India Relationship." *National Review*, February 1, 2018.
https://www.nationalreview.com/2018/02/india-united-states-relations-trade-military
-strategy-alliance/.

Morgenthau, Hans J. *In Defense of the National Interest: A Critical Examination of American
Foreign Policy*. New York: Knopf, 1951.

Nation, R. Craig. *Black Earth, Red Star: A History of Soviet Security Policy, 1917–1991*.
Ithaca, NY: Cornell University Press, 1992.

Nau, Henry R. "Ideas Have Consequences: The Cold War and Today." *International Politics*
48, nos. 4–5 (September 2011): 460–81. http://dx.doi.org/10.1057/ip.2011.19.

Naumkin, Vitaly V. "Russian Policy toward Kazakhstan." In *Thinking Strategically: The
Major Powers, Kazakhstan, and the Central Asian Nexus*. Edited by Robert Legvold. Cambridge, MA: MIT Press, 2003.

Nicolas, Françoise. "China and the Global Economic Order." *China Perspectives*, no. 2
(June 2016): 7–14. http://journals.openedition.org/chinaperspectives/6960.

Nikonov, Vyacheslav. "Back to the Concert." *Russia in Global Affairs*, November 16, 2002.
http://eng.globalaffairs.ru/number/n_12.

———. "Ot Kontserta derzhav k Kontsertu tsivilizatsii." *Strategiia Rossii*, no. 11 (November 2012), http://sr.fondedin.ru/new/fullnews_arch_to.php?subaction=showfull&id
=1352195650&archive=1354788090&start_from=&ucat=14&.

———. *Probuzhdenie BRIK (The Awakening of BRIC)*. Moscow, Russia, 2009. http://www
.nkibrics.ru/system/asset_publications/data/544c/e6f9/6272/6925/e86f/0000/original/%
D0%9F%D1%80%D0%BE%D0%B1%D1%83%D0%B6%D0%B4%D0%B5%D0%
BD%D0%B8%D0%B5_%D0%91%D0%A0%D0%98%D0%9A_The_Awakening_of
_BRIC.pdf?1414326008.

Nikonov, V. A., and G. D. Toloraya, eds. *Strategiia Rossii v BRIKS: tseli i instrumenty*. Moscow:
RUDN Universitet, 2013.

Norling, Nicklas, and Niklas Swanström. "The Shanghai Cooperation Organization, Trade, and the Roles of Iran, India and Pakistan." *Central Asian Survey* 26, no. 3 (September 2007): 429–44. https://doi.org/10.1080/02634930701702779.

Nursha, Askar. "Evolution of Political Thought in Kazakhstan on the Problems of Eurasian Integration: 'Eurasia-Optimists' and 'Eurasia-Skeptics.'" Working Paper, Institute of World Economy and Politics. 2014. http://iwep.kz/files/attachments/article/2014–06 –05/evolution_of_political_thought_in_kazakhstan_on_the_problems_in_kazakhstan _of_eurasian_integration-eurasia-optimists_and_eurasia-skeptics.pdf.

Obama, Barack. "Statement by the President on Ukraine." White House website, March 17, 2014. https://obamawhitehouse.archives.gov/the-press-office/2014/03/17/statement -president-ukraine.

———. "Statement by the President on Ukraine." White House website, March 20, 2014. https://obamawhitehouse.archives.gov/the-press-office/2014/03/20/statement -president-ukraine.

Okuneva, Liudmila Sergeevna, and A. A. Orlov, eds. *Voskhodiashchie gosudarstva-giganty BRIKS: rol v mirovoi politike strategii modernizatsii, sbornik nauchnykh trudov.* Moscow: MGIMO Universitet, 2012.

O'Neill, Jim. "Building Better Global Economic BRICs." Goldman Sachs, Global Economics Paper No. 66. November 30, 2001. http://www.goldmansachs.com/our-thinking /archive/archive-pdfs/build-better-brics.pdf.

———. *The Growth Map: Economic Opportunity in the BRICs and Beyond.* New York: Portfolio/Penguin, 2011.

Orlov, A. A. "BRIKS: Novaia realnost XXI veka." In Okuneva and Orlov, *Voskhodiashchie gosudarstva-giganty BRIKS: rol v mirovoi politike strategii modernizatsii, sbornik nauchnykh trudov.* Moscow: MGIMO Universitet, 2012.

Panda, Ankit. "The Asian Infrastructure Investment Bank Is Open for Business: What Now?" *Diplomat*, January 19, 2016. https://thediplomat.com/2016/01/the-asian-infra structure-investment-bank-is-open-for-business-what-now/.

Panova, Victoria. "BRIKS: Mesto Rossii v Gruppe, videnie i prakticheskie rezultaty, sovmestnaia deiatelnost 'piaterki' v ramkakh mnogostoronnikh institutov." In *Strategiia Rossii v BRIKS: Tseli i instrumenty.* Edited by V. A. Nikonov and G. D. Toloraya. Moscow: Rossiiskii Universitet Druzhby Narodov, 2013.

———. "Mesto Rossii v BRIKS: videnie i prakticheskie rezultaty. Vlianie vneshnikh igrokov vzaimodeistviia v 'klube.'" *Vsia Evropa i Luxemburg* 68, no. 7–8 (2012). http:// alleuropalux.org/?p=3927.

———. "Russia in the BRICS." Open talk, June 28, 2012. https://www.academia.edu /1922238/Russia_in_the_BRICS.

Pant, Harsh V. "Feasibility of the Russia-China-India 'Strategic Triangle': Assessment of Theoretical and Empirical Issues." *International Studies* 43, no. 1 (January 1, 2006): 51–72. https://doi.org/10.1177/002088170504300103.

———. "India-Russia Ties and India's Strategic Culture: Dominance of a Realist Worldview." *India Review* 12, no. 1 (March 2013): 1–19.

Pant, Harsh V., and Yogesh Joshi. "Indo-US Relations under Modi: The Strategic Logic Underlying the Embrace." *International Affairs* 93, no. 1 (January 2017): 133–46. https:// www.chathamhouse.org//node/27162.

———. "Russia: European or Not?" In *Europe Today: A Twenty-First Century Introduction.* Edited by Ronald Tiersky and Erik Jones. 4th ed. Lanham, MD: Rowman & Littlefield, 2011.

Paulson, Henry M. *On the Brink: Inside the Race to Stop the Collapse of the Global Financial System*. New York: Business Plus, 2010.

Payne, Anthony. "The G8 in a Changing Global Economic Order." *International Affairs* 84, no. 3 (May 2008): 519–33. https://doi.org/10.1111/j.1468–2346.2008.00721.x.

Pew Research Center. "Global Unease with Major World Powers." *47 Nation Pew Global Attitudes Survey*. The Pew Global Attitudes Research Project, June 27, 2007. http://assets.pewresearch.org/wp-content/uploads/sites/2/pdf/2007%20Pew%20Global%20Attitudes%20Report%20-%20June%2027.pdf.

PricewaterhouseCoopers. "The World in 2050." February 2017. https://www.pwc.com/gx/en/issues/economy/the-world-in-2050.html.

Putin, Vladimir. "Address by President of the Russian Federation." March 18, 2014, Moscow. http://en.kremlin.ru/events/president/news/20603.

———. "Address to the Federal Assembly of the Russian Federation." December 12, 2012, Moscow. http://en.kremlin.ru/events/president/news/17118.

———. "Address to the Federal Assembly of the Russian Federation." December 12, 2013, Moscow. http://en.kremlin.ru/events/president/news/19825.

———. "Address to the Federal Assembly of the Russian Federation." December 4, 2014, Moscow. http://en.kremlin.ru/events/president/news/47173.

———. "Address to Valdai International Discussion Club." XI Valdai International Discussion Club: The New World Order; New Rules or a Game without Rules, Sochi, Russia, October 24, 2014. http://en.kremlin.ru/events/president/news/46860.

———. "Mezhdunarodnyi forum 'Odin Poias, Odin Put.'" Speech at the opening of the Belt and Road International Cooperation Forum, Beijing, China, May 14, 2017. http://kremlin.ru/events/president/news/54491.

———. "Novyi integratsionnyi proekt dlia Evrazii—budushchee, kotoroe rozhdaetsia sigodnia." *Izvestiia*, October 3, 2011. http://izvestia.ru/news/502761.

———. "Obrashchemie Presidenta Rossiiskoi Federatsii." March 18, 2014, Moscow. http://kremlin.ru/events/president/news/20603.

———. "Poslanie k Federalnomu Sobraniiu Rossiiskoi Federatsii." Speech, July 8, 2000, Moscow. http://archive.kremlin.ru/text/appears/2000/07/28782.shtml.

———. "Poslanie k Federalnomu Sobraniiu Rossiiskoi Federatsii." Speech, April 3, 2001, Moscow. http://archive.kremlin.ru/text/appears/2001/04/28514.shtml.

———. "Poslanie k Federalnomu Sobraniiu Rossiiskoi Federatsii." Speech, April 18, 2002, Moscow. http://2002.kremlin.ru/events/510.html.

———. "Poslanie k Federalnomu Sobraniiu Rossiiskoi Federatsii." Speech, May 16, 2003, Moscow. http://archive.kremlin.ru/text/appears/2003/05/44623.shtml.

———. "Poslanie k Federalnomu Sobraniiu Rossiiskoi Federatsii." Speech, May 26, 2004, Moscow. http://archive.kremlin.ru/text/appears/2004/05/71501.shtml.

———. "Poslanie k Federalnomu Sobraniiu Rossiiskoi Federatsii." Speech, April 25, 2005, Moscow. http://archive.kremlin.ru/text/appears/2005/04/87049.shtml.

———. "Poslanie k Federalnomu Sobraniiu Rossiiskoi Federatsii." Speech, May 10, 2006, Moscow. http://archive.kremlin.ru/text/appears/2006/05/105546.shtml.

———. "Poslanie k Federalnomu Sobraniiu Rossiiskoi Federatsii." Speech, April 26, 2007, Moscow. http://archive.kremlin.ru/text/appears/2007/04/125339.shtml.

———. "Presidential Address to the Federal Assembly." Speech, December 3, 2015, Moscow. http://en.kremlin.ru/events/president/news/50864.

————. "Presidential Address to the Federal Assembly." Speech, December 1, 2016, Moscow. http://en.kremlin.ru/events/president/news/53379.

————. "Press Statement following the BRICS Summit." Fifth BRICS Summit, March 27, 2013, Durban, South Africa. http://en.kremlin.ru/events/president/transcripts /17756.

————. "Russia at the Turn of the Millennium." December 30, 1999. http://pages.uoregon .edu/kimball/Putin.htm.

————. "Speech at BRICS Summit Plenary Session." Speech, July 15, 2014, Fortaleza, Brazil. http://eng.kremlin.ru/transcripts/22677.

Raghavan, P. S. "BRICS: Still under Construction." Policy Brief. New Delhi, India: Ananta Aspen Center, September 2016. http://www.anantaaspencentre.in/pdf/BRICS _still_under_construction_10_10_2016.pdf.

Remnick, David. "Watching the Eclipse." *New Yorker*, August 11, 2014. http://www.new yorker.com/magazine/2014/08/11/watching-eclipse.

Research Centre for International Cooperation and Development. "Meeting with Vadim B. Lukov Ambassador-at-Large of the Russian Ministry of Foreign Affairs." July 6, 2010. http://en.rcicd.org/news/meeting-with-vadim-b-lukov/.

Riasanovsky, Nicholas, and Mark Steinberg. *A History of Russia since 1855*. Vol. 2. 8th ed. New York: Oxford University Press, 2010.

Roberts, Cynthia. "Building the New World Order BRIC by BRIC." *European Financial Review*, 2011, 8. http://www.mid.ru/brics.nsf/8aab06cc61208e47c325786800383727 /0076861093dc5f86c32578bc0045fca4/$FILE/Cynthia%20Roberts.pdf.

————. "Russia's BRICs Diplomacy: Rising Outsider with Dreams of an Insider." *Polity* 42, no. 1 (January 2010): 38–73. https://doi.org/10.1057/pol.2009.18.

Ruggie, John Gerard. Foreword to Thomas G. Weiss and Ramesh Thakur, *Global Governance and the UN: An Unfinished Journey*. Bloomington: Indiana University Press, 2010.

Sadovnichy, V. A., Y. V. Yakovets, and A. A. Akaev, eds. *Perspektivy i strategicheskie prioritety voskhozhdeniia BRIKS*. Moscow: SCII-INES-NCR BRICS, 2014.

Safranchuk, Ivan. "BRIC Agenda and Instruments." In *BRIC and the New World Order: Perspectives from Brazil, China, India and Russia*. Edited by Nandan Unnikrishnan and Samir Saran. New Delhi: Observer Research Foundation, with Macmillan Publishers India, 2010.

Sakwa, Richard. "The Problem of 'the International' in Russian Identity Formation." *International Politics* 49, no. 4 (July 2012): 449–65. http://dx.doi.org/10.1057/ip .2012.10.

Salzman, Rachel S. "From Bridge to Bulwark: The Evolution of BRICS in Russian Grand Strategy / De puente a fortaleza: La evolución de los países BRICS en la estrategia global de Rusia." *Comillas Journal of International Relations* 3 (2015): 1–13. http://revis tas.upcomillas.es/index.php/internationalrelations/article/view/5523.

————. "U.S. Policy toward Russia: A Review of Policy Recommendations." Designing U.S. Policy towards Russia. Cambridge, MA: American Academy of Arts & Sciences, May 2010. http://www.amacad.org/russia/recommendations.pdf.

Saran, Samir. "From Cold War to Hot Peace: Why the Mighty BRICS Matter." *National Interest*, July 16, 2015. http://nationalinterest.org/blog/the-buzz/cold-war-hot-peace -why-the-mighty-brics-matter-13349.

———. "India's Contemporary Plurilateralism." In *The Oxford Handbook on Indian Foreign Policy*, edited by David Malone, C. Raja Mohan, and Srinath Raghavan, 623–35. Oxford: Oxford University Press, 2015.

Saran, Samir, and Abhijnan Rej. "BRICS, Globalisms, and the Return of the State." Observer Research Foundation, *Raisina Debates*, August 31, 2016. https://www.orfonline .org/expert-speak/brics-globalisms-and-the-return-of-the-state/.

Saran, Samir, Ashok Kumar Singh, and Vivan Sharan. "A Long-Term Vision for BRICS." Submission to the BRICS Academic Forum. Observer Research Foundation, 2013. https://samirsaran.com/2013/09/02/a-long-term-vision-for-brics/.

Sarotte, M. E. "A Broken Promise? What the West Really Told Moscow about NATO Expansion." *Foreign Affairs* 93, no. 5 (September 2014): 90–97. https://doi.org/http:// www.foreignaffairs.com/archive.

———. *1989: The Struggle to Create Post-Cold War Europe*. Princeton, NJ: Princeton University Press, 2009.

Satter, David. *It Was a Long Time Ago, and It Never Happened Anyway: Russia and the Communist Past*. New Haven, CT: Yale University Press, 2012.

Scott, Robert L. "Cold War and Rhetoric: Conceptually and Critically." In Martin J. Medhurst, Robert L. Ivie, Philip Wander, and Robert L. Scott, *Cold War Rhetoric: Strategy, Metaphor, and Ideology*. East Lansing: Michigan State University Press, 1997.

Sergunin, Alexander. "Understanding Russia's Policies towards BRICS: Theory and Practice." In *Russian Politics*. Singapore: International Studies Association, 2015. http:// web.isanet.org/Web/Conferences/GSCIS%20Singapore%202015/Archive/55c376c8 -7911-42be-b13d-22867ff8ea2a.pdf.

Shambaugh, David, and Ren Xiao. "China: The Conflicted Rising Power." In *Worldviews of Aspiring Powers: Domestic Foreign Policy Debates in China, India, Iran, Japan, and Russia*. Edited by Henry R. Nau and Eepa Ollapally, 36–72. Oxford: Oxford University Press, 2013.

Shevtsova, Lilia. *Lonely Power: Why Russia Has Failed to Become the West and the West Is Weary of Russia*. Washington, DC: Carnegie Endowment for International Peace, 2010.

———. "Post-Communist Russia: A Historic Opportunity Missed." *International Affairs* 83, no. 5 (September 2007): 891–912. https://doi.org/10.1111/j.1468–2346.2007 .00661.x.

Shiraev, Eric, and Vladislav Zubok. *Anti-Americanism in Russia: From Stalin to Putin*. New York: Palgrave, 2000.

Shubin, V. G. "Ot BRIK k BRIKS: Rol IuAR v sostave gruppy i v kontinentalnom kontekste." In *Voskhodiashchie gosudarstva-giganty BRIKS: Rol v mirovoi politike, strategii modernizatsii—sbornik nauchnykh trudov*. Edited by L. S. Okuneva and A. A. Orlov. Moscow: MGIMO–Universitet, 2012.

Shuster, Simon. "Putin's Man in Crimea Is Ukraine's Worst Nightmare." *Time*, March 10, 2014. http://time.com/19097/putin-crimea-russia-ukraine-aksyonov/.

Silvius, Ray. "The Embedding of Russian State-Sanctioned Multipolarity in the Post-Soviet Conjuncture." *Globalizations* 13, no. 1 (January 2, 2016): 1–15. https://doi.org/10 .1080/14747731.2015.1102944.

Sin, Li. "Strany BRIKS: ukrepliaia sotrudnichestvo." *Mezhdunarodnaia zhizn* 2 (February 2012).

Singh, Manmohan. "Opening Remarks by the Prime Minister of India Dr. Manmohan Singh at the Plenary Session of the First BRIC Summit." Presented at the First BRIC

Summit, January 16, 2009, Ekaterinburg, Russia. http://archivepmo.nic.in/drmanmo hansingh/speech-details.php?nodeid=763.

———. "Opening Statement by the Prime Minister of India Dr. Manmohan Singh at the Plenary Session of the BRIC Summit." Presented at the Second BRIC Summit, April 15, 2010, Brasilia, Brazil. http://archivepmo.nic.in/drmanmohansingh/speech-details .php?nodeid=881.

———. "Prime Minister's Statement at the Plenary Session of the 5th BRICS Summit." Presented at the Fifth BRICS Summit, March 27, 2013, Durban, South Africa. http:// archivepmo.nic.in/drmanmohansingh/speech-details.php?nodeid=1296.

———. "Prime Minister's Statement at the Plenary Session of the Fourth BRICS Summit." Presented at the Fourth BRICS Summit, March 29, 2012, Delhi, India. http:// archivepmo.nic.in/drmanmohansingh/speech-details.php?nodeid=1156.

———. "Statement by the Prime Minister of India Dr. Manmohan Singh at the Plenary Session of BRICS Leaders." Presented at the Third BRICS Summit, April 14, 2011, Sanya, China. http://archivepmo.nic.in/drmanmohansingh/speech-details.php?nodeid =1012.

Singh, Nitya. "How to Tame Your Dragon: An Evaluation of India's Foreign Policy toward China." *India Review* 11, no. 3 (July 2012): 139–60. https://doi.org/10.1080/14736489 .2012.705632.

Smith, Martin A. "Russia and Multipolarity since the End of the Cold War." *East European Politics* 29, no. 1 (March 1, 2013): 36–51. https://doi.org/10.1080/21599165.2013 .764481.

"South Asia and the Gulf Lead Rising Trend in Arms Imports, Russian Exports Grow." Stockholm International Peace Research Institute, March 17, 2014. https://www.sipri .org/media/press-release/2014/south-asia-and-gulf-lead-rising-trend-arms-imports -russian-exports-grow-says-sipri.

Standish, Reid. "China and Russia Lay Foundation for Massive Economic Cooperation." *Foreign Policy*, July 10, 2015. https://foreignpolicy.com/2015/07/10/china-russia-sco-ufa -summit-putin-xi-jinping-eurasian-union-silk-road/.

Stapran, N. V. "'Treugolnik Primakova' v ramkakh BRIKS i ne tolko." In *Voskhodiashchie gosudarstva-giganty BRIKS: rol v mirovoi politike, strategii modernizatsii.* Edited by A. A. Orlov and L. S. Okuneva. Moscow: MGIMO Universitet, 2012.

Stent, Angela. *The Limits of Partnership: U.S.-Russian Relations in the Twenty-First Century.* Princeton, NJ: Princeton University Press, 2014.

———. "Reluctant Europeans." In *Russian Foreign Policy in the Twenty-First Century and the Shadow of the Past.* Edited by Robert Legvold. New York: Columbia University Press, 2007.

———. "Restoration and Revolution in Putin's Foreign Policy." *Europe-Asia Studies* 60, no. 6 (August 2008): 1089–106. https://doi.org/10.1080/09668130802161264.

Stuenkel, Oliver. *The BRICS and the Future of Global Order.* Lanham, MD: Lexington Books, 2015.

———. Connecting the Global South: Why the BRICS Academic Forum Matters." *Post-Western World*, May 23, 2015. http://www.postwesternworld.com/2015/05/23/connect ing-academic-matters/.

———. "Emerging Powers and Status: The Case of the First BRICs Summit." *Asian Perspective* 38, no. 1 (March 2014): 89–109. http://journals.rienner.com/doi/abs/10.5555 /0258-9184-38.1.89.

———. "The Financial Crisis, Contested Legitimacy, and the Genesis of Intra-BRICS Cooperation." *Global Governance* 19, no. 4 (October 2013): 611–30.

———. "The G7 and the BRICS in the Post-Crimea World Order." Valdai Paper presented at the Valdai Club, May 2015. https://www.scribd.com/doc/264366607/Valdai -Paper-14-The-G7-and-the-BRICS-in-the-Post-Crimea-World-Order.

———. "The Politics of Next Year's BRICS Summit in Russia." *Post-Western World*, October 31, 2014. http://www.postwesternworld.com/2014/10/31/politics-summit-russia/.

———. *Post-Western World: How Emerging Powers Are Remaking Global Order*. Cambridge: Polity Press, 2016.

———. "The Uncertain Future of IBSA." Carnegie Endowment for International Peace, February 18, 2015. https://carnegieendowment.org/2015/02/18/uncertain-future-of-ibsa -pub-59108.

Sutter, Robert G. *Chinese Foreign Relations: Power and Policy since the Cold War*. 4th ed. Asia in World Politics. Lanham, MD: Rowan & Littlefield, 2016.

Talbott, Strobe. "Dangerous Leviathans." *Foreign Policy*, no. 172 (May–June 2009).

Taylor, Brian D. *State Building in Putin's Russia: Policing and Coercion after Communism*. Cambridge: Cambridge University Press, 2011.

Thayer, Carlyle A. "Does Russia Have a South China Sea Problem?" *National Interest*, September 27, 2016. http://nationalinterest.org/blog/the-buzz/does-russia-have-south -china-sea-problem-17853.

"The Strategy for BRICS Economic Partnership." Ufa, Russia: BRICS, July 2015.

Titarenko, M., and V. Petrovsky. "Russia, China and the New World Order." *International Affairs* 61, no. 3 (2015): 13.

Titarenko, M. L., and S. V. Ulianaev. "Perspektivy formata BRIK: Vzgliad is chetyryekh stolits." *Aziia i Afrika segodnia*, no. 5 (May 2010): 2–8. http://dlib.eastview.com/browse /doc/22043433.

Tjalve, Vibeke Schou, and Michael C. Williams. "Reviving the Rhetoric of Realism: Politics and Responsibility in Grand Strategy." *Security Studies* 24, no. 1 (January 2, 2015): 37–60. https://doi.org/10.1080/09636412.2015.1003725.

Toloraya, Georgii, and Roman Chukov. "BRICS to Be Considered?" *International Organisations Research Journal* 11, no. 2 (June 21, 2016): 97–112. https://doi.org/10.17323/1996 -7845-2016-02-97.

Trenin, Dmitri. *From Greater Europe to Greater Asia? The Sino-Russian Entente*. Carnegie Endowment for International Peace, April 1, 2015. http://carnegieendowment.org /files/CP_Trenin_To_Asia_WEB_2015Eng.pdf.

———. "Russia Leaves the West." *Foreign Affairs* 85, no. 4 (July 1, 2006): 87–96. https:// doi.org/10.2307/20032043.

———. "Thinking Strategically about Russia." Policy Brief. Foreign Policy for the Next President. Washington, DC: Carnegie Endowment for International Peace, December 2008. http://carnegieendowment.org/files/thinking_strategically_russia.pdf.

Tsygankov, Andrei P. "Preserving Influence in a Changing World." *Problems of Post-Communism* 58, no. 2 (April 3, 2011): 28–44. https://www.tandfonline.com/doi/abs/10 .2753/PPC1075-8216580203.

———. *Russia's Foreign Policy: Change and Continuity in National Identity*. 2nd ed. Lanham, MD: Rowman & Littlefield, 2010.

———. *Whose World Order? Russia's Perception of American Ideas after the Cold War*. Notre Dame, IN: University of Notre Dame Press, 2004.

Ünay, Sadik. "Reality or Mirage? BRICS and the Making of Multipolarity in the Global Political Economy." *Insight Turkey* 15, no. 3 (Summer 2013): 77–94. https://www.insightturkey.com/article/reality-or-mirage-brics-and-the-making-of-multipolarity-in-the-global-political-economy.

United Nations. "General Assembly Adopts Resolution Calling upon States Not to Recognize Changes in Status of Crimea Region." Meetings Coverage and Press Releases, March 27, 2014. https://www.un.org/press/en/2014/ga11493.doc.htm.

United Nations General Assembly. "68/262. Territorial Integrity of Ukraine." United Nations, March 27, 2014. http://www.un.org/en/ga/search/view_doc.asp?symbol=A/RES/68/262.

Unnikrishnan, Nandan, and Uma Purushothaman. "Trends in Russia-China Relations: Implications for India." New Delhi, India: Observer Research Foundation, 2015. http://www.orfonline.org/research/trends-in-russia-china-relations-implications-for-india/.

Unnikrishnan, Nandan, and Samir Saran, eds. *BRIC in the New World Order: Perspectives from Brazil, China, India and Russia*. New Delhi: Observer Research Foundation, with Macmillan Publishers India, 2010.

Vice, Margaret. "Publics Worldwide Unfavorable toward Putin, Russia." Pew Research Center, August 16, 2017. http://www.pewglobal.org/2017/08/16/publics-worldwide-unfavorable-toward-putin-russia/.

Vinokurov, Evgeny. "Eurasian Economic Union: Current State and Preliminary Results." *Russian Journal of Economics* 3, no. 1 (March 1, 2017): 54–70. https://doi.org/10.1016/j.ruje.2017.02.004.

Vlaskin, G. A., S. P. Glinkina, and E. B. Lenchuk. "Sotrudnichestvo so stranami BRIKS v interesakh modernizatsii rossiiskoi ekonomiki." In *Strategiia Rossii v BRIKS: Tseli i instrumenty*. Edited by V. A. Nikonov and G. D. Toloraya. Moscow: RUDN Universitet, 2013.

Wallander, Celeste A. "Russia: The Domestic Sources of a Less-Than-Grand Strategy." In *Strategic Asia 2007–08: Domestic Political Change and Grand Strategy*. Edited by Ashley J. Tellis and Michael Wills. Seattle: National Bureau of Asian Research, 2007.

Ward, Steven Michael. "Status Immobility and Systemic Revisionism in Rising Great Powers." PhD diss., Georgetown University, 2012. https://repository.library.georgetown.edu/handle/10822/557606.

Weber, Steve. *The End of Arrogance: America in the Global Competition of Ideas*. Cambridge, MA: Harvard University Press, 2010.

Weiss, Thomas George, and Ramesh Thakur. *Global Governance and the UN: An Unfinished Journey*. Bloomington: Indiana University Press, 2010.

Weitz, Richard. "The Rise and Fall of Medvedev's European Security Treaty." Washington, DC: German Marshal Fund of the United States, May 2012. http://www.gmfus.org/publications/rise-and-fall-medvedev%E2%80%99s-european-security-treaty.

White House. "FACT SHEET: U.S. Missile Defense Policy: A Phased, Adaptive Approach for Missile Defense in Europe." Accessed May 6, 2015. https://www.whitehouse.gov/node/4873.

Wilson, Dominic, and Roopa Purushothaman. "Dreaming with BRICs: The Path to 2050." Goldman Sachs, Global Economics Paper No. 99. October 2003. http://www.goldmansachs.com/our-thinking/archive/archive-pdfs/brics-dream.pdf.

Wojczewski, Thorsten. "China's Rise as a Strategic Challenge and Opportunity: India's China Discourse and Strategy." *India Review* 15, no. 1 (January 2, 2016): 22–60. https://doi.org/10.1080/14736489.2015.1092748.

Woods, Ngaire. *Globalizers: The IMF, the World Bank, and Their Borrowers*. Ithaca, NY: Cornell University Press, 2006.

World Bank Group. "Global Economic Prospects, January 2015: Having Fiscal Space and Using It." January 13, 2015. http://documents.worldbank.org/curated/en/444361468127152333/Global-economic-prospects-January-2015-having-fiscal-space-and-using-it.

Xi Jinping. *The Governance of China*. Beijing: Foreign Languages Press, 2014. https://catalyst.library.jhu.edu/catalog/bib_5077942.

———. "Jointly Shoulder Responsibility of Our Times, Promote Global Growth." Keynote Speech by H. E. Xi Jinping President of the People's Republic of China at the Opening Session of the World Economic Forum Annual Meeting 2017, Davos, January 17, 2017. CGTN America. https://america.cgtn.com/2017/01/17/full-text-of-xi-jinping-keynote-at-the-world-economic-forum.

———. "Work Together to Build the Silk Road Economic Belt and the 21st Century Maritime Silk Road." Speech by H. E. Xi Jinping, President of the People's Republic of China, at the Opening Ceremony of the Belt and Road Forum for International Cooperation. Beijing, China, May 14, 2017. http://www.xinhuanet.com/english/2017-05/14/c_136282982.htm.

———. "Working Together to Usher in the Second 'Golden Decade' of BRICS Cooperation." Speech by H. E. Xi Jingping, President of the People's Republic of China, at the Opening Ceremony of the BRICS Business Forum, Xiamen, September 3, 2017. Ministry of Foreign Affairs of the People's Republic of China. http://www.fmprc.gov.cn/mfa_eng/zxxx_662805/t1489623.shtml.

"Xi Jinping Sends Letters to Leaders of Other BRICS Countries on China's Assumption of BRICS Presidency." Ministry of Foreign Affairs of the People's Republic of China, January 1, 2017. http://www.fmprc.gov.cn/mfa_eng/zxxx_662805/t1428185.shtml.

Xiang, Lanxin. "China and the International 'Liberal' (Western) Order." In *Liberal Order in a Post-Western World*. Edited by Trine Flockhart, Charles A. Kupchan, Christina Lin, Bartlomiej E. Nowak, Patrick W. Quirk, and Lanxin Xiang. Washington, DC: German Marshall Fund of the United States, 2014.

Ye Yu. "BRICS New Development Bank Moves Ahead Quietly." *Interpreter*, June 25, 2015. https://www.lowyinstitute.org/the-interpreter/brics-new-development-bank-moves-ahead-quietly.

Zagorski, Andrei. "Russian Approaches to Global Governance in the 21st Century." *Internationale Spectator* 45, no. 4 (2010): 27–42. https://doi.org/10.1080/03932729.2010.527099.

Zhao Suisheng. "Chinese Foreign Policy as a Rising Power to Find Its Rightful Place." *Perceptions* 18, no. 1 (Spring 2013): 101–28. http://sam.gov.tr/chinese-foreign-policy-as-a-rising-power-to-find-its-rightful-place/.

Zheng, Yongnian, and Liang Fook Lye. "China's Foreign Policy: Pursuing a More Active Foreign Policy while Upholding Its National Interests." *East Asian Policy* 6, no. 1 (January 1, 2014): 20–33. https://doi.org/10.1142/S1793930514000026.

Index

Figures and notes are indicated by f and n following the page number.

academic research on BRICS, 77–81, 82
Afghanistan, troop resupply routes, 71, 88
Aksyonov, Sergei, 91, 107
Amorim, Celso, 25, 83–84n23
Anti-Ballistic Missile Treaty (1972), 47–48
anticolonialism, in nonalignment, 121
anti-sanctions, xx
anti-Westernism, xix, 101–9, 118–19
Armenia, support for Crimean annexation, 96
arms and armaments: arms sales, 125, 129, 136n69; missile defense, 49, 72
Arms Control and International Security Working Group (Bilateral Presidential Commission), 71, 72
Asia, financial crisis (1997), 17
Asian Development Bank, 132
Asian Infrastructure and Investment Bank (AIIB): China's influence on, 137n93; China's use of, 43n77, 131, 132; democratic equity and, 126; NDB and, 33–34, 132
Association of Southeast Asian Nations (ASEAN), 121
Atlanticists, 6, 7

balance of power, multipolarity and, 14
Belarus: Crimean annexation, support for, 96; customs union with, 75; economic cooperation and, 12; security organizations, membership in, 13

Belgium, voting shares in IMF, 106
Belt and Road Forum for International Cooperation (2017), 133, 138
Belt and Road Initiative (BRI): China's influence on, 131, 132, 137n93, 140; Eurasian cooperation on, 109; India's concerns over, 133; Russia and, 125; sovereignty and, 126; Xi on, 138
Bilateral Presidential Commission (Arms Control and International Security Working Group), 71, 72
Brasilia Declaration (2003), 26
Brazil: BRIC, role in, 31; and BRIC, organization of, 27–28; GDP, 35f, 36, 37f; human rights concerns, 96; IBSA and, 26; O5 and, 27; political crisis in, 124, 125, 140
Brazil Russia India China South Africa. *See* BRICS
Brexit, 142
Brezhnev, Leonid, 54
BRI. *See* Belt and Road Initiative
BRIC (Brazil Russia India China): appearance as term, 24; balancing efforts by, 58; BRICS versus, 42n46; Foreign Policy Concept (2008) on, 69–70; global financial crisis and, 139; organization of, 27–29; Putin on, 67; Russian's foreign policy, role in, 59; Russia's inclusion in, 44–45; Survey on Russian Foreign Policy on, 51

BRICS (Brazil Russia India China South
Africa): antihegemonic nature of, 18;
anti-Westernism and, 101–9; BRIC versus, 42n46; conclusions on, 138–44;
concretization of Russian approach to,
99–101; Crimean annexation, response
to, 95–96; economic slowdown across,
124; effectiveness of, 39; establishment
of, role of anti-US sentiment in, 17;
focus of, in early 2010s, 64; hostilities
against, foreign ministers' response to,
88; implosion of, possibility of, 140–41;
institutional creation in, xix, 39–40,
97–98; intra-BRICS cooperation,
38–40, 79–80, 97, 123; intra-BRICS
practicalities, after Ukraine crisis,
96–101; origins of, xix, 25–27; overview
of, 13; political economy rationale for,
xviii; Putin on, 102; raising awareness
of, 101; rhetorical conception of, xx;
Russian conception of, 77; terms for, 24.
See also Ukraine crisis, BRICS and;
Russia after; additional entries beginning
"BRICS"
BRICS, in Russian foreign policy, 63–83;
BRICS in Russian intellectual circles,
77–81; conclusions on, 82–83; discussion of, 66–77; introduction to,
xix–xx, 63–65; Medvedev and, 65–66;
Russian desire to use BRICS as bridge,
81–82
BRICS, institutional history of, 23–40;
BRICS, beginnings of, 24–34; BRICS,
statistics on, 34–40; conclusions on,
40; introduction to, xix, 23–24
BRICS, non-Russian perspectives on, 118–
33; Chinese foreign policy, BRICS in,
127–33; conclusions on, 133; Indian
foreign policy, BRICS in, 119–27;
introduction to, xx, 118–19
BRICS, rhetorical foundation for, 44–60;
conclusions on, 59–60; introduction to,
xix, 44–45; Putin's rhetorical balancing, restoring balance to, 57–58;
Russia, civilizational discourse and,
55–57; Russia, evolving national

identity of, 51–55; sovereignty, inde-
pendence and, 45–51
BRICS Think Tank Network (China), 32
BRICS Think Tanks Council (BTTC),
32, 86n96
Britain. See United Kingdom
B20 (international business group), 32
budgetary institutions, 78
Bush, George H. W., 8
Bush, George W., 17, 66
Business Forum (BRIC/BRICS), 32, 74, 77

Carnegie Endowment for International
Peace, poll on attitudes toward Stalin,
55
Central Bank of Russia, 100
China: GDP, 35f, 36–37, 37f, 38, 127;
NDB, views on, 33; RIC, interest in, 26
China, BRICS and: BRICS events, 39;
BRICS presidency, 133; BRICS Think
Tank Network, 32; foreign policy of,
BRICS in, 119, 127–33; intra-BRICS
economic relations and, 38, 40
China, foreign relations: anti-Westernism,
118–19; India, relationship with, 123–
24; infrastructure lending, 43n77; O5
and, 27; Russia, relationship with, 71,
98–99, 112, 125, 128–30; Ukraine,
investments in, 107; UNSC expansion,
position on, 31; US, relationship with,
129–30; US securities holdings, 68;
West's relationship with, 144n11
China-Pakistan Economic Corridor, 126
China's Peaceful Development Road (Hu
foreign policy), 128
Civil Forum (BRICS), 97
civilizations, multiplicity of, 56
Clinton, Hillary, 71
Clunan, Anne, 4
Cold War, US rhetoric of, 3–4
Collective Security Treaty Organization
(CSTO), 13
color revolutions, 48, 75
Commonwealth of Independent States
(CIS), establishment of, 12
communism, Putin on, 52

Comprehensive Convention on International Terrorism (UN), 123
"Concept of Participation of the Russian Federation in BRICS" (policy document, 2013), 77, 99–100
"Concept of the Russian Federation's Presidency in BRICS in 2015–2016" (policy document), 99–100
Conference for Security and Cooperation in Europe (CSCE, later OSCE), 8
Congress (US), lack of action on IMF reforms, 31, 116n108
constructive cooperation, as future BRICS scenario, 141–42
Contingency Reserve Arrangement (CRA), 33, 97, 142
counterculturalism, 52, 56–57
Crimea, Russian annexation of, 90–91, 94–96
Customs Union, 12, 13, 76
Czech Republic, missile defense sites in, 49, 72

Davos World Economic Forum, 132
Davydov, Vladimir, 104–5, 111
Deep and Comprehensive Free Trade Area (DCFTA) agreement, 89–90
democracy, as political norm, 30
democratic equity, 125
Deng Xiaoping, 128
Deutsche Bank, 25
developing countries, India and, 121
development financing, China and, 33
"Dialogue among Civilizations" (Ministry of Foreign Affairs), 56
differentiated responsibility, 141
dilemma of rising powers, 131
Doklam Pass dispute, 141
domestic political pressures, impact of, 10
Duma, actions on BRICS, 110
Durban summit (BRICS), 76–77

Eastern Europe, US rhetoric on, 3
economics: economic development, 58, 74–75, 128, 132; economic norms, 30; economic policies, under Medvedev, 72–74; economic power, Russian appreciation of, 15; economic relations, among New Independent States, 12; economic relations, intra-BRICS, 38–40, 97; economic slowdown across BRICS, 124–25; global economic governance, 9–10, 15–16, 29, 106, 130, 132; global financial crisis (2008), 31–34, 64, 67–68, 71, 128, 139; India's economic crisis, 120; Pareto optimal solutions and, 116n106; world economy, BRICS and, 35–38, 35f, 36f, 37f
elites: BRICS, conception of, 82; foreign policy elites, 4–5, 6–7; multiplicity of opinions of, 66; political elite, Western orientation of, 57, 103; on Russian foreign policy goals, 11
emerging economies, underrepresentation in IMF, 17–18
Eurasian Economic Community, 12
Eurasianists, Atlanticists versus, 6
Eurasian Union (EEU), 75–77, 89, 109–10, 129
Euro-Atlantic order, Russian conflicts with, 89
Euromaidan Revolution, 82–83, 89–90
European Bank for Reconstruction and Development, 132
European Security Treaty (EST), 70
European Union (EU), 29, 94–95, 105, 142

Federal Assembly, presidential addresses to: meaning of, 5; by Medvedev, 67, 72, 74; by Putin, 46–47, 52–53, 76, 102, 109–10
financial/economic global governance. See economics, global economic governance
foreign direct investments, 38, 71, 123–24
Foreign Policy Concepts: (2000), 14, 45, 52, 69; (2008), 65, 69; (2013), 76; (2016), 110; under Putin, 5
Foreign Policy Survey (2007), 56, 59
Fortaleza Declaration, 97, 139
Fortaleza summit (BRICS), 32–33, 96

fortress Russia mentality, 47, 143
France, GDP, 17, 36*f*, 37*f*

G7 (Group of Seven), 10, 35–36, 36*f*, 37*f*, 38
G8 (Group of Eight), 27, 53, 57, 81–82
G8+5 (Outreach 5, O5, Heiligendamm Process), 27
G20 (Group of Twenty), 27, 31, 57, 86n109
G77 (group of developing countries), 122
Gaddafi, Muammar, 75
Gaidar, Yegor, 9
Geithner, Timothy, 31
General Agreement on Tariffs and Trade, 9
geo-economics, 28, 108, 119, 130
Georgia, Russian war with (2008), 15, 67
globalization, Survey on Russian Foreign Policy on, 51
global norms: established powers and, 108; role of BRICS in challenging, 30, 110, 119, 122; Russia and, 9, 11, 15, 74, 77, 140; sources of, 30
global order: BRICS's impact on, 139–40; global development, BRI and, 138; global economic governance, 9–10, 15–16, 29, 106, 130, 132; global financial crisis (2008), 31–34, 64, 67–68, 71, 128, 139; global governance, 29–31, 68, 131, 140, 143; global institutions, 9–10, 81–82; global multipolarism, as Russian strategy, 13–14; international law, 22n100, 93; international security, 8; international stability, perceived threats to, 108; Putin on, 92–93; strategic uncertainty in, 138–44. *See also* international system, post-Soviet Russia and; World Trade Organization; *specific organizations, e.g., NATO*
global order, disruption of, Russia and BRICS and: BRICS, in Russian foreign policy, 63–83; BRICS, institutional history of, 23–40; BRICS, non-Russian perspectives on, 118–33; BRICS, rhetorical foundation for, 44–60; conclusions on, xx–xxi, 138–44; international system, post-Soviet Russia and, 1–19; introduction to, xviii–xxi;

Ukraine crisis, BRICS and Russia after, 88–112
Goldman Sachs, 24–25
Gorbachev, Mikhail, 8, 13
gosudarstvennosti (statehood), 47
Greater Eurasian Partnership, 109–11, 112, 132, 140
Great Patriotic War, 53–55
Great Power Balancers (Pragmatic Nationalists), 6–7
gross domestic product (GDP), of BRICS versus G7, 35–36, 35*f*, 37*f*, 38

Hu Jintao, 128, 129, 131, 133

IBSA (India-Brazil–South Africa Dialogue Forum), 26
IMF (International Monetary Fund): BRICS' demands on, 30–31; and economic power, changes in distribution of, 17–18; quota formula, bias of, 22n121; Russia's integration into, 10, 81; voting shares, revision of, 106–7; WTO, comparison with, 15–16
independence (in Russian foreign policy), sovereignty and, 45–51
India: anti-Westernism, 118–19; BRICS events and, 39; China, relationship with, 123–24; foreign policy of, BRICS in, 119–27, 133; GDP, 17, 35*f*, 36, 37*f*, 38; IBSA and, 26; O5 and, 27; Parliamentary Forum, reaction to, 108–9; RIC, interest in, 26; Russia, relationship with, 121, 125; SCO, membership in, 13; United States, relationship with, 126–27, 132–33, 140; West's relationship with, 144n11
Indo-Crimean Partnership, 107
Indo-Soviet Treaty of Cooperation and Friendship (1971), 120
institutional creation (Russia), post–Cold War, 12–13
institutionalization, of BRICS, xix, 39–40, 97–98, 109, 133, 141
integration dilemmas, 8
intellectual Russian circles, BRICS in, 64–65, 77–81

international ___. *See entries beginning* "global"

International Monetary Fund. *See* IMF

international system, post-Soviet Russia and, 1–19; conclusions on, 18–19; international system, post-1991 changes to, 16–18; introduction to, xix, 1–2; political rhetoric, meaning of, 2–5; post–Cold War order, Russian responses to, 11–16; Russia, the West and, 7–11; Russian foreign policy orientations, 6–7. *See also* global order

Iran, SCO and, 13

Iraq War, 48

Kamath, Kundapur Vaman, 33

Kashmir, territorial dispute over, 126

Kasyanov, Mikhail, 46

Kazakhstan: customs union with, 12, 75; security organizations, membership in, 13

Klitschko, Vitali, 93

Kosovo, war in, 17

Kozyrev, Andrei, 4, 7, 11

Kudrin, Alexei, 9, 68

Kyrgyzstan: economic cooperation and, 12; security organizations, membership in, 13

Lavrov, Sergei, 12, 42n58, 63, 68–71, 73, 109

Lehman Brothers, collapse of, 67

Libya, NATO intervention in, 75

Look East policy (India), 120–21

Lukov, Vadim, 79

Lukyanov, Fyodor, 103

Lula (Luiz Inácio Lula Da Silva), 23, 25, 41n34

Martynov, Boris, 104, 110–11

McFaul, Michael, 75

Medvedev, Dmitry, 63–67, 69–75, 78, 79

Memorial (organization for Stalin's victims), 55

Mezhdunarodnaia zhizn (*International Affairs*, journal), articles about BRICS, 79

Millennium Manifesto ("Russia at the Turn of the Millennium," Putin), 51–52, 56

Ministerstvo innostranykh del. *See* Ministry of Foreign Affairs

Ministry of Economic Development and Trade, 71

Ministry of Education and Science, 78

Ministry of External Affairs (India), 120–21

Ministry of Foreign Affairs (Ministerstvo innostranykh del, MID): authority of, 28; China, cooperation with, 125; on leaked foreign policy survey document, 72–73; Survey on Russian Foreign Policy (2007), 49, 50, 56–57; on US-Russian relations, 72

missile defense, 49, 72, 75

Modi, Narendra, 118, 121, 123, 126–27

Molotov–Ribbentrop Non-Aggression Pact, 54

Moscow State Institute of International Affairs (MGIMO), 79

multialignment, in India's foreign policy, 121

multipolarity: India and, 122; Medvedev and, 64; National Security Concept on, 52; Putin on, 50; as Russian foreign policy goal, 14, 45; Russian views on, 143

Munich Security Conference, Putin's speech at, 49–50, 59, 68, 70

National Committee for BRICS Research (NKI BRIKS), 32, 57, 79

national identity: modern, Putin's actions in constructing, 54; nature of, 1, 51–55; Putin on, xix, 52; rhetorical limitations on, 4. *See also* BRICS, rhetorical foundation for

National Security Agency (US), spying programs of, anger at, 106

National Security Concept (Russia) (2000), 45, 52

national sovereignty. *See* sovereignty

Nazarbayev, Nursultan, 76

Nehru, Jawaharlal, 120

New Development Bank (NDB), 32–34, 126, 132, 142
new world order, Russia's call for, 50
Nikonov, Vyacheslav, 78–79, 79–80
nonalignment, 120–22
non-Western world, idea of rise of, 24–25
norms, political, 30. *See also* global norms
North Atlantic Treaty Organization (NATO), 8–11, 13, 60n23
Northern Distribution Network, 71, 88
North Korea, support for Crimean annexation, 96
Novaya gazeta (newspaper), leaked articles on seizure of Crimea, 90–91
Nuclear Security Summit (2014), 95
Nuland, Victoria, 93

O5 (Outreach 5, G8+5, Heiligendamm Process), 27
Obama, Barack, and Obama administration, 66, 71, 72, 94, 116n114, 127
Observer Research Foundation (India), 32
O'Neill, Jim, 1, 18, 24, 28, 29
optics, of BRICS: importance of, 98–99, 130, 133, 141; India and, 122, 123, 127
Organization for Security and Cooperation in Europe (OSCE, formerly CSCE), 8, 12

Pakistan: China's support for, 123; Russia, joint military exercise with, 136n46; SCO, membership in, 13
Parliamentary Forum (BRICS), 97, 108–9
Paulson, Henry, 68
Poland, missile defense sites in, 49, 72
political elite, Western orientation of, 57, 103
political norms, 30
political rhetoric, xviii, 2–5, 101–5
polycentrism, 21n93
post–Cold War order, Russian responses to, 11–16
power, Russian conception of, 15
presidential speeches, role of, 5. *See also* Federal Assembly, presidential addresses to

Primakov, Evgenii, 13–14, 25, 48, 68
purchasing power parity (PPP), as measure of China's economy, 127
Putin, Vladimir: anti-sanctions, 99; and BRIC, organization of, 27–28; BRICS, impact on, 41n34, 64; Bush (George W.), relationship with, 47–48; Crimea annexation, justification for, 91–93; CSTO and, 13; economic development, emphasis on, 58; Eurasia, focus on, 110; Federal Assembly, presidential addresses to, 46–47, 52–53, 76, 102, 109–10; Foreign Policy Concept documents, 5; Great Patriotic War, invocation of memory of, 53–54; Medvedev, relationship to, 65; Munich Security Conference speech, 49–50, 59, 68, 70; return to presidency, 75–77; rhetoric of, 44–45, 51–52, 57–58, 101; ruling elites and, 66; sovereign globalization under, 15; stabilization, early focus on, 46. *See also* Federal Assembly, presidential addresses to
Putin, Vladimir, views of: anti-Westernism of, 101–5, 116n101; on communism, 52; on facing difficulties, 88; global economic governance values, agreement with, 9; on Parliamentary Forum, 97; on RIC, 26; on Russian-US relationship, 48; on Stalin, 55; the West, perceptions of, 143
Pyatt, Geoffrey R., 93

Rao, Narasimha, 120
regional security cooperation, 12
Responsibility to Protect (2005), 30
rhetoric, xviii, 2–3. *See also* BRICS, rhetorical foundation for; political rhetoric; Putin, Vladimir, rhetoric of
Rice, Condoleezza, 48
Right Sector (Ukrainian nationalist coalition), 92
rising powers, dilemma of, 131
Rosneft (state oil company), 71
Rousseff, Dilma, 96, 124

Russia: anti-sanctions, xx; anti-Westernism, xix, 105–9; and BRIC, organization of, 27–28; civilizational discourse and, 55–57; as distinct civilization, 57; global governance, views on, 143; international law, attitude toward, 22n100; leadership, event-driven nature of, 98; post-Soviet, international system and, 1–19; as revolutionary actor, xviii; Russian world, 55–57; sanctions against, 94–95, 99, 107–8; security organizations, membership in, 13; Ukraine crisis, impact of, 96–101, 140; UNSC and, 31, 114n44. *See also* national identity; Putin, Vladimir; Soviet Union; Ukraine crisis, BRICS and Russia after; *entries beginning "BRICS"*

Russia, BRICS and: BRICS, concretization of approach to, 99–101; BRICS chairmanship, impact of, 98; BRICS policy (2008), 66–71; BRICS policy (2009–11), 71–75; BRICS policy (2012–13), 75–77; BTTC, government chartering of members of, 86n96; intellectual circles, BRICS in, 77–81; post-Ukraine political rhetoric, BRICS versus West in, 101–5; Russia's desire to use BRICS as bridge, 81–82; Russia's real goal regarding BRICS, 80–81

Russia, economy: economic cooperation and, 12; economic downturn (2014), 97; GDP, 35f, 36, 37f, 38, 46, 67, 73; global financial crisis's impact on, 68

Russia, foreign relations: alliances, preference for informal, 14–15; China, relationship with, 71, 98–99, 112, 125, 128–30; domestic context, link with, 14–15; foreign policy orientations, 6–7; foreign policy process, rhetoric's role in, 4–5; foreign policy rhetoric, persistent themes in, 45; foreign policy weaknesses, 139; India, relationship with, 121, 125; multipolarity as goal of, 14; Pakistan, joint military exercise with, 136n46; political rhetoric and, 2;

post–Cold War order, responses to, 11–16; US, relationship with, xviii, 47–49, 60, 67, 71–72, 75, 138; US securities holdings, 68; West, relationship with, xvii, xx, 7–11. *See also* Ministry of Foreign Affairs

Russia India China (RIC): "Strategic Triangle," 25–26, 48, 130; Troika, 69

Russian Academy of Sciences (RAN), 78, 86n95

sanctions, against Russia, 94–95, 99, 107–8

Sanya Declaration (BRICS), 74

Saran, Samir, 125

Shanghai Cooperation Organization (SCO), 13, 102, 109–10

Shanghai Five, 13

Silk Road Economic Belt, 109, 129

Silk Road Fund, 131, 132

Singh, Manmohan, 123, 126–27

Slavophiles, Westernizers versus, 6, 7

soft power, Russia's experiments with, 56

South Africa: BRIC, membership in, 28; GDP, 35f, 36, 37f; IBSA and, 26; O5 and, 27; political crisis in, 124–25, 140

South China Sea, China's activities in, 125, 128, 130

sovereignty: independence and, 45–51; national sovereignty, Putin's narrative on, 93; Putin's redefinition of, xix; Russian understanding of, 14, 47; sovereign democracy, 14–15; sovereign globalization, 15; sovereign preponderance, 125; sovereign states, interference in domestic affairs of, 48; Surkov on, 49

Soviet Union (USSR): IMF and, 20n51; impact of WWII on, 53; India, trade with, 120; Western response to dissolution of, 7. *See also* Russia

"special path" debate, 6, 7

Stalin, Joseph, 54–55

stasis, as future BRICS scenario, 142

statistics, on BRICS, 34–40

Strategic Arms Reduction Treaty, 71

strategic autonomy, in India's foreign policy, 121
Stuenkel, Oliver, 108
Surkov, Vladislav, 44, 49
Survey on Russian Foreign Policy (2007), 49, 50
Syria: conflict in, 88; Crimean annexation, support for, 96

Tajikistan: economic cooperation and, 12; security organizations, membership in, 13
Temer, Michel, 124
Toloraya, Georgii, 29
trade: arms sales, 125, 129, 136n69; BRICS-EU, 105; BRICS-United States, 105; BRICS-the West, 38, 40; India-China, 123–24; India-Soviet Union, 120
Transneft (state oil transit company), 71
Trubnikov, Vyacheslav, 28
Trump, Donald, and Trump administration, 127, 142–43
Turkey, SCO and, 13

Ukraine: China, relationship with, 107, 136n69; economic cooperation and, 12
Ukraine crisis, BRICS and Russia after, 88–112; annexation of Crimea, global responses to, 94–96; BRICS versus West, in post-Ukraine Russian political rhetoric, 101–5; BRICS versus Western response to crisis, 139–40; conclusions on, 111–12; Greater Eurasian Partnership, 109–11; intra-BRICS practicalities, 96–101; introduction to, xx, 88–89; Putin's justification for annexation of Crimea, 91–93; Russian anti-Westernism, 105–9; Ukraine crisis, discussion of, 89–91
unipolarity, 16. See also multipolarity
United Nations (UN): BRICS's actions in, 100; Comprehensive Convention on International Terrorism, 123; Russia's role in, 11; "Territorial Integrity of Ukraine" (UN Resolution 68/262),

95–96; UN General Assembly, on Crimean annexation, 95; UN Security Council, 11, 30–31, 114n44
United States: Cold War rhetoric, 3–4; Congress, lack of action on IMF reforms, 31, 116n108; Crimean annexation, response to, 94; dominance, after Cold War, 16–17; Eastern Europe, rhetoric on, 3; GDP, 36f, 37f; global governance and, 142; global hegemony of, BRICS as constraint on, 140; international leadership of, discontent with, 25; isolationism, possibility of, 142–43; leadership of, distrust of, 17; on missile defense system in Europe, 72; political powers, post–Cold War, 11; Putin on, 49, 67, 92–93, 102–5; UNSC resolution on Crimea, actions on, 114n44
United States, foreign relations: BRICS countries' trade with, 105; China, relationship with, 129–30; India, relationship with, 126–27, 132–33, 140; Russia, relationship with, xviii, 47–49, 60, 67, 71–72, 75, 138
USSR. See Soviet Union
Uzbekistan, membership in security organizations, 13

Valdai International Discussion Club, 102, 103, 104, 115n77, 116n95

Warsaw Treaty Organization, 8
the West: anti-Westernism, xix, 101, 105–9, 118–19; BRICS trade with, 38, 40; BRICS versus, in post-Ukraine Russian political rhetoric, 101–5; China's and India's relationship with, 144n11; Crimean annexation, response to, 94–96; as global norm setter, presumptions of, 140; internal dynamics in, impact of, 142–43; Medvedev's interest in, 70; receptivity to BRICS proposals, 141–42; relationship with Russia, Putin on, 93; Russia, attempted isolation of, 96, 100;

Russian anti-Westernism, xix, 101, 105–9; Russia's failure to engage with, 7–11; Russia's relationship with, xvii; Western hegemony, ideational objections to, 30. *See also* United States
World Bank, 18, 132
World Trade Organization (WTO), 9–10, 15–16, 34, 76
World War II: Great Patriotic War, 53–55; veneration of, 62n60, 92, 101

Xi Jinping: on BRICS, 118; on China's foreign relations, 138; foreign policy under, 119, 128–30; Hu Jintao versus, 131, 133; Russia and, 109

Yanukovych, Viktor, 89–90
Yatsenyuk, Arseniy, 93
Yeltsin government, 10, 11, 45

Zuma, Jacob, 28–29, 124

About the Author

Rachel Salzman is a visiting scholar at the Paul H. Nitze School of Advanced International Studies (SAIS) at Johns Hopkins University. She previously held a postdoctoral fellowship at the Center for Russian, Eurasian and East European Studies at Georgetown University. In 2014 Salzman was awarded a Cosmos Scholars grant and a Boren Fellowship for dissertation research and language study in Moscow. Before beginning her doctorate, Salzman worked as the assistant director for the Euro-Atlantic Security Initiative at the Carnegie Endowment for International Peace. She holds a BA in European History from the University of Pennsylvania, an MPhil in Russian Studies from the University of Cambridge, and a PhD from SAIS at Johns Hopkins.

www.ingramcontent.com/pod-product-compliance
Lightning Source LLC
Chambersburg PA
CBHW030332270326
41926CB00010B/1591